The Material Culture of Steamboat Passengers

Archaeological Evidence from the Missouri River

The Plenum Series in Underwater Archaeology

Series Editor:

J. Barto Arnold III

Institute of Nautical Archaeology
Texas A&M University
College Station, Texas

Maritime Archaeology: A Reader of Substantive and Theoretical
   Contributions
Edited by Lawrence E. Babits and Hans Van Tillburg

The Material Culture of Steamboat Passengers: Archaeological
   Evidence from the Missouri River
Annalies Corbin

The Persistence of Sail in the Age of Steam: Underwater
   Archaeological Evidence from the Dry Tortugas
Donna J. Souza

A Continuation Order Plan is available for this series. A continuation order will bring delivery of each new volume immediately upon publication. Volumes are billed only upon actual shipment. For further information please contact the publisher.

F
598
.C67
2000

Library of Congress Cataloging-in-Publication Data

Corbin, Annalies
   The material culture of steamboat passengers: archaeological evidence from the
Missouri River/Annalies Corbin.
      p.   cm. — (The Plenum series in underwater archaeology)
      Includes bibliographical references (p.   ) and index.
      ISBN 0-306-46168-4
      1. Missouri River—Antiquities.   2. Excavations (Archaeology)—Missouri River.   3.
Underwater archaeology—Missouri River.   4. River steamers—Missouri
River—History—19th century.   5. Material culture—Missouri River—History—19th
century.   6. Material Culture—West (U.S.)—History—19th century.   7. Immigrants—West
(U.S.)—History—19th century.   8. West (U.S.)—Emigration and
immigration—History—19th century.   I. Title.   II. Series.

F598 .C67 1999
978'.01—dc21   99-048649

Cover photograph: The steamer *Helena* at the Milk River Landing in 1880 loaded with passengers.
F. Jay Hayes, photographer, # H-316, courtesy of the Montana Historical Society, Helena.

ISBN: 0-306-46168-4

©2000 Kluwer Academic / Plenum Publishers
233 Spring Street, New York, N.Y. 10013

http://www.wkap.nl/

10 9 8 7 6 5 4 3 2 1

A C.I.P. record for this book is available from the Library of Congress

Printed in the United States of America

The Material Culture of Steamboat Passengers

Archaeological Evidence from the Missouri River

Annalies Corbin

University of Idaho
Moscow, Idaho

Kluwer Academic / Plenum Publishers

New York • Boston • Dordrecht • London • Moscow

This book is for Ed, Niki, Bill, and Daisy
and is dedicated to the memory of Dr. E. B. Trail,
dentist, historian, and the first Missouri River steamboat buff to make
an active call for the protection of western river steamboats

Foreword

For many years, one of my favorite classroom devices in historical archaeology was to ask the students to imagine that they had to make the choice between saving—from some unnamed calamity—all master's theses or all doctoral dissertations in anthropology, but not both. Like good students, they usually looked to their Ph.D.-holding professor and chose the dissertations. Much to their surprise, I would respond that the theses would win without even taking time to ponder the issue. The issue is clearly one of often naïve and rarely eloquent theses full of good primary data versus sometimes more sophisticated and better written works full of irrelevant theory and meaningless statistics. Perhaps this is an overstatement of the situation, but it is not too far off the mark.

The University Microfilms International efforts to make the titles of dissertations in North America and the English-speaking portions of Europe available through *Dissertation Abstracts* is commendable. With only one minor exception, dissertations in historical and underwater archaeology in the United States are to be found listed in *Dissertation Abstracts* and thus are available for purchase.

Unfortunately, there is no comparable source for the multitude of institutions producing masters' theses in historical and underwater archaeology. If the subject matter is clearly anthropological and predates 1977, the title might be in McDonald (1977). If by chance the work was conducted in Virginia, it would probably be listed in Wittkofski (1991). What is needed in the field of historical and underwater archaeology is a current finding aid for titles in graduate studies. This is a worldwide problem, not one just involving Great Britain, Australia, and English- and French-speaking North America. One fortunate enough to find a likely title must then face the frustrating task of obtaining a copy through interlibrary loan, which involves the strangely possessive charter of the librarian controlling the thesis. "We cannot send a copy because it might be lost " (in spite of having two copies). "No, we cannot make a copy because that might damage the original" (why not use the second copy?). Ultimately, one finds a colleague who finds a student to go to the library in question and make a copy on the multitude of copy machines available on every floor. If this sounds all too familiar, it is because we have all been through the process in one way or another. For the agency archaeologist in a small town who must depend on the local public library for interlibrary loan, the frustration is increased many times over.

Is there a solution beyond going after a federal grant to compile a bibliography every few years? One solution is to publish quickly those theses worthy of publication. Every so often, a thesis comes along that contains not only the useful and extensive data of a typical thesis but is written in a mature way with reasonable theoretical elements more typical of a dissertation. The thesis written by Annalies Corbin is one such work. We clearly need to publish more theses of this quality. This work is doubly useful because it involves and is valuable to both terrestrial and underwater archaeology.

There are several factors making this thesis unusual and valuable in historical and underwater archaeology. The most obvious is the difficulty in assigning it to one or the other of the two fields. The rich array of artifacts so thoroughly enumerated is typical of a terrestrial site, yet it was the hazards of shallow water navigation that put them in storage for later excavation. The preservation was not bits and pieces, as we so often find in terrestrial sites, but the complete contents of the various boxes and trunks, labeled "artifact sets." What makes this compilation even more useful and of inestimable value not only to archaeologists but to social anthropologists working with nineteenth century culture is the ability to identify the people who lost the various containers. Corbin has not only been able to identify all but one of the numerous individual owners but has gleaned facts of their "social persona" (Goodenough, 1965:7) including traveling family groupings. As she expresses it, this is a study of the "types of people who used river transportation for westward migration."

The generous use of photographs, a full listing of the artifacts from both the *Bertrand* and the *Arabia,* and the excellent artifact preservation make this volume a valuable contribution that will become a standard reference manual for many years to come. The artifact descriptions contained in Appendixes A–G include data often neglected in archaeological reports such as the precise size and the manufacturer when known. In many cases, grouping the artifacts into the "sets" contained in one box tells a great deal about what a craftsman or homemaker of that period considered necessary for his or her work. The use of a typological classification created from two complementary systems and a knowledge of the occupation of the owners have resulted in a very high degree of artifact identification. This has been viewed in terms of a series of clearly stated, predictive hypotheses. This analysis has predictive value to others; it is not pursued just to prove a pet theory as is so typical today of many archaeological dissertations.

Another major consequence of this publication is the additional research that it will spawn. The questions answered are far outnumbered by the questions that this work asks. Appendix H—a listing of Missouri River shipwrecks—should help to further research of other sites in what is in reality the interior of a major land mass. Corbin shows that even at the upper reaches of navigation on the Mississippi–Missouri system there are important resources that need to be identified, protected, and investigated. Even more important, these resources are vital to our study of material culture in general and to the study of the frontier in detail.

To return to the original question, why save all master's theses? The work published here provides a clear and concise example of why all theses in underwater and historical archaeology should be available in published form.

REFERENCES

Goodenough, Ward H., 1965, Rethinking "Status" and "Role." In *The Relevance of Models for Social Anthropology, ASA Monographs,* pp. 1–24. New York, Praeger.

McDonald, David R., 1977, *Masters' Theses in Anthropology: A Bibliography of Theses from United States Colleges and Universities.* New Haven, HRAF Press.

Wittkofski, J. Mark, 1991, Theses and Dissertations Relevant to Virginia Archaeology, Architecture, and Material Culture. *Virginia Department of Historic Resources, Bibliography Series,* No. 3, revised. Richmond.

RODERICK SPRAGUE
University of Idaho
Moscow, Idaho

Preface

At the annual meeting of the Society of Historical Archaeology in Atlanta in 1998, I was honored by an invitation from Plenum Press to submit my M.A. thesis for publication in its series on underwater archaeology. The invitation was especially gratifying for four reasons.

First, publication of my thesis highlights the importance of the steamboat era in the opening of the American West. Steamboats made possible, at low cost and with efficiency, the transport of persons, their possessions, and goods of commerce to the nation's interior. The study, then, deals with the transcontinental migration, which as an event helped define the American character.

Second, as a report on historical archaeology, my study of the *Bertrand* and the *Arabia,* two substantial steamboats that were in operation from 1856 to 1865, is instructive. Although Petsche (1974) and G. Hawley (1998) wrote important works on both vessels, neither linked the material remains with emigrant migration patterns. My study does precisely that. To establish a profile of the passengers, I analyzed the content of passenger boxes with a view toward gender, group dynamics, and socioeconomic status. I used documentary sources, photographs, and archaeological artifacts to help posit hypotheses about nineteenth-century emigrant travel. I suggest, on the basis of my interpretation of the evidence, a profile of the persons who used steamboats for migrating westward.

Third, I believe that my thesis will be a useful reference manual. Petsche and Hawley did not specifically focus on the artifacts on the *Bertrand* and the *Arabia.* My work, by contrast, gives detailed archaeological and historical information about the artifact sets from the two vessels. That information is the heart of my work. Often, when archaeologists excavate sites in the American West, they find only fragments of many artifacts, and those material remains often leave the researcher with more questions than firm answers. Very fragile items—clothing, for example—rarely survive in situ. Thanks, however, to the high moisture content at both sites, the physical remains were well preserved. In the holds of the two vessels were garments, tool handles, complete containers, and the preserved foodstuffs of the American West. The intact artifacts, numbering in the thousands, are an archaeologist's treasure trove.

Fourth, Appendix H, which is new for this publication, is part of a much larger project. From 1993 onward, I have collected information about vessels of all descriptions (barges, keelboats, mackinaws, ferries, steamboats, and early motorboats) in operation on inland rivers in the nineteenth century. The material makes up a database (presently 1,400 vessels) that I hope continues to grow with additional research and, when reasonably complete, will be published as a reference work. For the present, Appendix H contains a portion of that database to suggest the volume of steamboat activity on the Missouri River and the potential value of the database for historical archaeological sites.

The organization of my study is straightforward. Chapters 1 and 2 serve as introductions to my work. Chapter 1, drawing upon established authorities, aims at providing a basic understanding of how and when steamboating came to the Missouri River; Chapter 2 reviews the salient details in the history of the *Bertrand* and the *Arabia*. Chapter 3 explains my research methodology and introduces a set of hypotheses about the types of people who used river transportation for westward migration. Chapters 4–8 contain detailed descriptions of the artifacts that I studied. Chapter 9 has a quantitative analysis of the artifact sets. Chapter 10, the conclusion, revisits the questions raised about the emigrants who were traveling west and suggests directions for further work on those issues. Appendixes A–G detail the artifact sampling from the two wrecks.

ACKNOWLEDGMENTS

My research would not have been possible without assistance from many people. I thank Sarah Tuttle, James O'Barr, and the staff at the DeSoto National Wildlife Refuge for their suggestions and help with research on the *Bertrand* collection. I also thank Gregory, David and Robert Hawley, and Lynn Jenkins for their assistance with the collection at the *Arabia* Steamboat Museum, and for housing during my stay there I thank Carol Siegel and Chrissy and Danny Pearson.

The staff at the Montana Historical Society were especially helpful as were the staffs at the St. Louis Mercantile Library, the Missouri Historical Society, and the National Archives in Washington, D.C. I also thank Jay Gaynor and D. Allen Saguto for their answers to my carpenter- and cobbler-related inquiries, and I thank Roderick Sprague and Karlis Karklins for their expertise about beads. Jack Scott is responsible for having created the beautiful map of the Missouri River region on page 4. Special thanks goes to Pay Guyette and the staff at Inter-Library Service at East Carolina University's library for finding obscure printed sources and to Edward and Niki Corbin, Wendy Coble, Kent Hackmann, and Cynthia Schwenk for their suggestions and unfailing support.

I express my appreciation to Bradley Rodgers, Donald Parkerson, and John Tilly for their help in the revision of my original M.A. thesis. I am especially indebted to Lawrence Babits and Douglas Scott for directing my research, patiently reading the early drafts of my thesis, and offering support and suggestions for turning it into a book.

I acknowledge valuable support in my collection of information for my steamboat database. East Carolina University's program in Maritime History and Nautical Archaeology helped in the infancy of the project, and the Department of History at the University of Idaho has more recently encouraged it. Kenneth Karsmizki at the Museum of the Rockies assisted with research in various printed and manuscript collections, and volunteers at the museum provided clerical help. My good friend Mike Cassler shared his steamboat research with me and provided hours of debate concerning Upper Missouri River steamboating issues. Financial support has come from Sons and Daughters of Pioneer Rivermen, who administered the J. Mack Gamble Fund, and from the Honorable John Calhoun Smith Memorial Fund, at the University of Idaho, for subventions for my doctoral dissertation research on steamboats on the Missouri River.

A special acknowledgment goes to J. Barto Arnold III, the series editor, and Eliot Werner, editor at Kluwer Academic/Plenum. Both played a crucial role in encouraging this publication and took a great leap of faith in imagining it would be possible. I appreciate their guidance and suggestions.

Finally, this text would have been impossible without the support and understanding of my family. Nelson and Anna were most patient with this process, even though it interfered with family activities for several months. I must thank them both for keeping me on track by asking each day, when they got off the school bus, "So how many pages do you have now?" What a reminder to keep on task. My husband Chip deserves the greatest thanks of all. He was gentle and patient with a very tedious and consuming process. His constant faith that I could juggle my family, a book, and a dissertation was admirable. Without his support, this book would not have been attempted in the first place.

Contents

Contents

Chapter 1

Introduction
Westward Expansion toward Fort Benton, Montana Territory

An "empty" North American continent seemed to pull new inhabitants ever westward. Since the Jamestown settlement, Anglo-Americans had moved closer to the Pacific Ocean. The West was equated with opportunity, an opportunity that was not halted in 1763 by the Appalachian Mountains or by English legal proclamation. Likewise, expansion was not stopped almost a century later by the midcontinent's river systems, Great Plains, Rocky Mountains, or Native American resistance. As stated by John O'Sullivan, America's "manifest destiny" was to occupy all of North America. The New York journalist wrote "It was the nation's obvious fate to expand from sea to sea for God and nature intended Americans to possess the North American continent" (Merk, 1963; O'Sullivan, 1839; Pratt, 1933; Weinberg, 1935).

The apex of American westward emigration was from the 1840s through the 1870s. The post–Civil-War movement of people was part of the second mass exodus experienced in American history. The first migration occurred between 1763 and 1800 with waves after 1763 and 1783. The second large-scale migration westward occurred between 1840 and 1870, again with two waves, the first between 1840–1850 and the second after 1865. During these years, a quarter of a million people crossed the central United States (Schlissel, 1982). Some sought free land in the Oregon and California Territories; others went to make their fortunes in the gold and silver mines. When gold was discovered in California (1848), Nevada (1849), and Montana (1858), many saw an opportunity to strike it rich and start over. Once again, repeating the familiar pattern practiced by their parents before them, American families picked up their belongings and moved west (ibid.; Conlin, 1993).

1

1.1. OVERLAND OR BY SEA

During the large-scale American migration, the vast majority of emigrants traveled by wagon train along trails such as the Oregon, the Sante Fe, and the California. The overland route was slow, filled with many hazards, and almost 2,000 miles long. The journey often lasted six to eight months with emigrants traveling in springless wagons or walking alongside through drenching rains, summer storms, and sometimes even snow (Schlissel, 1982).

Overland, however, was not the only way to travel to America's Pacific Coast. Another option was sea travel from a port on the Atlantic or Gulf coast to California. The ocean route could be made in two ways; travelers could go by steamboat to the Isthmus of Panama where they would unload and caravan with their belongings overland to another vessel waiting on the Pacific side, or they could travel by sea around South America's Cape Horn. This journey involved 6,000 miles of sea travel and was impractical for most emigrants, owing to its high expense (Mullan, 1865).

Because of the cost of sea travel and the time spent traveling overland, there was a great need to identify a water route where sea travel was eliminated and land travel kept to a minimum. In 1865, Captain John Mullan noted that the trans-Mississippi geography demonstrated that these goals were achievable. By ascending the Missouri River to its highest point, Fort Benton, Montana Territory (Figure 1.1), and then crossing to the navigable waters of the Columbia River, land carriage to California was reduced to only 624 miles (ibid.).

1.2 REALIZING MULLAN'S VISION: STEAMBOATS ON THE MISSOURI RIVER

Steamboat operations on the Missouri were directly related to developments in the Missouri River valley and the northern Rocky Mountain regions. Factors contributing to the flow of steamboats up the Missouri included the upper river fur trade, military operations, mining in the Rockies and Montana, settlement in various plains regions, the Sante Fe trade, and the Pike's Peak gold rush of 1858 (Corbin, [in press]; Peterson, 1945; Winther, 1964).

Steamboating began on the Missouri River in May 1819 when the ninety-eight-ton steamer, the *Independence*, ascended a distance of 250 miles to Franklin and Chariton, Missouri. The vessel was carrying a cargo of flour, whiskey, sugar, and iron castings from St. Louis, Missouri (Corbin, 1998; Corbin, in press; Hunter, 1949; Peterson, 1945). Major Steven H. Long of the Corps of Topographical Engineers also traveled up the Missouri by steamboat in 1819. His steamer, the *Western Engineer*, transported troops and military supplies to Fort Lisa, a trading post located a few miles above present-day Omaha. This fort was the farthest

Figure 1.1. Early Fort Benton by J. M. Stanley, a product of the Isaac I. Stevenens Survey.
Photo courtesy of the Montana Historical Society, Helena.

north a steamboat had been on the Missouri River (Corbin, in press; Jackson, 1985; Peterson, 1945). Despite grand beginnings, the 1820s and 1830s proved to be a lackluster time for lower Missouri River steamboating (the lower river was the 660 miles between St. Louis, Missouri, and Council Bluffs, Iowa) (Figure 1.2). There were few boats on the river during the earlier period, and those that were operated on irregular schedules because of a lack of settlement and limited commerce.

The first regular service between St. Louis and Fort Leavenworth, a distance of 425 miles, began in 1829 (Hunter, 1949; Jackson, 1985). After 1829, the number of steamboats on the lower Missouri slowly increased. The 1830s and 1840s saw an escalation in steamboat traffic on the river from St. Louis to Omaha. Five steamboats were reported in 1831, twenty-six in 1842, twenty-eight in 1857, and fifty-nine by 1858 (Chappell, 1905; Chittenden, 1903; Hunter, 1949). By 1857, twenty-three boats were offering regular service between St. Louis and the village of Sioux City; the freight value for that season was estimated at $1,250,000.00 (Chittenden, 1903). In 1857, there were 174 steamboat arrivals registered at Omaha, 123 of which occurred between May and August (*The Nebraskian*, 1857).

While steamboat operations on the lower Missouri were progressing, operations on the upper Missouri (from Council Bluffs, Iowa, to Fort Benton, Montana) moved much more slowly. The first steamboats to travel the upper river belonged to the American Fur Company. The company's 120-foot, 144-ton, side-wheel steamer the *Yellow Stone* was the first to make the journey. In 1831, the

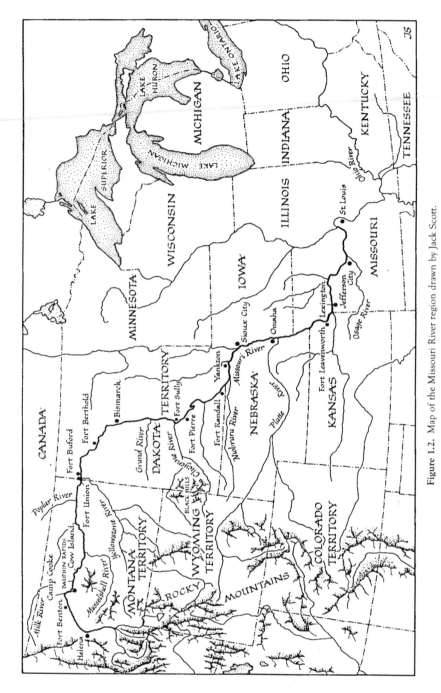

Figure 1.2. Map of the Missouri River region drawn by Jack Scott.

vessel carried supplies to the fur company's post, Fort Tecumseh, opposite what is now Pierre, South Dakota. By 1832, the *Yellow Stone* had traveled as far as Fort Union at the mouth of the Yellowstone River (Corbin, 1998; Corbin, in press; Hunter, 1949; Jackson, 1985; W. J. Peterson, 1945).

It was nearly three decades later, in 1859, when the American Fur Company's stern-wheel steamer, the *Chippewa*, ascended the Missouri to Brule Bottom, fifteen miles below Fort Benton (Chittenden, 1903). The *Chippewa* finally reached the fort in 1860 accompanied by the steamer *Key West*. This trip set a new distance record in the history of steamboat navigation. Fort Benton, 3,300 miles from St. Louis, became the world's innermost port—the farthest port by water from ocean or sea served by regularly scheduled powered craft (Chittenden, 1903; Corbin, 1998; Lass, 1962; Overholser, 1987).

Steamboat traffic at Fort Benton soon became commonplace. After 1858, when gold was discovered in Montana, upper Missouri River traffic increased dramatically. The gold rush spawned a rush of miners, speculators, and suppliers to the Fort Benton area (W. J. Peterson, 1945). From 1860 to 1867, Fort Benton experienced a boom of steamboat activity. Joseph LaBarge, a long-time steamboat captain, estimated that approximately 1,000 passengers and 6,000 tons of freight traveled up the Missouri in 1865 (Figure 1.3). Thirty-one boats arrived at Fort Benton in 1866 and discharged 4,686 tons of freight; thirty-nine arrived in 1867 (Chittenden, 1903; Corbin, in press; Lass, 1962; W. J. Peterson, 1945; Petsche, 1974).

1.3. THE DEVELOPMENT OF THE "MOUNTAIN BOAT"

Most Missouri River steamboats were packet boats, combination passenger and freight haulers. The boats that made the long journey to Fort Benton were also known as "mountain boats" (Bates, 1968). Initially, any steamboat making the trip to Fort Benton was called a mountain boat. By the 1870s, however, a specific hull design emerged on the upper Missouri River (Petsche, 1974). This new hull design greatly impacted the future of the Upper Missouri River. Dr. E. B. Trail, a dentist and noted Missouri River steamboat collector, argued that "mountain steamboating" was the greatest steamboating the country ever knew (Corbin, in press; Trail, 1940s).

Mountain boats were shallow-draft craft with sturdy hulls and powerful high-pressure engines. They were smaller than the Mississippi River packets and lacked the elaborate "gingerbread" work commonly seen on southern rivers (W. J. Peterson, 1945). General Phillippe Regis de Trobriand, an 1867 passenger on the *Deer Lodge* (an early Mountain prototype), noted that the Missouri River steamers were quite simply constructed. He described them as flat hulled, almost without a keel. When fully loaded, a well constructed mountain boat drew, at most,

Figure 1.3. Freight stacked high at the Fort Benton levee in 1879 after unloading a steamboat. Unknown photographer, Montana subject file, courtesy of the Montana Historical Society, Helena.

four feet of water. The vessel had a large cargo hold in which the cargo was stacked up to two thirds of the length of the vessel. The forward deck was almost always open, while the stern contained a closed room to protect the engines as well as an onboard repair shop. The furnace and boilers sat directly on the deck, slightly forward of the engines. Cord wood was piled port to starboard, front to back, leaving only walkways for the crew between. In front of the huge furnaces was a stairway that led to the upper deck, which was supported, the length of the boat, by cast iron columns. This deck included the dining room or saloon and the cabins or staterooms. The great paddle wheel was as wide as the whole stern. The pilothouse, which contained the wheel, was located above the upper deck between two large smokestacks. Often these boats were armed with fieldpieces, and they usually carried a carpenter and blacksmith on board (Kane, 1951).

Mountain boats, therefore, were specifically built for the extreme conditions of the upper Missouri. The boats used in the early years of the Fort Benton trade were based on lower river designs and had "model bows," whereas the mountain boats developed a bowl-like or "spoonbill bow" (Figures 1.4 and 1.5). Model-bowed boats had bows with slightly V-shaped hulls; spoonbill bows were rounded with flat bottoms, thus distinguishing upper Missouri River boats from those used on the Mississippi and Ohio Rivers (Bates in Petsche 1974; Fenn in Petsche 1974).

Other differences were in the paddle wheels. Earlier vessels used side-wheels typical of the Ohio–Mississippi River steamboats. The original *Yellow Stone*, for example, was a side-wheel steamboat. Side-wheel steamers were limited primarily to the lower river trade because of the number of obstructions in the upper river. Stern-wheel boats were designed to handle the extreme conditions in the river's upper regions; they were better able to get over sandbars, although they lacked some of the maneuverability of their side-wheeled cousins. In addition, stern-wheelers had only one wheel that could be entangled or damaged by snags in the river, and the stern-wheel was also partially protected by the vessel's hull in front of the paddle wheel (Bates, 1968).

Figure 1.4. The model-bowed steamer the *Keokuk* (no date or location). Unknown photographer, #955-137, courtesy of the Montana Historical Society, Helena.

Figure 1.5. The spoon-bill-bowed steamers *Benton* and *Western* with the *Far West* and *Nellie Peck* unloading freight and passengers at the Bismark levee in 1877. F. J. Hayes photographer, #H-56, courtesy of the Montana Historical Society, Helena.

Missouri River steamers were generally much smaller than those on the Mississippi. Upper Missouri River vessels carried less than 100 to as much as 500 tons of cargo depending on the size of the vessel; the average carried between 300 and 400 tons. The dimensions ranged from 132 feet to 216 feet in length and from 24 feet to 36 feet in beam (Winther, 1964).

1.4. TIME ON THE RIVER

Steamboats began operation each season on the Missouri River when the ice broke upriver. This might be as early as March in some years but, usually, was not until late April or early May. Most steamboat activity logged in at Fort Benton occurred between May and August, but there are rare accounts of vessels making runs downriver as late as early December (Hunter, 1949).

The time it took to reach Fort Benton depended on many factors: weather, the water level of the river, vessel load, movement of sandbars, and the number of snags in the rivers. Generally, vessels did not travel at night because of the inability to see submerged obstacles in the water. In 1865, H. D. Upham mentioned that he left St. Louis on April 19 and was seventy-two days on the way to Fort Benton (Upham, 1865). Upham did not mention that the trip seemed unusually long, and his story is typical of other accounts. Stuart Granville wrote in his 1866 journal that the same trip took him fifty-four days (Granville, 1867).

1.5.   TRAVLEING WEST BY STEAMBOAT: THE PASSENGER EXPERIENCE

At present, it is impossible to accurately estimate the number of people who traveled up the Missouri River by steamboat. Fragmentary accounts from newspapers, personal journals, and a few rare steamboat logs provide only limited clues. For example, we know that in 1869 the *Henry M. Shreve* left St. Louis with sixty cabin passengers and twenty deck passengers (W. J. Peterson, 1945).

Packet companies advertised several weeks before departures for Fort Benton so that potential passengers could gather in steamboat towns along the route. Potential passengers could select from two types of passage on steamboats, deck or cabin passage. Cabin passage included board, lodging, and transportation. Passengers received full hotel accommodations on most boats until they reached their destination, regardless of delays (Hunter, 1949). Cabin passengers were generally considered the steamboat aristocracy, and fares depended on the "grandness" of the boat, the time of year, and the final destination. Downriver fares were usually less than upriver fares.

Travel costs in the mountain trade were considerably higher than on the Mississippi or Ohio River during the same time. In 1866, Cornelius Hedges took the *Lady Parkinson* down from Fort Benton and paid $100.00 in gold for his cabin passage late in the season. Hedges noted that, in addition to the $100.00 fee, all male passengers were expected to pick bull berries during wood stops along the way (Brazier, 1953). In that same year, passage on the *Peter Balen* to Fort Benton was reported at $300.00 (*Missouri Republic,* 1867).

Deck passage was far more commonly used. Not all Missouri River boats had enough passenger cabin space, and many emigrants could not afford cabin fare. Most passengers traveled second class as deck passengers where deck fares were generally one fourth the cost of cabin passage. Ohio and Mississippi fares could be as low as $6.00–$10.00; Missouri rates were proportional to cabin passage on the Missouri (Hunter, 1949).

Unlike cabin passengers, deck passengers fended for themselves. They brought their own food and utensils and prepared their own meals. Provisions were selected for convenience in handling and preparation and for the avoidance of spoilage. "As a rule bologna sausage, dried herring, water crackers, cheese and a bottle of whiskey was the usual fare" (Hunter, 1949). Many described deck conditions as lamentable. Passengers found accommodations where they could, on or about the freight and sometimes with the livestock. Despite the inconvenience, most emigrants preferred to travel by steamer rather than overland. It was better to sleep on a bench or a sack of grain than in a wagon or stagecoach (Winther, 1964).

1.6. CONCLUSION

Ultimately, many steamboats plied the Missouri River. Thousands of emigrants used Captain Mullan's method for traveling across the continent, and many more used steamboats and the river system as a daily resource for moving supplies, products, and people in and out of a quickly developing region. Long before the railroad, the steamboat and adjoining wagon and stagecoach roads reigned supreme (Schwantes, 1999). Evidence of this fact is found in the abundance of romantic literature about travel on the Missouri River and is also buried in shipwrecks scattered across the river landscape.

Chapter 2

The Steamboats
Arabia and *Bertrand*

Fortunately for archaeologists and historians alike, all steamboats that traveled on the Missouri River did not survive their journeys. Many were wrecked and became embedded cultural resources. Although public fascination with steamboats is immense, only two archaeological examples of Missouri River steamboats have been reported to date: the *Bertrand*, excavated in 1968, and the *Arabia*, salvaged in 1989. These two vessels provide insights into the use of steamboat transportation in the American westward movement. The first "modern" Missouri River steamboat excavation was of the steamer *Bertrand*.

2.1. THE BUILDING OF THE *BERTRAND*

The *Bertrand*'s hull was manufactured by Dunlevy and Company of West Virginia (*Daily Inteligencer*, 1864; Petsche, 1974). The formal enrollment record listed the vessel's original owners as George Fellow and Thomas W. Aird (also documented as Thomas H. Reed), both of Wheeling, West Virginia, and George Laing, Lewis W. Cochran, and Jeremiah Cochran, all of Monroe County, Ohio. The boat was listed at 251 tons, 161 feet in length, 32 feet 9 inches in beam, with a 5 foot 2 inch mean depth of hold (Figure 2.1) (National Archives, RG 41, PE 72).

The stern-wheeler's maiden voyage was from Wheeling to St. Louis where the boat entered the mountain trade. In March 1865, St. Louis newspapers advertised the *Bertrand*'s upcoming departure for the Montana Territory (Figure 2.2). Now part of the Montana and Idaho Transportation Line, the steamboat was under new ownership (*Daily Missouri Democrat*, 1865). The *Bertrand* was part of the company's "Mountain Fleet," which also included the *Benton*, the *Yellowstone*, the *Fanny Ogden*, and the *Deer Lodge* (Petsche, 1974).

11

Figure 2.1. Unknown artist's interpretation of the steamboat *Bertrand*. Courtesy of DeSoto
National Wildlife Refuge, U. S. Fish and Wildlife Service, Missouri Valley, Iowa.

2.2. A DISASTROUS VOYAGE

The *Bertrand* left St. Louis on its ill-fated maiden voyage with Captain James A.
Yore in command (*Daily Missouri Democrat*, 1865). The steamboat's fate was
reported to the *Davenport Gazette* (1865) by a *Bertrand* passenger, W. Burrows:

> Our old friend W. Burrows, Esq. returned Tuesday evening from the Missouri
> River, where he was wrecked on the steamer Bertrand, on the first day of
> April, being bound for Fort Benton and having on board his daughter Mrs.
> Millard, and children, and several other lady passengers, some from the city.
> Mr. B.[urrows] says the Bertrand was snagged about twenty-five miles above
> Omaha and sunk in five minutes carrying down a cargo of groceries valued
> at $300,000, and becomes a total loss. Most of the effects of the passengers
> were saved, and the cargo was generally fully insured.

A second eyewitness was William Houston Gallaher of St. Charles, Missouri. Mr. Gallaher was a passenger on board the steamer *St. Johns* and wrote an
account of the *Bertrand*'s sinking in his journal after his own steamer came upon
the wreck of the *Bertrand*:

> At 10½ Oclock reached the wreck of "Bertrand." Badly sunk to cabin floor,
> total loss except light freight from upper deck which was taken ashore, and

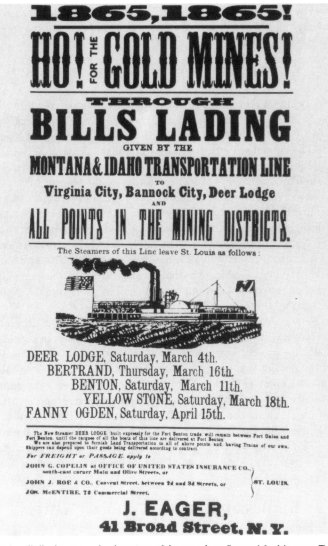

Figure 2.2. A handbill advertising the departure of the steamboat *Bertrand* for Montana Territory in 1865. Courtesy of DeSoto National Wildlife Refuge, U. S. Fish and Wildlife Serivce, Missouri Valley, Iowa.

built into shanties for the protection of the crew. Passengers all up at "DeSoto" eight miles above. While laying at the "Bertrand" Fannie & Annie Campbell came down to the wreck. Very much surprised to see us. They had all arrangements made for going on the "Genl Grant." "St. Johns'" left "Bertrand" at half past eleven." (Moss, 1963)

These two accounts of the *Bertrand*'s loss are invaluable because they mention passenger names and describe what happened to some of the cargo.

2.3. THE EXCAVATION OF THE *BERTRAND*

The wreck of the *Bertrand* was found on DeSoto National Wildlife Refuge, approximately twenty-five miles north of Omaha, in 1968. The wreck was discovered by two Omaha salvors, Jesse Pursell and Sam Corbino. In January 1968, they signed a contract with the federal government's General Services Administration, a requirement when attempting to salvage treasure on federal land. The contract stipulated that the salvors would receive 60 percent of any "treasure" specified as mercury, whiskey, and gold. The federal government was to receive the remaining 40 percent. The contract further provided that the salvors would be "guided during any excavation by the advice of the Chief, Midwest Archaeological Center, National Parks Service." The salvors were, therefore, subject to provisions of the Act for Preservation of American Antiquities. This law provided that "any artifact or other valuable items that may be recovered, must remain the properties of the United States Government and shall be given into the custody of the Refuge Manager" (Petsche, 1974).

The *Bertrand* excavation (Figures 2.3. and 2.4), therefore, differed from the *Arabia*'s recovery in that it was subject to government and archaeological control. Initially, the project was supervised by Wilfred D. Logan, but in 1969 supervision of the project was turned over to Jerome E. Petsche of the Midwest Archaeological Center (Petsche, 1974). After excavations were completed in 1968–1969, the hull of the *Bertrand* was reburied on the refuge. Artifacts recovered from the site were conserved at DeSoto National Wildlife Refuge's conservation facilities, and the collection is now on public display at the refuge museum. The *Bertrand* represents an important segment of western America's history. It is not, however, the only example of a Missouri River steamboat to survive.

2.4. BUILDING THE STEAMBOAT *ARABIA*

The *Arabia* (Figure 2.5) was a side-wheel steamboat built in Brownsville, Pennsylvania, in 1853. The vessel measured 181 feet in length with a 29-foot beam and could carry 222 tons of freight. Adam Jacob of Brownsville, Pennsylvania, originally owned most of the vessel, along with Nicholas Shringer of Pittsburgh and George Reed of Sampeace.[1] John Woodburn was the steamboat's first master

---

[1] On Public Enrollment #3 of the Port of Pittsburgh in January 1855, Nicholas Shringer's ownership was replaced with the letter D, which was not clearly readable in the written document. Z. Brickle of Pittsburgh (National Archives, RG 41, PE 3).

Figure 2.3. The *Bertrand* being excavated in 1969. In this overall view of the hull near the end of the excavation, cargo in the center is still being removed. Photographer unknown, courtesy of DeSoto National Wildlife Refuge, U. S. Fish and Wildlife Service, Missouri Valley, Iowa.

(National Archives, RG 41, PE 42). The group operated the *Arabia* out of Pittsburgh on the Ohio and Mississippi until March 1855.

In 1855, the Port of St. Louis enrollments noted that John Shaw of St. Charles, Missouri, had become the boat's master and that the Pittsburgh enrollment was surrendered in a change of ownership (National Archives, RG 41, PE 12). Enrollment records for March 1856 listed the *Arabia*'s new owners as J. W. Terrill of St. Louis, George W. Boyd of St. Louis, and John S. Shaw of St. Charles, Missouri. J. W. Terrill became the steamboat's new master (National Archives, RG 41, PE 17).

Figure 2.4. The excavation team working to remove boxes from the hull of the steamboat *Bertrand* in 1969. Archaeologist Jerome E. Petsche in a dark shirt, stands at far right. Photographer unknown, courtesy of DeSoto National Wildlife Refuge, U. S. Fish and Wildlife Service, Missouri Valley, Iowa.

2.5. THE *ARABIA* ON THE MISSOURI RIVER

Other than enrollment records, little historical information about the *Arabia* exists today. Most information about the vessel comes from a few newspaper accounts. The Jefferson, Missouri, *Inquirer* (1856) reported that the steamer *Arabia* made her first arrival from St. Louis in the week of March 8, 1856. That same month, the Columbia, Missouri, *Statesman* (1856) printed an article warning would-be passengers that the owners of *Arabia* had cheated a gentleman of his fare from Jefferson City to Providence. The paper went on to suggest that "all honest men avoid this boat the balance of the season." The next reference to the *Arabia* came

Figure 2.5. Painting by Gary R. Lucy of the Steamboat *Arabia*.
Courtesy of the *Arabia* Steamboat Museum.

six months later when the vessel sank. The Kansas City *Enterprise* (1856) reported on September 6, 1856, that the *Arabia* sank the night before while carrying settler supplies for local mercantile stores and a few passengers bound for Council Bluffs, Iowa. The vessel hit a snag about a mile below Parkville, Missouri, and sank up to the boiler deck.

The *Arabia*'s sinking was reported by several newspapers including the St. Louis, Missouri, *Republican*, the Jefferson *Inquirer*, and the Liberty *Weekly Tribune*. The St. Joseph *Commercial Cycle* added that the *Arabia* was insured by the St. Joseph's Insurance Company. Able D. Kirk, a passenger on the side-wheeler, reported that the vessel was loaded with freight but did not have many passengers. Kirk described how some passengers escaped in a lifeboat. Eventually, all the passengers got off the boat with much of their baggage; they were then taken to Parkville by wagon (D. Hawley, 1995; G. Hawley, 1998). Shortly after the *Arabia*'s sinking, the steamer *Cataract* went alongside and removed cabin furniture and freight from the boiler deck and left those items in Parkville (St. Louis *Republican*, 1856). After September 6, 1856, the steamer was slowly covered by sand and eventually disappeared into a newly formed bank of the river. The *Arabia*

Figure 2.6. *Arabia* being salvaged in 1989. Illustration by David Hawley, *Arabia* Steamboat Museum.

seemed unsalvageable, and by September 10, 1856, the insurance companies began the task of paying off claims (G. Hawley, 1998).

2.6. SALVAGING THE *ARABIA*

There were, however, several attempts to salvage the *Arabia* over the next century. Like many steamboats, the vessel was rumored to be carrying barrels of
whiskey (four hundred) as well as gold and silver (G. Hawley, 1998). The Kansas
City *Times* (1871) reported that the *Arabia* was discovered protruding out of the
river bank in December 1871. The paper said that local residents removed a few
barrels of rye and a crate of dishes. The rumor of gold and four hundred barrels of
whiskey continually spurred several attempts to find the *Arabia*.

Robert Treadway and Henry Tobener of Kansas City attempted a salvage in
1877. The pair spent an estimated $2,000.00 trying to salvage the boat by using a
wooden coffer dam. They abandoned the effort after four months with only a box
of felt hats to show for their effort (G. Hawley, 1998). In 1896, the Kansas City
Star reported, that a company from Parkville was attempting to salvage the whiskey from the boat. The article mentioned a Mr. George R. Collins of Kansas City,
who said that he had investigated the wreck two years before. He claimed that in

1894 the *Arabia* was "buried in thirty feet of quicksand and [was] one hundred yards from the river bank." Mr. Collins did not believe the company from Parkville was capable of finding the wreck, much less of salvaging the *Arabia*. In March 1896, the same newspaper reported the salvors had found no trace of the boat.

A third nineteenth-century attempt proved most successful. In 1897, Gale Henson of Holt, Missouri, attempted to salvage the *Arabia* by using a long steel caisson six feet in diameter to reach the vessel's hull. After Henson's team had reached the hull on three occasions without finding the valuable whiskey, the crew stopped digging. After Henson's failed salvage attempt, the *Arabia* lay undisturbed for almost eighty years.

The first twentieth-century salvage attempt was made in 1975. Jessie Pursell and Sam Corbino (the same men who successfully found the *Bertrand*) were the first to attempt a fully open excavation of the *Arabia*. They attempted to salvage the vessel for several weeks but ultimately abandoned the effort before they reached the vessel (G. Hawley, 1998).

Finally, in 1988 and 1989 a group from Independence, Missouri, River Salvage, Incorporated, found the remains of the *Arabia*. The vessel was located under forty-five feet of earth in a Kansas soybean field, a half mile from the river (D. Hawley, 1995). The sand overburden was removed with heavy equipment (Figure 2.6), and several parts of the side-wheeler and all the cargo (Figure 2.7) were

Figure 2.7. The diversity of cargo found in the *Arabia*. Illustration by David Hawley, *Arabia* Steamboat Museum.

ultimately removed. The recovered items are now being conserved, and many are on display at the *Arabia* Steamboat Museum in Kansas City (Corbin, in press).

2.7. CONCLUSION

The *Bertrand* and *Arabia* are important elements of American history. In many ways, they are unique; they are the only Missouri River steamboats viewed recently by means other than photographs. These vessels provide archaeologists, historians, and laypersons with an opportunity to study western river steamboat operations. There is great interest in hull structures, engine configurations, the history of packet companies, the cities where the vessels landed, and the people who used steamboats as vehicles for westward movement. There is considerable need for more study in these areas, and, as is evidenced by the short life of these Missouri River mountain steamboats, there are also many wrecks yet undiscovered.

Chapter 3

Methodology

In 1977, Leland Ferguson suggested that material culture was not just a reflection of everyday human behavior, but was part of every aspect of human behavior. For more than a century, scholars have been debating the meaning and application of the term *material culture*. Most important, the debate still continues as we discover more and more sites each year and more previously unknown artifacts or aspects of human life.

3.1. INTRODUCTION:
MATERIAL CULTURE STUDIES IN AMERICA

Material culture studies in America draw from many diverse fields. Material culture, primarily recognized as physical remains or artifacts, is heavily emphasized in the study of archaeology, anthropology, art history, cultural geography, history of technology, and folklife studies. These different fields often ask different questions of similar artifacts, but they rely on objects as a primary source of cultural information. The study of artifacts constitutes fieldwork where material culture is collected, identified, compared, and categorized (Schlereth, 1982).

For well over a century, archaeologists and philosophers have struggled to find an appropriate working definition of culture. In 1871, Sir Edward Tylor asserted that culture, when taken in its widest ethnographic sense, was "that complex whole which included knowledge, belief, art, morals, laws, customs, and other capabilities and habits man acquired as a member of society" (Thomas, 1990). Tylor's definition was quickly modified to stress relationships between environment and human thoughts and actions. His philosophy was expanded in the twentieth century to form the building blocks for modern cultural theory. Leslie White (1959) attributed culture to the "extrasomatic, temporal continuum

21

of things and events dependent on symboling." Julian Steward (1976) expanded on White and argued that culture is a learned mode of behavior transmitted from one generation to the next and from one society to the next.

James Deetz (1977) later defined culture as unique to humans and as socially transmitted rules of behavior. These rules, as defined by Deetz, govern how we think and what we do. Culture is not a function of genetics but is learned from one's elders or peers or through personal interactions in one's established community. It includes characteristics of a social group's language, belief system, mores, and laws that govern that society. Many facets of "learned" human behavior are reflected in the often subtle yet important ways in which we shape, alter, or manipulate our physical world to adapt to an ever-changing personal environment (Deetz, 1977). Human adaptability to the environment appears in the form of recognizable patterned behavior. The residue of cultural behavior, including artifacts, is also patterned and therefore recognizable.

Evidence of human existence in, and the use of, the physical world appears as material culture. Material culture is usually synonymous with artifacts, the physical manifestations of culture (Adams, 1977). It should be noted, however, that the term *material culture* refers to a very broad, but not unrestricted range of objects, which can be modified or made by patterned human activity. Ian Hodder (1984) asserted that material culture is "meaningfully constituted," the direct result of deliberate endeavors by individuals whose thoughts and actions should not be overlooked. Material culture includes tools, clothing, and sculptures; it also includes written works and how one plows a field, rides a horse, or performs a folk dance. All represent direct products of human activity, and all, when preserved as archaeological remains, constitute the archaeological record (Renfrew, 1984).

3.2. THE ARTIFACT SET

In this study, *material culture* is defined as the objects attributed to passengers traveling west on board the nineteenth-century steamboats *Bertrand* and *Arabia*. The *artifact assemblages* or *sets* are defined as boxes containing personal belongings of a particular passenger or group of passengers. In some cases, a single box is associated with an entire family. Therefore, items in the box may belong to different family members of a recognizable family unit. The boxes served as luggage, enclosing passengers' belongings in a single container that kept their possessions separated from other passengers' belongings.

3.3. PROJECT GOALS

The goal of this study is to analyze the contents of the artifact sets (boxes) to gain information about the gender and socioeconomic background of individual passengers. This information is used to test my hypotheses about the types of people traveling on western rivers in the nineteenth century. Each box was analyzed as a separate unit to facilitate comparisons in the conclusion of the study. Descriptive artifact analysis makes up Chapters 4, 5, 6, 7, and 8.

3.4. ARTIFACT CLASSIFICATION

In each assemblage, individual artifacts are organized in a ranked classification system based on a structured taxonomy. A *structured taxonomy* is a method of organization in which artifacts are defined by hierarchical ranking of formal properties based on an individual artifact's relative importance. The method of formal classification chosen for this study is based on two interrelated models articulated by Lyle Stone and Roderick Sprague. Stone's basic taxonomy is primarily used. It must be modified, however, to be statistically evaluated (Chapter 9). The modifications are based on Sprague's classification of nineteenth century western historic sites.

Stone suggested that classification of historic artifacts must first be based on observed physical properties despite any presumed cultural significance. This approach is limiting in that it does not consider function and use in a cultural context. It is useful, however, if the approach is varied to maintain strict control between separate artifact sets for statistical analysis. Second, classification is useful when evaluating significance of variation in a particular site (Stone, 1974). When applied to a self-contained artifact set (a box), each box can be evaluated as an independent unit and compared with other boxes (units) for similarities and differences. If artifact associations are not clear, such as in a garbage or refuse site, this methodology does not work.

Sprague's classification scheme specifically defines artifacts based on a functional category and defines artifacts in that category (Sprague, 1981). Sprague's classification system is especially adaptable for quantitative analysis (Chapter 9) because it provides a baseline for artifact distinctions such as personal, domestic, industry-related, and group-based activities.

In this analysis, each box or set was analyzed as an independent unit, both historically and archaeologically, and then applied to analytical statistical analysis. The artifacts in each box were placed in specific artifact categories based on general use as observed in this study. The categories used here are not all inclusive and exclude artifact types not present in the collection. For example, there are no tobacco pipes; therefore, no category including pipes is used.

General use categories included *personal utilization, household utilization, child utilization,* and *occupational utilization. Personal utilization* includes clothing and shoes, adornment such as beads and jewelry, personal grooming devices, and billfolds or purses. *Household utilization* includes linens, rugs, decorative items, illumination devices, sewing supplies, books, family bibles, and medicinal items. *Child utilization* includes toys and games, books specific to children, and education-related items such as maps, slates, and schoolbooks. *Occupational utilization* includes tools, trade supplies, and products for sale.

Artifacts from each box were subdivided into types in utilization categories. For example, the personal utilization category is subdivided into types differentiated as clothing and footwear, adornment, and personal hygiene. If an artifact is identified as clothing, it is further divided by gender, male or female, and by age, child or adult. In the quantitative analysis, artifacts are further specified; clothing is distinguished as outer garments (coats, hats, gloves, capes, and shawls), woman's clothing (including dresses, blouses, and skirts), men's clothing (pants and shirts), shoes, buttons, and beads. Specific subdivisions of each category are specified in the quantitative analysis (Chapter 9). A complete list of all artifacts, corresponding to each box in each assemblage, is located in appendixes A, B, C, D, and F.

3.5. A FEW EXPLANATIONS

Because of the acidity of the Missouri River, vegetable fibers including cotton and linens did not survive, whereas animal fibers including fur, wool, and silks did (differential preservation). Therefore, no clothing items made of vegetable fibers survived, and there are hundreds of loose buttons, beads, and metal fasteners such as hooks and eyes in several of the artifact boxes. In this study, these items are not considered independent artifacts but pieces of another, larger artifact that did not survive. These items are only briefly described in tabular form.

I have not carried out an in-depth bead analysis in this study because there are a number of comprehensive works on North American trade beads. I followed Sprague and chose not to repeat earlier analyses (Sprague, 1984). For a complete analysis of North American glass trade beads, see Karklins (1992), Kidd and Kidd (1970), Ross (1990), and Sprague (1991).

3.6. HYPOTHESES

Archaeological assumptions can be combined with historical information to form hypotheses. It is therefore essential to acquire information about emigrant travel, homesteading, and settlements. Hypotheses in this study were derived from three sources. First, I carefully examined historical records for nineteenth century western settlements, travel journals, and historic photographs to make assumptions about what should be found in the passengers' boxes. For example, records showing the variety and availability of items being shipped to supply houses in the upper Missouri region suggest that passengers did not take items such as heavy farming or mining equipment with them because these items were readily available for sale in the region. Photographs were especially invaluable for determining styles and practices about clothing.

There are no other western steamboat sites to consult for comparison with passenger materials on the *Bertrand* and *Arabia*. There are, however, several upper Missouri River sites, now historic sites, museums, or both, which were frequently used by emigrants during the height of western expansion. These sites provide a second body of material. From these, I formulated a list of potential artifacts, including items present in households, shops, or toolkits. Forts Laramie and Kearny were resupply locations for overland travel. Both forts were partially supplied via the river, and supplies were also carried overland. Both forts were frequently mentioned in emigrant travel journals in which the kind of supplies available was noted (Schlissel, 1982). Forts Benton and Campbell were steamboat destinations and the recipients of a majority of passengers and supplies from the 1850s through the 1870s. The Buffalo Bill Historical Center and Museum in Cody, Wyoming, has one of the largest collections of western material culture available. The museum provides researchers with a wealth of examples from western settlements. The collections from all these sites provide a baseline for what might be carried in each passenger box. These sites, however, represent a time frame spanning several decades, whereas a shipwreck represents a collection deposited at a single moment.

A third source of information comes from product catalogs dating from the mid- to late nineteenth century. As the western frontier expanded and its population grew, demand for manufactured or store-bought goods increased. A direct result of opening the upper Missouri River was the availability of manufactured goods. Goods were brought to frontier communities from larger manufacturing centers in the east, Europe, and port cities such as St. Louis, New Orleans, or Chicago. Many manufacturers of clothing, shoes, household items, and tools produced catalogs to promote sales in remote regions. Their catalogs provide a wealth of information for identifying artifacts in several of the boxes and for generating hypotheses about what might be found in the boxes.

Hypotheses are predictions to be tested against the reality of a set of variables, in this case, artifacts. These predictions determine how researchers structure their data collection and interpret the data. To help eliminate research bias, several possible hypotheses are presented. The use of multiple hypotheses allows for the refutation of some hypotheses when compared with the data. This disproving of hypotheses tends to amplify the validity, or lack thereof, of each hypothesis (Chamberlin, 1965). The combination of information from these three research sources allows the researcher to formulate hypotheses, not only about what should be found in the passenger boxes, but also about the passengers who used steamboats as a mechanism of western travel.

3.6.1. Hypothesis A

Single men and family groups commonly used steamboats for western travel, whereas single or individual women did not make the journey unaccompanied. The overland journey was rarely made by single women. Journals written about steamboat travel confirm this trend. Brazier specifically differentiated between single male passengers and family groups traveling the Missouri River (Brazier, 1953). Therefore, the contents of passenger boxes should reflect the presence of single men and family units but not single women.

3.6.2. Hypothesis B

Family groups have a greater frequency of household goods, personal items, female and child items, and luxury items than do single males. A common occurrence in archaeological literature is the correlation between female-specific items such as clothing, perfume bottles, jewelry, and decorated ceramics associated with households. The turn of the century also saw an increase in child status, which gave children a visible material culture of their own. Small-size clothing and toys, including dolls, blocks, and marbles, are good diagnostic indicators of the presence of children (Blee, 1991; Hardesty, 1988).

3.6.3. Hypothesis C

Single men have a higher frequency of occupational-based items associated with their boxes and fewer personal and household items. In the nineteenth century, single men were typically more mobile and less likely to establish roots than men who were part of an organized family unit (Blee, 1991). As a result of their added mobility, single men tended to travel lighter. It was common on the overland journey for men to sign on to drive extra wagons for families or to hire out as drivers on freight trains (Settle, 1971). Similarly, the American Fur Company often sent trappers and tradesmen back and forth from supply posts at the beginning and end of each season (Jackson, 1985; Sunder, 1965). These men traveled with the tools needed for success in their trade and a few personal items such as clothing and cooking supplies. They rarely took nonessential items on their journey.

3.6.4. Hypothesis D

Children are more likely to be associated with groups that include a definite female presence rather than an association with single men. It was uncommon for men to travel great distances alone with small children. Men with families who traveled west often left their wives and children at home to be sent for later. Men did not typically take their small children on this journey unless there was no one to leave the children with. It was not, however, uncommon for older boys to accompany their fathers while wives, sisters, and younger siblings stayed behind. Older male children helped drive wagons, handle stock, or assist with their father's trade. Because of their size and age, it is often difficult to distinguish between one adult male and two, or between a father and older son.

3.3.5. Hypothesis E

A statistical method can be devised to demonstrate gender and socioeconomic differences across an artifact population. Logistic regression analysis determines the amount of impact of one artifact characteristic on another. In other words, logistic regression analysis predicts the amount of influence of one variable on another. For example, it is possible to statistically demonstrate that the gender associated with an artifact is directly related to whether or not the artifact is also personal and age specific. Chapter 9 specifically addresses this idea.

3.7. CONCLUSION: ARTIFACT CATALOGING

Artifacts from the *Bertrand* collection are referenced in two ways. Artifacts were initially identified by an excavation lot prefix assigned to cargo items as they were removed from the boat. The alphabetic prefix (SSC— stern cargo, starboard side) refers to a general location in the holds. Boxes were generally opened only in the conservation laboratory where individual artifacts were assigned a catalog number as the box was emptied and recorded in the lab. The *Bertrand* reference numbers, therefore, are static about the collection and can be used as reference numbers in the collection files.

The *Arabia* collection was not recovered with a similar control for accuracy. No assigned numbers or provenance records were kept during the vessel's salvage (D. Hawley, 1995). It is often impossible to establish artifact associations. The *Arabia* Steamboat Museum has assigned catalog numbers to artifacts used in this study. It should be noted that the museum is currently reorganizing its cataloging system, and artifact catalog numbers presently associated with this study may be changed by museum staff.

The *Arabia* box used in this study is referred to as the "Carpenter's Box" (D. Hawley, 1995). Artifacts associated with this box were identified by means of a photograph taken when the box was opened in the field. Specific artifacts were identified in the photograph. Other artifacts were associated with this box through personal recollection by participant observers (particularly members of the Hawley family) of the salvage.

Chapter 4

Bertrand Box 74

In the earliest stage of the *Bertrand* excavation, only test samples of the cargo were taken. The goal of the salvors was profit. It was quickly discovered that little "treasure" was to be found on board. The initial cargo test samples were assigned "box" or "barrel" numbers only. At the end of the July 1969 excavations, it was decided to excavate the entire vessel for public display. More stringent provenance references were assigned to each box determined by the location from which it was removed in the vessel. *Bertrand* Box 74 was removed from the boat's hull between June 30 and July 4, 1969. It was located in the midship's cargo section on the port side. The box measured 17 ½ inches by 22 inches by 36 inches. Unfortunately, the box pieces or fragments were discarded sometime after the excavation. The only references to the box were in field notes where the box's dimensions were recorded. There was no mention in the notes of how the box was constructed.

4.1. THE JOHN S. ATCHISON FAMILY

Box 74 was identified as belonging to members of the John S. Atchison family. Atchison family members traveling on board the *Bertrand* were Mary S. (age 24), Charles (age 5), and Emma (age 4). The *Montana Post* (1865) reported that Mrs. Atchison and her children escaped the sinking, but lost all their baggage. Local newspapers indicated that John S. Atchison preceded his family to Montana, where he eventually became involved with several banks and later became the owner of Atchinson's Trading Post, a trading company that sold mining supplies (Fort Benton *Press*, 1882).

Existing catalog records suggest that a single box contained all of the Atchisons' belongings. Letters written by Jerome Petsche on file at DeSoto National Wildlife Refuge, however, clearly indicate two boxes containing Atchison family items. Petsche mentioned that the two box exteriors were marked "TO J. S. ATCHISON, V. CITY" and "TO J. S. ATCHISON, VIRGINIA CITY, M.T." (Petsche, 1974). It is unclear today whether these were two completely independent boxes or whether one box was packed inside the other.

4.2. BOX 74 ARTIFACTS

The Atchison family belongings offer a unique look at items specifically associated strictly with women and children on the American frontier. The box contained a wide variety of household and personal items representing many different material types that typically disintegrate on many terrestrial sites. Of particular note is the variety of clothing items in this artifact set.

4.2.1. Personal Utilization

4.2.1.1. Clothing and Footwear. *4.2.1.1a.* The Atchison *Fur Stole* (Cat. #3160) was remarkably well preserved. The stole is a soft fur shoulder style with a rounded oblong shape. It is brownish-black in color and probably mink. Unfortunately, no lab tests were performed to determine the exact type of fur, and none is planned for the future. Silk cloth lines both ends of the stole where it would pass over the wearer's shoulders. No lining is evident on the central sections of the stole. Several types of loose buttons and beads were found lying on the fur stole. Because of differential preservation, most buttons and beads that were originally sewn on garments were no longer attached at the time of the excavation. Loose items are therefore examined separately because a direct association to a particular item of clothing is usually impossible.

4.2.1.1b. A roughly circular handsewn *Black Silk Cape* (Cat. #66), made of five sections of finely woven black silk was also in this box (Figure 4.1). The cape measures 153 inches in circumference along the bottom with a 50 3/4-inch neck opening, which does not appear to have been finished. The cape's main body is in two pieces, labeled sections four and five, sewn together with a seam down the back. These sections were essentially semicircular with seven convex scallops (ranging in width from 5 1/2 inches to 6 3/4 inches) cut from the top of each semicircular section. The scallop edges are turned under and topstitched onto section three, the neck yoke. Section three is semicircular with two flat ends. The piece is wide enough to drape off the shoulders. The flat ends are sewn to sections one and two. A row of stitch marks is located 4 3/4 inches to 4 5/8 inches from the hem. These marks may indicate that a binding was once sewn to the cape edge. Either it was removed before the cape was packed, or it was made of a material that did not survive.

The cape is decorated with seven crocheted circular medallions located in

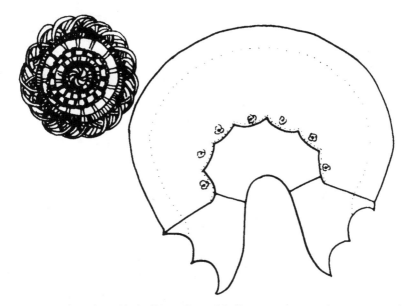

Figure 4.1. The Atchison black silk cape (Cat. #66). Illustration courtesy of DeSoto National Wildlife Refuge, U. S. Fish and Wildlife Service, Missouri Valley, Iowa.

the curve of each scallop in sections four and five. The medallions are made of thin wire frames 2 1/4 inches in diameter. Each had a 3/8-inch center with radiating wire arms, covered with black crocheting in five different crochet patterns. This cape appears to have been handmade and altered in style several times, as indicated by several different rows of stitching and by the cape's unfinished state.

4.2.1.1c. The box also included an excellent example of a *Child's Frock Coat* (Cat. #3298). The coat is made of black wool and was probably worn by a boy. This style of coat appears on boys in many trade catalogs and pattern books of the period (McClellan, 1977). The coat is 35 1/3 inches in length (without collar) and has a 14 1/2-inch shoulder seam. The garment is made of twenty-five finished pieces (Figure 4.2). The coat is heavy, well made, and machine sewn. It has a square-cornered collar made to fold down and includes a heavy braided hanging tab on the inside of the collar.

The coat front is double breasted with pointed lapels. There are three buttonholes on the lapel and two rows of buttons on the breast (three buttons each). Impressions left by buttons that are no longer attached indicate that the buttons were 5/8 inch in diameter. There is a breast pocket on the coat's inner left side.

The coat hem is unfinished, and black silk lines the bodice and skirt but not the sleeves. The lining is machine patterned and may have been interfaced with brown wool. This jacket shows few signs of wear; it was probably new when

Figure 4.2. Child's wool frock coat found in the Atchison box (Cat. #3298). Illustration courtesy of DeSoto National Wildlife Refuge, U. S. Fish and Wildlife Service, Missouri Valley, Iowa.

packed for the move to Montana. The measurements are typical of those of a modern boy's size 5–6. The coat was probably a little large for the Atchison boy but would allow for growth or the layering of clothes under it.

4.2.1.1d. There was a full and long *Woman's Jacket or Smock* (Cat. #3296) with an overall length of 39 1/2 inches (without collar) found in the box. The jacket is made of lightweight brown wool with a black stripe composed of lines of close, small diagonal striations in the weave (Figure 4.3). The jacket pieces are

FIgure 4.3. Lady's wool jacket or smock from the Atchison box (Cat. #3296). Illustration courtesy of DeSoto National Wildlife Refuge, U. S. Fish and Wildlife Service, Missouri Valley, Iowa.

machine sewn with heavy black wool thread. This same thread is used to make a simple decoration along many of the edges. There are four basic pieces to the jacket: a front, back, sleeves, and collar. The jacket hem is turned under twice (1/8 inch, then 5/8 inch) and double machine stitched. The jacket was mended many times.

4.2.1.1e. The box contained blue, red, and black *Plaid Silk Dress Pieces* (Cat. #2924) with a smooth satin weave. A satin weave is a form of common twill weave in which the fibers are interlaced in such a manner that the twill pattern is invisible. The result is a smooth, lustrous surface. Satin weave is commonly used with silks and wools (Woman's Institute, 1926). The dress was not completed. Many of the pieces are only roughly cut out and not to their finished sizes as the plaids would not match. The bodice front is in two pieces and would have had a scooped front neckline, eleven buttonholes, and three rows of darts extending up from the waist when completed. The bodice back is in three pieces. The seams on the front and back are sewn with large even stitches, and the edges are finished. *Silk and velvet ribbon fragments* (Cat. #3159) were associated with the unfinished folded dress pieces.

Silk dresses were not common everyday wear for most individuals. The cost of a complete ready-made silk dress was approximately $100.00 in the late 1850s. Silk dresses during this time were commonly plaid. Brown and white plaids were as common as greens and pinks and blues and whites. The dresses often had floral patterns worked into the stripes, and they were often made with basque or bell sleeves and had tight fitted waists (McClellan, 1977). These dress types were typically shown in popular woman's magazines such as the *Godey's Lady's Book,* which depicted fashions for the well-to-do from New York or Europe. The editor recognized that few women who read the magazine could afford such fine clothes, but many styles were commonly copied in cotton or wool (Blum, 1985). Most of the silk clothes that were found in the Atchison box, therefore, are "finer" than common everyday wear made of fabric other than silk. The high preponderance of silk suggests that perhaps the Atchisons were more than just middle class.

4.2.1.1f. There was a pair of well-worn *Boy's Wool Trousers* (Cat. #67) in the box. The trousers are dark red in color with a vertical black stripe set every 5/8 of an inch (Figure 4.4). There are several tears in the garment, which shows signs of alterations. At some point, the waist was altered on both sides, and the waistband was extended. The waistband has five evenly spaced 3/4-inch buttonholes across the front. Unlike modern pants with a fly that opens at the center front, these pants open at the side seams. The back half of the waistband wraps to the inside of the front section of the waistband and is secured with a button on each side. The additional buttons across the front were for attaching the pants across the front of the child's shirt (York, 1984).

Trousers with this style of button placement were often referred to as "railroad breeches" (Worrell, 1979). The leg bands are fastened shut with homemade

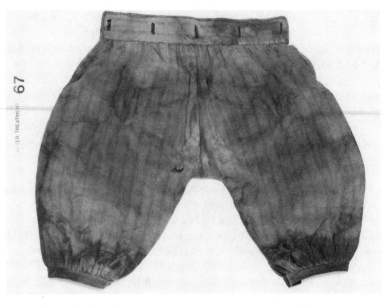

Figure 4.4. Boy's silk railroad breeches found in the Atchison box (Cat. #67). Photograph courtesy of DeSoto National Wildlife Refuge, U. S. Fish and Wildlife Service, Missouri Valley, Iowa.

brass hooks and eyes (not of uniform size). There are also several loose pieces of bands, perhaps additional leg bands, associated with the trousers. The garment has a maximum waist measurement of 23 2/3 inches and an 8 3/4-inch inseam. Railroad breeches were common wear for small boys. The breeches were let out in the waist as the child grew. Originally, they would not have had banded bottoms, but as the child grew taller and the pants became shorter, the bands were added to create knee breeches for middle-sized boys. This flexible style of pants was an economically feasible way to deal with a child's rapid growth (York, 1984).

  4.2.1.1g. A *Knitted Wool Cap* (Cat. #63) made of reddish-brown and black yarn was in the box (Figure 4.5). The main body of the cap is semicircular and knitted in a striped socknet pattern. A socknet pattern is made by knitting the first and every alternate (odd) row and purling the second and every alternate (even) row (Brittain, 1979). There is evidence of much wear as the cap is well stretched. The cap is meant to be tied on the head with two hanging tassels, only one of which survives.

  4.2.1.1h. There were 148 unattached *Buttons* found in this box. The buttons are made of glass, brass, wood, ceramic, tin, and textile in a variety of styles, sizes, colors and textures (Figures 4.6, 4.7, and 4.8). Table 4.1 provides brief descriptions of each kind of button found in the Atchison box.

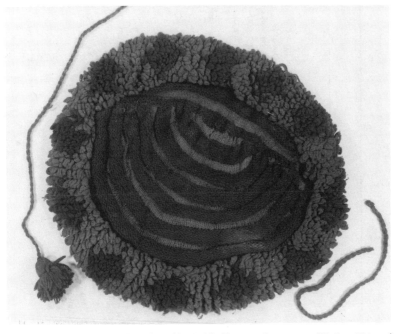

Figure 4.5. Women's knitted wool cap (Cat. #63). Photograph courtesy of DeSoto Naitonal Wildlife Refuge, U. S. Fish and Wildlife Service, Missouri Valley, Iowa.

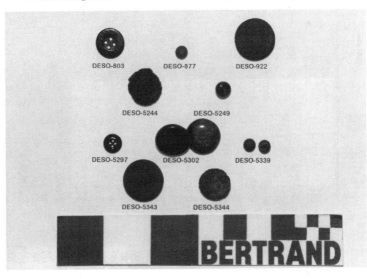

Figure 4.6. A variety of buttons found among the Atchison family belongings. The buttons were probably sewn to garments that did not survive the acidic conditions of the Missouri River. Photograph courtesy of DeSoto National Wildlife Refuge, U. S. Fish and Wildlife Service, Missouri Valley, Iowa.

Table 4.1. Bertrand Box 74: Buttons

Catalog number	Total number	Material	Color	Diameter × thickness	Description
803	01	Wood	Black	16mm × 3mm	Wood covered with black lacquer. Flat and circular with 4 small holes set in recess 9mm diameter. Back convex.
877	02	Brass	Brass	6mm × 5mm	Molded brass button top, convex with flat bottom. Has a brass shank 2mm thick.
922	06	Textile, cotton	Black	23mm × 21mm	Button fronts are covered with tightly woven thread, 6 threads per 26mm. Backs are cardboard rings covered with black lacquer. Lab results verified that these buttons were cotton covered. Some cotton samples survived in this collection owing to differential preservation. These buttons were found lying on the fur wrap, which may have helped preserve them.
3160	01	Textile	Brown	29mm	Cloth covered with woven design. Back is cardboard with an iron ring. Found on fur wrap.
3160	02	Ceramic (china)	White	11mm × 3mm	Plain, circular, 4 holed. Relatively flat.
3160	01	Textile	Black	15mm	Has a cardboard back. Found on fur wrap.
3160	01	Wood	Natural	Unknown*	4-holed, circular wood. Found on wrap.
3160	02	Glass	Black	19mm	Circular, shiny fronts, round backs, brass loop shank pressed into cooling glass.
3763	13	Ceramic, porcelain	White	11mm × 3mm	Porcelain with 4 holes set in 5mm concavity on front. Remaining surface slants down to edge 1mm thick. Convex back. Mold seams on some edges from 2-piece mold. Fired and glazed.
3766	01	Ceramic, porcelain	Unknown*	15mm × 3mm	Porcelain with 4 holes set in concavity 6mm in diameter. Remaining surface slants to edge 2mm. Convex back.
3767	01	Ceramic, porcelain	White	11mm × 3mm	Same button as #3763.
5216	01	Ceramic, porcelain	White	11mm × 3mm	Porcelain with 4 holes in 5mm concavity. Remaining surface is flat to edge. Convex back.
5244	02	Textile	Black	16mm × 3mm	Circular felt-cored, textile-covered buttons. 2 pieces of felt, glued on each other, covered with black textile brocade on 2/3 of diameter.

Cat. No.	Qty	Material	Color	Dimensions	Description
5249	09	Glass	Black	6.5mm × 6mm	Circular glass gaiter buttons with brass shanks. Glass tops made in single mold, circular brass shanks pushed into glass while still hot. Smooth doming tops. Convex back with spiral ridges where shanks are placed.
5292	36	Ceramic, china	White	11mm × 3mm	Same as #3763.
5293	01	Ceramic, porcelain	White	12mm × 3mm	Circular 2-piece mold, seams visible on backs. Fired and glazed. 9mm concavity at center with 4 holes. Outermost rim decorated with small triangles with apex toward center.
5294	01	Ceramic, porcelain	White	11mm × 3mm	Circular, 4 holed. Made in two-piece mold, glazed and fired. 6mm concavity at center. Flat outer rim. Convex back.
5295	01	Ceramic, porcelain	White	17mm × 5mm	Circular, 4 holed. 2-piece mold, glazed and fired. 6mm concavity. Flat rim, aspirin shaped. Convex back.
5296	01	Ceramic, porcelain	White	9mm × 3mm	Circular, 4 holed. 2-piece mold, glazed and fired. 9mm concavity with flat outer rim. Convex back.
5297	01	Ceramic, porcelain	Black	9mm × 3mm	Circular, 4 holed. 2-piece mold, glazed and fired. 5mm concavity. Rim slants to center. Convex back.
5298	01	Ceramic	White	11mm × 16mm	Circular ceramic gaiter button. 2-piece mold, meeting at back. While clay is still hot a brass plate and shank are pushed into back. Glazed, then fired. Convex doming front and convex back. Shank ends pass through 2-holed plate secured with solder.
5302	10	Glass	Black	19mm × 9mm	Irregular, opaque glass with brass-shanked buttons. Before the glass hardened, 3mm bent brass wire is pressed into glass. Buttons are roughly circular with flat front faces. Backs and side are convex. Often called charm buttons.
5339	25	Brass	Brass	6mm × 3mm	2-piece molded, circular, flat gaiter buttons with 2 parallel slits cut into center. The brass between slits is forced upward forming a shank. A molded domed top is crimped over shank.
5343	02	Textile	Brown/Black	21mm × 3mm	Flat-topped, circular, disc button. Flat tin bottom topped with felt and then fabric covered. The tin bottom is covered with a convex filler (cardboard).
5344	01	Textile	Brown	16mm × 3mm	High domed sphere with flat bottom. Dome top covered with checkered textile over a donut-shaped felt center held in place with a lacquered tin ring. The back is now missing.

* = Actual sample is missing from collection.

Figure 4.7. Buttons from the Atchison box. Photograph courtesy of DeSoto National Wildlife Refuge, U. S. Fish and wildlife Service, Missouri Valley, Iowa.

4.2.1.2. Adornment. *4.2.1.2a.* There were 818 unattached or loose *Beads* in the Atchison Box (Figure 4.9). The beads represent a variety of sizes, shapes, and colors and are classified as adornment in this case because they were probably purely decorative in nature and did not have a functional purpose. The loose beads may have been sewn on garments that did not survive; there is no way of establishing whether the beads came off three items, a single item, or ten. Nor is there any way of positively stating that identical beads were on the same garment although this is a likely assumption. Table 4.2 provides a partial description of the beads.

4.2.1.2b. Beadwork Fragment (Cat. #5349). A highly fragmentary piece of beadwork composed of textile, brass, glass, and feathers was found in the box. The piece consists of feather and fabric remains interlaced with beads in an indiscernible pattern. Portions of the beadwork indicate a combination of white glass

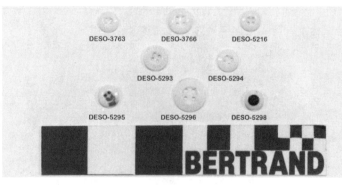

Figure 4.8. White china buttons from the Atchison box. Photograph courtesy of DeSoto National Wildlife Refuge, U. S. Fish and Wildlife Service, Missouri Valley, Iowa.

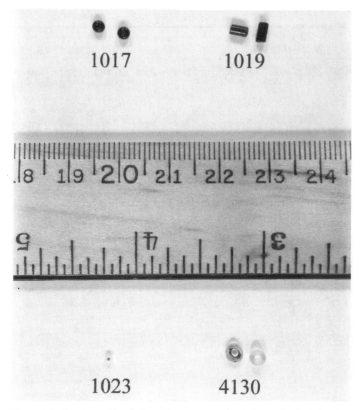

Figure 4.9. A variety of beads found loose among the Atchison family belongings.

and brass seed beads strung on brown wool thread. The white beads outnumber the brass beads two to one. Between these strings of beads were small, round, wire spring-like, beads strung on the same thread. Also found among the fabric, beads, and feathers were three longer, flat-braided wire spring beads.

4.2.1.3. Accessories. *4.2.1.3a. Umbrella Covering* (Cat. #3294). The Atchison box also contained an umbrella covering made of black silk. It is composed of seven identical triangular sections measuring 9 inches across the base edge and 14 inches across each angled side. All the pieces are still attached with machine-stitched seams. The umbrella rib attachment points are still visible, and the cloth exhibits extensive use and wear. The covering is badly rust stained, presumably from rusted and now disintegrated iron ribs or braces.

4.2.1.3b. Parasol (Cat. #4063). The Atchisons carried with them one complete parasol and several pieces of a second. The complete parasol is composed

Table 4.2. *Bertrand Box 74:* Beads

Catalog number	Number	Material	Color	Diameter × thickness	Description
1017	122	Glass	Black	3mm × 2mm	Circular, opaque beads with smooth round edges.
1018	23	Glass	Dark gray	2mm × 2mm	Circular, donut-shaped, opaque beads with smooth round ends.
1019	75	Glass	Red-brown	2mm × 5mm– 3mm length	Tubular beads with circular cross-section. Straight sides with flat ends. Iridescent patina. Appear opaque black but are transparent red-brown in the light.
1020	12	Glass	Black	3mm × 2mm	Same as #1017.
1021	10	Glass	Red-brown	2mm × 5mm– 3mm length	Same as #1019.
1022	04	Glass	Dark gray	2mm × 2mm	Sam as #1018.
1023	04	Glass	3 white 1 tan	2mm × 3mm	Flat, opaque circular beads in plan view, sides and ends are round and smooth.
3166	100	Glass	Gray	2mm × 2mm	Same as #1018. Found lying on fur wrap.
3166	30	Glass	Gray	2mm × 5mm– 3mm	Tubular beads with circular cross section. Straight sides with flat, rough, ends.
4130	325	Glass	203 black & 121 gray	1mm–3mm × 3mm	Flat, round seed beads. Sides are round, tops and bottoms are flat. Made by breaking off thin, hollow glass tubes. Gray beads are slightly smaller than black ones.
5351	1–3	Glass	Black to dark blue	2mm × 3mm– 6mm length	Circular beads with smooth sides. Ends are not uniform. Manufactured like #4130, using hollow glass tubes.

of wood, silk, brass, and steel. The parasol handle or "fit-up" is four pieces of carved wood with a total shaft length of 41 inches. In the umbrella trade, the central stick (handle today) was called a *fit-up,* which could be composed of single or multiple pieces. A number of ribs, usually eight, were attached to the fit-up. The ribs supported the cover and were in turn supported by stretchers from the central rib-centering ring or tubular runner where it runs up and down the fit-up (Farrell, 1985). In this example, the slender wooden shaft ends with a small, turban-shaped, brass cap. One inch below the brass cap is a U-shaped metal projection that kept the rib-centering ring from moving too far up the parasol shaft. Wooden ribs and a corresponding metal stabilizer helped to extend the parasol.

The parasol canopy consists of eight triangular sections, each with rounded, finished bottom edges. The parasol silk is brown and black and has a parallel striped pattern across each section. Each section has at least one tear in the silk, and some sections show signs of mending.

4.2.2. Household Utilization

4.2.2.1. Medicinal. *4.2.2.1a. Drake's Plantation Bitters* (Cat. #1789). A case containing twelve bottles of Drake's Plantation Bitters was in the Atchison box. The bottles measure 9 7/8 inches in height with base dimensions of 2 3/4 inches by 2 3/4 inches (Figure 4.10). All the bottles are nearly square, and amber colored and have a distinctive log cabin shape. The bottles are corked and contained 17 percent alcohol (Switzer, 1974:36–37). Drake's Plantation Bitters is St. Croix rum, which made its first appearance during the American Civil War (Carson, 1961).

4.2.2.2. Illumination Devices. *4.2.2.2a. Lamp Chimneys* (Cat. #1646, 1647). There were twelve clear glass, thick-walled lamp chimneys among the Atchisons' belongings (Figure 4.11). The lamps have a short flaring rim at the bottom, with a mid-bulge that reaches its maximum diameter near the base. The lamps taper near the top. On most chimneys, the top edges are thick, flat, and flared. Their height ranges from 7 1/4 inches to 7 7/8 inches, with a maximum diameter at the top flare of 2 7/8 inches. The chimneys are handblown and have few flaws or bubbles in the glass.

4.2.2.3. Rugs. *4.2.2.3a. Carpet Runner* (Cat. #2870). The box also contained a wool carpet runner measuring 26 feet 2 1/2 inches in length and 21 inches

Figure 4.10. Drakes' Plantation Bitters bottles (Cat. #1789) that were being carried into Montana by the Atchisons. Photograph courtesy of DeSoto National Wildlife Refuge, U. S. Fish and Wildlife Service, Missouri Valley, Iowa.

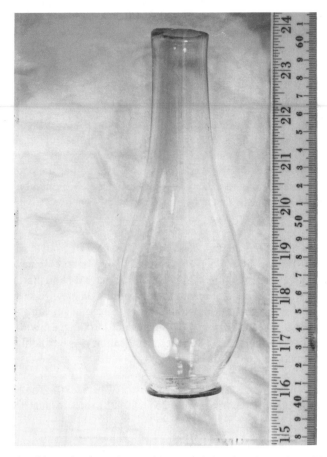

Figure 4.11. A handblown glass lamp chimney (Cat. #1646) found in the Atchisons' belongings. Photography courtesy of DeSoto National Wildlife Refuge, U. S. Fish and Wildlife Service, Missouri Valley, Iowa.

wide (Figure 4.12). The runner is thick and heavy with patterned lengthwise stripes in three colors: black, brown, and maroon.

4.2.2.4.   Linens.   *4.2.2.4a.   Table Cloth/Fabric Bolt* (Cat. #3295). A section of black and white wool fabric was found in Box 74. The piece measures 42 inches by 42 inches and has a pattern of parallel black stripes intersecting parallel stripes of black and white, making a checked pattern. There is no indication that the edges were ever finished. This square piece cannot be positively identified as a tablecloth as the museum catalogs it, but its shape makes this suggestion fea-

Figure 4.12. A wool carpet runner (Cat. #2870). Photograph courtesy of DeSoto National Wildlife Refuge, U. S. Fish and Wildlife Service, Missouri Valley, Iowa.

sible. Another possibility is that the piece was from a bolt of uncut fabric taken on the journey to be used at a later time.

4.2.2.5. Sewing Supplies. *4.2.2.5a. Straight Pins.* The box contained seventy-five brass and steel straight pins assigned to nine catalog numbers (Figure 4.13). The straight pins are considered sewing notions and are therefore household in nature. Table 4.3 provides a brief description of the straight pins.

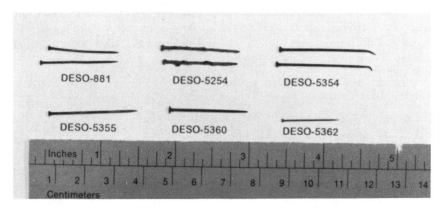

Figure 4.13. A variety of straight pins found among the Atchison belongings. Photograph courtesy of DeSoto National Wildlife Refuge, U. S. Fish and Wildlife Service, Missouri Valley, Iowa.

Table 4.3. *Bertrand* Box 74: Straight Pins

Catalog number	Number	Material	Dimensions	Description
881	02	Brass	2mm head dia. × 24mm– 28mm long	Pins have circular heads, convex in profile that slant slightly to a 1mm dia. pointed shaft.
5254	60	Steel	2mm × 28mm	Cast from single mold, poured from head. Slender 1mm diameter pointed shaft emerging from inverted conical head.
5255	02	Steel	3mm × 19mm	Description same as #5254.
5354	02	Brass	3mm × 36mm	Cast from single mold poured from head. Slender 1mm pointed shaft emerging from inverted conical domed head. Head has four striations radiating from center.
5355	02	Brass	3mm × 6mm	Description the same as #5354 except top of head is smooth.
5356	03	Brass	3mm × 27mm	Description same as #5355.
5360	01	Brass	3mm × 27mm	Made in 2-piece mold. Pointed 1mm dia. shaft and bottom portion of head in one mold. Domed conical head in 2nd mold. Mold marks appear around head circumference.
5361	02	Brass	3mm × 24mm	Description same as #5255.
5362	01	Brass	1mm × 23mm	Description same as #5255.

4.2.2.5b. Hooks and Eyes. Twenty-one loose hooks and seventeen loose eyes were found in the Atchison box (Figure 4.14). Like the beads, they were probably sewn on garments at one time. They were made of both iron and brass, and all are machine manufactured (Table 4.4).

4.2.2.5c. Brass Shoe Eyelets. (Cat. #5340). Thirteen brass shoe eyelets were also found in the box. They are donut-shaped rings with deep grooves around the outer circumference that attach them to a textile shoe quarter that did not survive because of differential preservation. The eyelets have a 5/16-inch outer diameter and are 1/8 inch thick.

4.2.3. Child Utilization

4.2.3.1. Toys. *4.2.3.1a. Alphabet Blocks* (Cat. #330). There were twelve flat, rectangular wooden alphabet blocks in the box (Figure 4.15). The blocks measure 1 13/16 inches by 15/16 inch per side and are 9/16 inch thick. The blocks are painted gray-green on one side and pale red on the opposite side. Black letters are painted on the top and bottom of each block. The letters A through M are painted on the gray sides, with N through Z on the red sides. All the blocks have one letter on each painted side except for the letters I and J, and Y and Z, which are paired on a single side. The letters are paired as follows: A on one side, N on

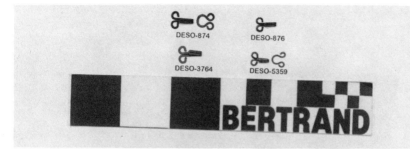

Figure 4.14. Various hooks and eyes that were found loose in the Atchison box. Photograph courtesy of DeSoto National Wildlife Refuge, U. S. Fish and Wildlife Service, Missouri Valley, Iowa.

the other; B/O; C/P; D/Q; E/R; F/S; G/T; H/U; I and J with V; K/W; L/X; and M with Y and Z.

4.2.3.1b. Alphabet Blocks (Cat. #72). Another set of twenty wooden blocks measuring 1 11/16 inches per side was also in the box. The blocks are painted pale red on the top and bottom and gray on the four sides. Each side has a painted border of small black squares that measure 1/16 inch by 1/16 inch and are spaced 1/4 inch apart. The blocks have letters, numbers, and Roman numerals painted on their surfaces in black block letters (Table 4.5).

Table 4.4. *Bertrand* Box 74: Hooks and Eyes

Catalog number	Number of hooks	Number of eyes	Material	Dimensions hooks/eyes	Description
874	09	15	Brass	12mm × 9mm 9mm × 9mm	Flat, machined brass hooks and eyes. Eyes are bent loops with the ends al most touching, then curved into small circles on either side. Hooks are same metal, folded double with each end separating to form a circle on either side of hook.
875	01	00	Brass	9mm × 3mm	Descriptions the same as #874 but smaller.
3764	02	00	Brass	9mm × 4mm	Machined, round wire hooks. Metal is folded double with ends separating to form circle on either side of hook. The wire making the hook is flattened.
5358	06	01	Iron	11mm × 24mm 9mm × 24mm	Description the same as #874 but finished with black lacquer.
5359	03	01	Brass	9mm × 24mm 24mm × 24mm	Description the same as #5358.

Figure 4.15. A sample of the various child's alphabet blocks (Cat. #330) found in this box. Displayed with the blocks is a tin toy pony and cart (Cat. #449) that shows signs of much use. Photograph courtesy of DeSoto National Wildlife Refuge, U. S. Fish and Wildlife Service, Missouri Valley, Iowa.

Table 4.5. *Bertrand* Box 74: Alphabet Blocks

Block	Top	1	2	3	4	Bottom
1	A	9	—	O	Z	F
2	B	S	—	X	M	H
3	C	—	M	E	X	T
4	D	A	B	C	—	E
5	E	—	1	Y	M	U
6	G	C	7	1	S	L
7	H	T	O	N	R	D
8	I	U	VI	N	—	G
9	J	F	2	H	G	I
10	K	C	—	J	O	—
11	L	P	W	B	—	Q
12	N	—	M	L	3	O
13	O	K	—	G	9	E
14	P	E	VIII	K	F	W
15	Q	T	IX	D	I	P
16	R	P	Q	S	4	T
17	S	J	III	T	—	Y
18	T	H	E	N	—	W
19	V	—	VII	R	H	L
20	Y	U	5	N	—	W

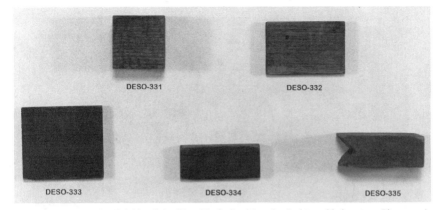

DESO-331   DESO-332

DESO-333   DESO-334   DESO-335

Figure 4.16. A sample of children's building blocks found in the Atchisons' belongings. Photograph courtesy of DeSoto National Wildlfe Refuge, U. S. Fish and Wildlife Service, Missouri Valley, Iowa.

4.2.3.1c. There are several sets of building blocks in the Atchisons' belongings (Figure 4.16). *Building Blocks* (Cat. #331) represent four blocks 7/8 inch on a side. The blocks are made of lightweight wood. Two sides are painted pale red, two sides are gray, and the remaining sides are not painted.

4.2.3.1d. Building Blocks (Cat. #332). Two flat rectangular blocks of lightweight wood compose a second set of blocks. On each block, three of the four sides are painted a dark red-brown. One block has this color streaked across a portion of one face. The remaining sides and faces are uncolored. The blocks measure 1 7/16 inches by 15/16 inch by 1/4 inch.

4.2.3.1e. Building Blocks (Cat. #333). This catalog number contains two flat rectangular blocks of light weight wood similar to Cat. #332. The blocks are dark red-brown on one face and on three sides. The remaining side and face are uncolored. Each uncolored face has a colored streak across the face. The blocks measure ·1 7/16 inches by 1 1/4 inches and are 1/4 inch thick.

4.2.3.1f. Building Blocks (Cat. #334). This number contains two red-brown rectangular blocks made of lightweight wood. All surfaces are colored except for one face and one long side each. The blocks measure 1 1/2 inches to 1 7/16 inch in length; they are 9/16 inch wide and 1/4 inch thick.

4.2.3.1g. Building Block (Cat. #335). This number represents one pale red rectangular block with a sharp V shaped end. The block measures 1 1/2 inches by 1 1/8 inches by 9/16 inch. The V is 1/4 inch deep and not painted. This piece may have been a chimney for a toy block house. Catalog # 332, 333, 334, and possibly 335 may have made up a single set of blocks. The color scheme supports this assumption when compared with the other sets of blocks.

4.2.3.1h. School Building Blocks (Cat. #107). This remarkable set of blocks includes thirty lightweight wood building blocks (Figure 4.17). The blocks are painted gray on one side and pale red on the other. They have black building

Figure 4.17. A remarkable set of child's blocks. These schoolhouse blocks (Cat. #107) might have been a favorite of the Atchison children, evidenced by the amount of wear on the blocks. Photograph courtesy of DeSoto National Wildlife Refuge, U. S. Fish and Wildlife Service, Missouri Valley, Iowa.

patterns on both sides. The blocks make a reversible building without a roof. Twenty-four rectangular blocks measure 1 13/16 inches by 9/16 inch by 5/8 inch. Of the twenty-four blocks, sixteen are building sides, while eight are building ends. The set also contains four rectangular corner posts measuring 3 11/16 inches by 13/16 inch by 13/16 inch; two are painted red, the other two gray. Two blocks are triangular gables that measure 5/8 inch by 5 3/8 inches by 3 13/16 inches. The red gable face has "HILL'S" painted over three small windows with Gothic arches and "UNION COLLEGE" beneath the windows. The gray gable face has "HILL'S" painted over a window section with "VILLAGE SCHOOL" beneath the windows. There are nail holes on either side of the gable edge.

The school blocks were associated with a *wooden box* (Cat. # 899). The box measures 10 7/8 inches by 8 1/8 inches by 2 inches. The bottom of the box is nailed to the sides with small machine-cut nails. The top slides in routed grooves along the inside upper edge of the side pieces.

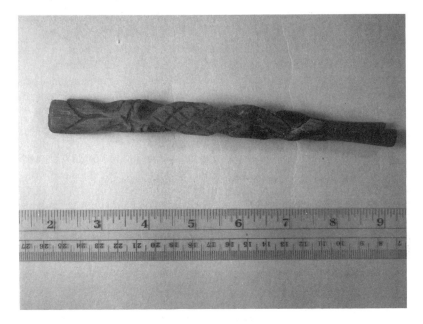

Figure 4.18. The wooden whistle (Cat. #982) seems delicately hand carved. Photograph courtesy of DeSoto National Wildlife Refuge, U. S. Fish and Wildlife Service, Missouri Valley, Iowa.

4.2.3.1i. Wooden Whistle (Cat. #982). The box contained a hand-carved wooden whistle (Figure 4.18) measuring 7 1/4 inches in length. The whistle is in five pieces and has warped from a combination of extended emersion and conservation in acetone. The whistle is cylindrical and curved from end to end.

4.2.3.1j. Pony Cart (Cat. #449). The Atchisons brought along a tin trotting pony attached to a two-wheeled tin cart (Figure 4.15). The pony is cut from two pieces of tin, each forming a side, fastened together along the midline to give the pony a three-dimensional shape. The pony (4 inches long by 2 3/4 inches high) is painted dark gray with spots of red-orange paint along the back and nose. The cart is made by folding up the sides of a piece of sheet tin. The cart measures 2 1/2 inches wide across the top of the sides and 3 1/4 inches in length. A 1/2-inch-wide strip is attached horizontally along the bottom to connect the wheels. Only one wheel (measuring 1 5/8 inches in diameter with eight spokes), not attached, was present at the time of excavation. The cart is thin and heavily rusted. The back end of the cart has an irregular shape, which may indicate it was once longer. The outside of the cart is painted red-orange, and this toy appears well used. There are several dents in the tin as well as several gouges or scrapes in the .metal.

4.3. CONCLUSION

Archaeologically, this box indicates the presence of at least one adult woman and one male child. The size of the boy's clothing suggests an age of four or five. The abundance of toys in the box may indicate the presence of another child. The silk clothing in combination with well-worn woolen garments may be indicative of an upper middle class family unit.

Noticeably missing from this box are ceramics, cooking utensils, pots, and pans; and there are few sewing notions. Ceramics of all kinds were available at supply houses as were cooking items so that these heavy and often fragile items may have been left behind. It is unlikely that these items were sent ahead with Mr. Atchison. Sewing supplies and items such as hairbrushes, cosmetics, and other personal items were probably packed in a bag carried on board with Mrs. Atchison. The archaeological information is supported by the historical information, which verifies that Mrs. Atchison was traveling with a son.

Chapter 5

Bertrand FPC-8

Bertrand box FPC-8 was excavated between August 11 and August 17, 1969, from the forward cargo spaces on the port side. The box measured 34 inches by 32 inches by 16 inches and contained several smaller boxes. The box was marked "J. A. CAMPBELL" (the A may have been misread; it should be J. B.).

5.1. ANNIE AND FANNIE CAMPBELL

Box FPC-8 is attributed to Annie and Fannie Campbell (Figures 5.1 and 5.2), daughters of James B. and Sarah (Kaen) Campbell. James Blackstone Campbell moved his wife and four children from Chicago to St. Louis in 1855. Three Campbell sisters, Helen, Annie, and Fannie, were placed in a Catholic boarding school in the St. Charles area. In 1862, Mr. and Mrs. Campbell, their son Gurdon, and daughter Helen, left St. Louis for Montana Territory. Fannie and Annie were left in the convent school; they would join the family after they completed school. In 1865, Annie, age 19, and Fannie, age 16, left for Montana on the *Bertrand* (Moss, 1963; Petsche, 1982).

5.2. FPC-8 ARTIFACTS

5.2.1. Personal Utilization

5.2.1.1. Clothing and Footwear. *5.2.1.1a. Silk Cape* (Cat. #2918). A black and brown lady's circular silk cape was found in the Campbell sisters' box. The cape is in poor condition and in many pieces (Figure 5.3). After cleaning and drying, the cape pieces were attached to laminate. Originally the cape was composed of ten vertically oriented sections. Exact dimensions are not available be-

Figure 5.1. *Betrand* passenger Annie Campbell. Photograph courtesy of the Three Forks Historical Society, Montana.

Figure 5.2. Annie's younger sister Fannie Campbell, who also traveled on the ill-fated *Bertrand*. Photo courtesy of the Three Forks Historical Society, Montana.

cause of the cape's fragmentary nature. Extra fabric at the back of the neck may indicate the garment had an attached hood at one time. There is evidence of a 1 3/4-inch brown wool edging along the bottom of the cape.

    5.2.1.1b. Silk Coat (Cat. #2965). The box contained a highly decorative lady's black silk overcoat. The coat is 47 inches long and is composed of eleven pieces (Figures 5.4 and 5.5). The coat is semifitted through the body with a widely flaring skirt. It has a simple Peter Pan style collar measuring 2 inches wide. The back of the collar is slightly rounded with a triangular shape at the center, which mea-

Figure 5.3. A black silk cape (Cat. #2918) found among the Campbell sisters' belongings on the *Bertrand*. Illustration courtesy of Desoto National Wildlife Serivce, U. S. Fish and Wildlife Serivce, Missouri Valley, Iowa.

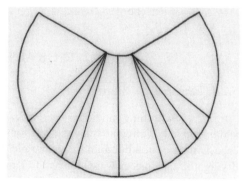

Figure 5.4. The Campbell black silk coat (Cat. #2965) is one of the finest textile pieces in the entire *Bertrand* collection. Photograph courtesy of DeSoto National Wildlife Refuge, U. S. Fish and Wildlife Service, Missouri Valley, Iowa.

sures 3 1/2 inches at the widest point. The outer edges of the collar are edged with 1/4-inch black piping.

The bodice of the coat is highly decorative. An upside-down pear-shaped applique is sewn on the front with one half of the applique on either side of the bodice. The applique starts at the base of the collar and is 14 inches in overall length. The outside edges of the applique are finished with piping. The applique is further decorated with small cloth-covered buttons (see button description). There are three additional buttons sewn along a piping seam on either side of the applique. Two decorative pockets are attached to the front of the skirt. Each pocket is placed 21 1/2 inches above the front hem, and both are decorated with a plain 1-inch silk button stitched at the apex of the pocket flaps. This silk garment was

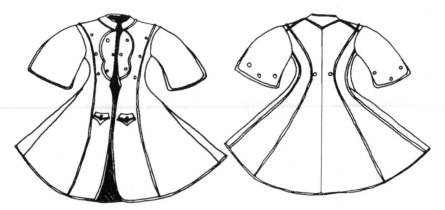

Figure 5.5. A line drawing of the Campbell coat (Cat. #2965) that shows detail not visible in the photograph. Illustration courtesy of DeSoto National Wildlife Refuge, U. S. Fish and Wildlife Service, Missouri Valley, Iowa.

machine sewn and as evidenced by the elaborate decoration was probably very expensive. It was found inside a black-lacquered Chinese box (Cat. #142).

5.2.1.1c. Gloves (Cat. #3698). Three small, child's size, brown wool gloves (Figure 5.6) were found in the box. All three gloves are made in the same style.

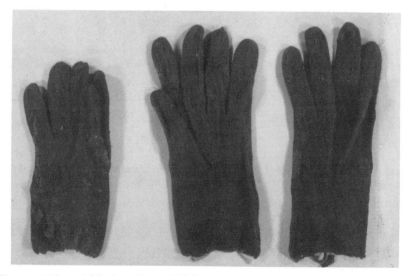

Figure 5.6. Three child's gloves (Cat. #3698) found in the Campbell box. Photography courtesy of DeSoto National Wildlife Refuge, U. S. Fish and Wildlife Service, Missouri Valley, Iowa.

One left glove measures 4 7/8 inches in length, and the other two were a pair 6 inches in length from the wrist to the longest fingertip. The glove wrists are edged in elastic with a seam running from the wrist to the tip of the little finger with additional seams along the inside edge of each finger. The back of each glove is decorated with three stitched vertical lines. These seem to be heavy, everyday-wear gloves.

5.2.1.1d. Wrist Warmer Cuff (Cat. #2915). This is a single, knitted wrist warmer cuff made of brown wool (Figure 5.7). The cuff is closely knit, with the top portion more loosely knit and displaying a knit, purl, knit pattern. On the inside of the cuff, three rows of crossstitches are worked over two ribs each to prevent the cuff from stretching. The cuff measures 7 inches in length, 3 inches in width at the narrowest point, and 5 3/4 inches at the widest point.

5.2.1.1e. Girl's Mitt (Cat. #2912). One black silk crocheted mitt was also in the box. The mitt is crocheted in a diamond-shaped mesh and has four different designs across the back of the hand. There are three rows of hearts, an intertwined circular design below the hearts, and a four-petal flower design below the circles with a wider intertwined circular design below the flowers. The mitt has gathered elastic at the wrist. It measures 3 1/8 inches by 3 4/8 inches (Figure 5.7). During this period, black net or crocheted mitts or mittens were commonly worn with semiformal evening dress (Cumming, 1982).

5.2.1.1f. Dress (School Uniform) (Cat. #2846). Two identical blue wool

Figure 5.7. The box also contained a girl's wrist warmer cuff (Cat. #2915), a girl's hand mitt (Cat. #2912), and blue silk ribbons associated with the girls' school uniforms (Cat. #2846). Photograph courtesy of DeSoto National Wildlife Refuge, U. S. Fish and Wildlife Service, Missouri Valley, Iowa.

dresses were found in the box. Each dress consists of a bodice, sleeves, and skirt each made of several pieces. Each dress has a single-piece bodice with six pleats. The bodice fronts are in two pieces. Each opens down the middlefront; there are five buttonholes down the left front, but no buttons are attached. The bodices have a single waistband 1 1/2 inches wide, which will accommodate a 23-inch waist. The band is not attached to the skirt and appears to have been worn over the skirt rather than attached to the skirt. The skirts are composed of four sections measuring 36 inches from selvage to selvage and 34 inches from the waist to the bottom of the finished hem.

The dresses exhibit extensive wear. They have bleach and sweat stains and are mended in several places. The dresses may have been passed down from one wearer to another and were probably altered in size each time they were given to a new owner or were passed from girl to girl as they were outgrown. Because there are two of these dresses and it is known that the Campbell girls were traveling from a boarding school, a likely assumption is that these are the girls' school uniforms.

5.2.1.1g. Leather Shoes (Cat. #87). One pair of high laced black leather shoes was in the box (Figure 5.8). The shoes have ten pairs of brass eyelets 1/4

Figure 5.8. A pair of high laced black leather boots (Cat. #87) found among the sisters' belongings. Photograph courtesy of DeSoto National Wildlife Refuge, U. S. Fish and Wildlife Service, Missouri Valley, Iowa.

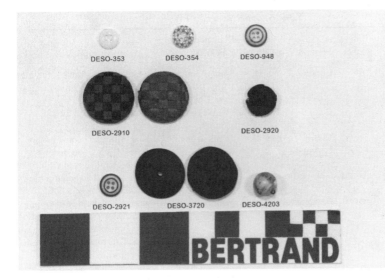

Figure 5.9. A variety of buttons found loose in the Campbell box. Photograph courtesy of DeSoto National Wildlife Refuge, U. S. Fish and Wildlife Service, Missouri Valley, Iowa.

inch in diameter. The eyelet row is 1/2 inch wide with a thin leather strip on either side of the thicker body of the shoe.

5.2.1.1.h. There were 118 unattached Buttons and twenty-one buttons still sewn to the black silk coat. The buttons are made of glass, wood, ceramic, and textile (Figure 5.9) in a variety of styles, sizes, colors, and textures (Table 5.1).

5.2.1.2. Adornment. *5.2.1.2a. Hat Pins* (Cat. #725). Two gilt brass hat pins 5 3/16 inches long adorned with hollow ornamental balls were found among the girls' belongings. The two pins are similar except that one has a round ball 1 inch in diameter and the other has an oval ball 1 1/8 inch high by 7/8 inch wide (Figure 5.10).

5.2.1.2b. Beads. There were 131 unattached glass beads (Figure 5.11) of various sizes and shapes in the Campbell box (Table 5.2).

5.2.1.3. Body Ritual and Grooming. *5.2.1.3a. Toiletry Vials* (Cat. # 710, 711, 712). There were twenty-one clear glass toiletry vials in the Campbell box. The vials have flat bases, cylindrical bodies, and slightly constricted necks with flared lips (Figure 5.12). The vials represented three types and varied in size and capacity (Table 5.3). These vials were still corked when found, and their contents were identified as perfume (Switzer, 1974). These vials were associated with a jewelry box (Cat. #148).

Table 5.1. *Bertrand* Box FPC-8: Buttons

Catalog number	Total number	Material	Color	Diameter × thickness	Description
353	66	Ceramic	White	9mm × 3mm	Circular, 4 holed chinas set in a 5mm concavity. Front slants to 1mm edge. Convex back.
354	22	Ceramic	Turquoise	9mm–11mm × 3mm	Same as #353 except for color.
933	21	Textile/ wood	Black	26mm × 6mm	Circular with planoconvex wood centers. Each wood disk has a hole in its center. Covered with tightly woven silk and gathered at back with wool thread.
948	01	Ceramic	White/ red	11mm × 4mm	Circular, 4-holed china with 6mm con cavity. Front slants to 2mm. Convex back. 2 circular bands of red trim.
2910	19	Textile	Brown/ black	26mm × 10mm	Circular, flat, round edge buttons. Covered with silk in a checkered pattern. 3 alternate brown and black squares, 16 are all brown. Cardboard backs covered with lacquer.
2920	06	Textile	Black	16mm × 3mm	Circular, silk covered. Pattern of diamond inside a square. There are triangles in the middle of the diamonds with a tight checked pattern. Cardboard backs.
2921	01	Ceramic	White/ brown	11mm × 4mm	Same as #948 except with brown trim instead of red.
3720	02	Textile/ wood	Black	26mm × 6mm	Same as #933. Covered with silk.
4203	01	Glass	White	1mm diameter	Spherical white glass with brown surface paint. Has metal shank.

5.2.2. Household Utilization

5.2.2.1. Decorative Items. *5.2.2.1a. Glass Heart* (Cat. #4033). A tiny, transparent, yellow-green glass heart measuring 3/8 inch by 1/2 inch by 5/16 inch was in the box. The top face of the heart is slightly smaller than the bottom face. The top face has a frosted appearance caused by minute striations. Both faces have beveled edges and "YOURS / TRULY" is incised backward on a center diagonal in Roman boldface type on the bottom face (Figure 5.13). The words are meant to be read through the upper face. The heart is slightly longer on one side than the other.

5.2.2.2. Containers. *5.2.2.2a. Jewelry Box* (Cat. #148). A small (7 3/4 inches by 5 1/16 inches by 3 5/16 inches) rectangular jewelry box was also found

Figure 5.10. Two intricately designed brass hat pins (Cat. #725), one of the finer pieces of adornment found in the *Bertrand* collection. Photograph courtesy of DeSoto National Wildlife Refuge, U. S. Fish and Wildlife Service, Missouri Valley, Iowa.

Table 5.2. *Bertrand* Box FPC-8: Beads

Catalog number	Number	Material	Color	Dimensions	Description
1041	01	Glass	Black	16mm × 15mm	Spherical with flat ends, covered with black paint.
1042	39	Glass	Black	3mm × 2mm	Circular, opaque, donut shaped with round edges. Same as #1017.
1043	27	Glass	Black	2mm × 5mm–3mm length	Tubular beads with circular cross-section. Straight sides with flat ends. Iridescent patina. Appear opaque black but are transparent red-brown in the light. Same as #1019.
2911	64	Glass	Black/gray	round: 9mm & 3mm tubular: 5mm diameter	37 are opaque, donut shaped, and black in 2 dia. 9mm & 3mm. 24 are circular and tubular with ends broken off. Some are gray and some black.

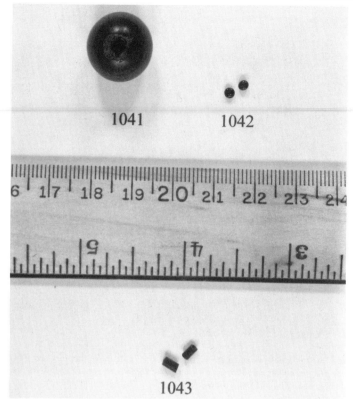

Figure 5.11. Like the Atchison box, a variety of loose beads was found in the Campbell sisters' packing crate. Photography courtesy of the author.

in the Campbell box (Figure 5.14). The lid is attached with two yellow brass hinges (Cat. #745). The hinge plates measure 3/8 inch by 5/8 inch with a hinge shaft 5/32 inch in diameter. The lid top has a recessed, flat-bottomed circle 5/8 inch in diameter in the center of the lid. Each corner of the lid has a similar circle 3/8 inch in diameter. The four corner circles are connected by a groove to form a rectangle with circles at the corners. The box lid is covered with a piece of black veneer. The circular holes and groove are not covered by the veneer. The box has a small *circular lock,* 5/8 inch in diameter, on its front face (Cat. #747). The lock plate is an L-shaped yellow brass plate with a steel locking mechanism.

The box contains a small rectangular *tray* (Cat. #147) made of smoothly finished, fine-grained, light brown wood. The tray has a single bottom piece 5 9/16 inches by 3 1/2 inches by 1/16 inch and four side pieces 5 7/16 inches and 3 7/16 inches in length. The ends of the tray sides are beveled to produce finished mitered corners. Catalog numbers 454 and 875 are thin sheets or strips of thin wood.

Figure 5.12. Three sizes of glass toiletry vials (Cat. #710, 711, and 712) found to contain perfume. Photograph courtesy of DeSoto National Wildlife Refuge, U. S. Fish and Wildlife Service, Missouri Valley, Iowa.

These pieces are associated with the jewelry box and may represent another divided tray. Some pieces are fragmentary, and the configuration is only speculative.

    5.2.2.2b. Black Chinese Box (Cat. # 142). A black lacquered box with Chinese characters painted on both the inside and outside was in the Campbell shipping crate (Figure 5.15). The box measures 14 1/8 inches by 9 3/4 inches by 11 inches. The lid, base, and four sides are each made of three boards. The corners are dovetailed and nailed through each tenon (except those at the very bottom). The *nails* (Cat. #700 and 999) are cut nails tapering to the tip.

Table 5.3. *Bertrand* Box FPC-8: Toiletry Vials

Vial type	Number	Total height	Base diameter	Neck diameter inside/outside	Capacity
Type 1	17	1 3/8"	3/8"	1/4" / 7/16"	0.1 oz.
Subtype 1a	02	2 3/8"	5/8"	3/8" / 5/8"	0.3 oz.
Subtype 1b	02	1 3/8"	5/16"	1/4" / 3/8"	0.07 oz.

Figure 5.13. Perhaps a parting gift from a sweetheart? The Campbell box contained a tiny frosted glass heart (Cat. #4033) that has raised much speculation about its meaning. Photograph courtesy of DeSoto National Wildlife Refuge, U. S. Fish and Wildlife Service, Missouri Valley, Iowa.

The box has a *lock* (Cat. #746) on the front center with a small keyhole cut through the wood. The lock is housed behind a rectangular yellow brass plate that measures 1 1/2 inches long by 15/16 inch wide. The steel locking mechanism is semicircular in shape and situated in the middle of the brass plate. The mechanism is 1/4 inch long and 3/32 inch in diameter.

Figure 5.14. The Campbell sisters' packing box contained several smaller boxes or containers, identified as a jewelry box (Cat. #148). Photograph courtesy of DeSoto National Wildlife Refuge, U. S. Fish and Wildlife Service, Missouri Valley, Iowa.

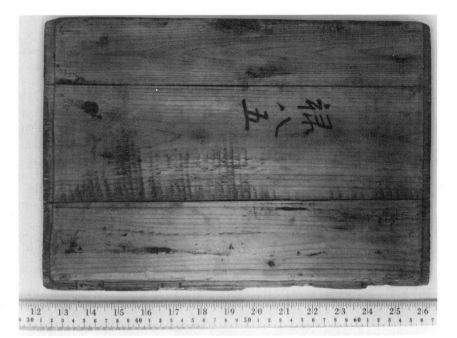

Figure 5.15. Another small container in the larger Campbell packing crate was a black lacquered Chinese box (Cat. #142). This photograph shows writing on the inside of one of the box sides. Photograph courtesy of DeSoto National Wildlife Refuge, U. S. Fish and Wildlife Service, Missouri Valley, Iowa.

A flat lid attached with four rectangular yellow brass hinges (Cat. #744) serves as the top. Each hinge has four 3/16-inch-diameter holes on either side of the hinge that is attached with a center pin. The hinge edges are beveled. The lid closes flush with all four top edges of the box.

Three Chinese characters are painted on the inside of the lid and on the front of the box under the lock. The characters were identified as the numerals 6, 8, and 5 (Fontenoy, 1995). There are also several pieces of loose *black lacquer* (Cat. #906) with Chinese writing, which were removed from the box because of their fragile state. The pieces are black with a red and gilt border consisting of two parallel lines. The black silk coat (Cat. #2965) was found in this box.

5.2.2.2c. Green Chinese Box (Cat. #3915) A tall, green, rectangular box with dovetailed corners was also in the shipping crate. The boards are connected to each other by means of two 1/8-inch-diameter wooden pegs inserted in the top and bottom of each joint. The joints are made solid by cut nails. The box sides and top are painted deep green with a square red outline 1/8 inch wide starting 1 5/8 inches from each edge. The box's outer edges are painted with a black square border 1 1/4 inches wide. The lid, painted like the box sides, has large Chinese characters painted on it. There are four words or meaningful groups on the box lid. The first two were identified as KING and FATHER. The second two were not identifiable owing to their fragmentary nature (Ostasien, 1983). The box bottom is plain and unpainted. The box is 16 7/8 inches long, 16 7/8 inches wide, and 18 3/8 inches tall.

The two Chinese boxes are unique in this collection. Petsche suggested that the boxes were associated with a servant traveling with the girls, but there is no documentary evidence to support this assumption (Petsche, 1974). In my opinion, there was no logical reason for the girls to have a servant while attending school.

5.2.2.3. Ritual. *5.2.2.3a. Bible Cover* (Cat. #146). A hand-tooled leather bible cover was found in the box. The rectangular cover is stained dark brown and has mitered corners. The spine of the cover (11 3/8 inches by 7 3/8 inches) is 2 1/4 inches wide and has "HOLY BIBLE" stamped horizontally in 1/4-inch gilt letters. The spine also has five rectangular panels with simple floral and scroll figures on a stippled background. The front and back of the cover are finely tooled in a symmetrical foliage pattern on a stippled background (Figure 5.16).

Figure 5.16. An ornate bible cover (Cat. #741) found among the Campbell sisters' belongings. Photograph courtesy of DeSoto National Wildife Refuge, U. S. Fish and Wildlife Service, Missouri Valley, Iowa.

5.2.2.4. Sewing Supplies. *5.2.2.4a. Leather Packet* (Cat. #741). This item is a thin, brown leather packet, which may have been a billfold or a sewing kit (Figures 5.17 and 5.18). The piece has small stitch holes along all edges and is in two pieces. The small piece is rectangular and measures 3 7/16 inches long by 2 7/8–2 3/4 inches wide. The larger piece has straight parallel sides, one square end, and one end that is triangular with the top squared off. This piece is 10 7/16 inches long and 3 7/16–3 5/16 inches wide. This item is lined with deteriorated fabric. The smaller piece may have been sewn onto the squared end of the rectangular piece to form a pocket. The billfold would be folded, forming a square with the triangular end serving as the front flap. The piece may also have been a "housewife" or compact sewing kit.

5.2.2.4b. Hooks and Eyes (Cat. #2922). There were seventeen brass hooks and nineteen brass eyes found loose in the Campbell box (Figure 5.19). Both the hooks and eyes are made of flat, bent wire. The eyes are U-shaped curves with both ends curved outward forming loops. The hooks are made by doubling over the wire and then bending a portion back. Like the eyes, the ends of the hooks are

Figure 5.17. A leather billfold (Cat. #741), inside view. Photograph courtesy of DeSoto National Wildlife Refuge, U. S. Fish and Wildlife Service, Missouri Valley, Iowa.

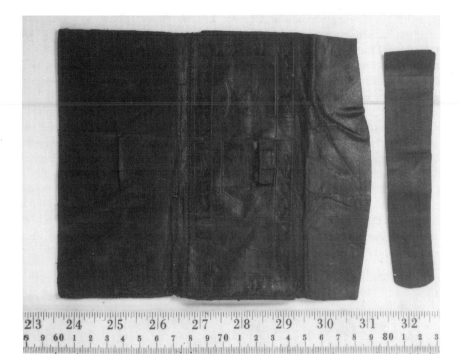

Figure 5.18. Outside view of the leather billfold (Cat. #741). Note the design work on what would be the front surface of the folded packet. Photography courtesy of DeSoto National Wildlife Refuge, U. S. Fish and Wildlife Service, Missouri Valley, Iowa.

bent to form loops on either side of the hook. The hooks are 5/16–1/2 inch long, and the eyes are 3/16–1/4 inch wide.

    5.2.2.4c. Straight Pins (Cat. #s 1206 and 2923). There were sixty-seven brass straight pins associated with this box. The pins ranged in size from 13/16 inch to 1 3/16 inches in length (Figure 5.19). They have sharp pointed shafts with domed circular heads. The lower edges of the head slant slightly toward the shaft. Mold seams at the top of the head indicate that they were made in a one-piece mold.

    5.2.2.5. Miscellaneous.   5.2.2.5a. *Reed Mat* (Cat. #145). A circular reed mat measuring 5 3/8 inches in diameter was also found in the Campbell box. It has sixteen radiating ribs 1/16 inch thick, which cross the center with four ribs crossing on either side at right angles by four other ribs. The ribs are woven with a simple over/under pattern with a single strand of lighter reed material. This item has not been identified. It may be a center to a larger piece, possibly a basket bottom.

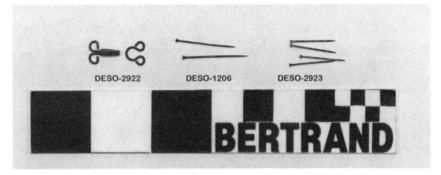

DESO-2922   DESO-1206   DESO-2923

BERTRAND

Figure 5.19. Like the numerous buttons and beads found loose in the Campbell box, there were also many loose hooks and eyes and straight pins (Cat. #2922, 1206, and 2923) among the other artifacts. Photograph courtesy of DeSoto National Wildlife Refuge, U. S. Fish and Wildlife Service, Missouri Valley, Iowa.

5.2.3. Child Utilization

5.2.3.1. Educational Supplies. *5.2.3.1a. World Map* (Cat. #1843) A 19-by-29-inch map of an unknown place was found in the box. The paper map is attached to a piece of blue-green plate glass. The paper is brown and tan with some green- and red-checkered patterning in places. The map has a brown leaf border along its edge. "DIA" is printed to the right of the map center. The map has many solid and dotted lines along its surface. The map was broken and may have been in several large pieces when packed in the box. It is possible that this is a portion of a map of India.

5.2.3.1b. Artist's Pastels (Cat. #738). Eighty-three loose sticks of artist's pastels were found in the crate. The pastels are dark gray in color and square in cross-section. The lengths varied depending on wear; the unused sticks had lengths from 2 5/8 inches to 2 7/8 inches. There are two different manufacturers represented: LEMOINE NO. 1 (also No. 3) and CONTE A PARIS N. 1 (also N. 2 and N. 3) with the numbers referring to the degree of hardness (Johnson, 1994).

5.2.3.1c. School Slate (Cat. # 150). A rectangular school slate made of thin plate steel covered on both sides with black lacquer was in the crate. The steel plate measures 10 1/16 inches by 7 5/16 inches. The slate has a simple wooden frame made of four pieces (11 5/8 inches by 1 inch and 8 13/16 inches by 1 inch). Cut lightly into the top of the frame was FANN_E[2] in letters 5/16 inch high (Figure 5.20).

---

[2]Two types of abbreviations are used in this study: A dash (_) is used to indicate an unidentifiable or missing letter in a marking. If a letter is present but questionable, it is enclosed in parenthesis (x).

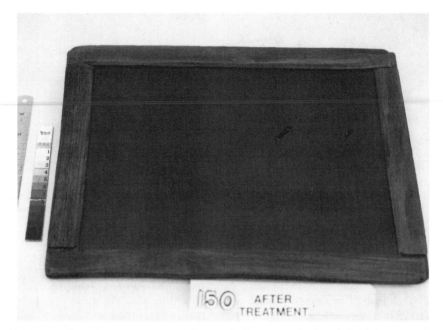

Figure 5.20. Despite newspaper accounts that specifically mention the Campbell girls by name, we would have known that someone named Fannie lost belongings on the *Bertrand*. Although barely visible in the photography, the name FANNIE is scratched into the top of this school slate (Cat. #150).

5.2.3.1d. Book Bindings. Several leather book bindings were found in the packing crate. None of the bindings was attached to pages. A *Music Book Binding* (Cat. #144) 13 1/2 inches long and 3 1/2 inches wide with a 15/16-inch-wide spine was found. The spine is divided into six horizontal sections by raised gilt ridges. The gilt word "MUSIC" (1/4 inch tall) is stamped on the binding.

A second book binding, *Herbarium Book Binding* (Cat. #482), measures 17 1/2 inches long and is 4 1/4 inches wide. It accommodates a book that is 15 1/2 inches by 1 1/8 inches, discernable by fold marks left by the book. The spine has eleven horizontal gilt lines across it. Printed vertically in 3/16-inch gilt letters is the word "HERBARIUM."

Book Back Binding (Cat. #483). There was one book binding with no printed title. It measures 7 5/16 inches by 2 1/8 inches wide . It once accommodated a book that measured 6 1/4 inches by 7/8 inch wide. The binding is decorated with four panels divided by pairs of raised lines.

Geography Book Binding (Cat. #484). This book binding was well used. It has numerous holes and tears in the leather. The binding measures 7 3/8 inches high and 2 1/4 inches wide. The binding once accommodated a book measuring 6 1/4 inches by 1 1/4 inches. "MITCHELL'S/SCHOOL/GEOGRAPHY" is printed horizontally in 3/16-inch gilt letters in a square panel on the binding top. The letters "H. [C]. & CO." appear in raised letters along the bottom of the binding.

5.2.3.1.e. Leather Book Cover (Cat. #485). One complete leather book cover was also in the Campbell sisters' packing crate. The book cover is rectangular with one square end and one end with a flap. It has long straight sides measuring 11 3/16 inches long and 5 7/8 inches wide. The cover is divided into five decorative panels by groups of narrow lines stamped vertically into the leather. The cover has a stippled background surface and a heavily stamped scrolled pattern covers its entire surface.

5.3. CONCLUSION

Archaeologically, this box suggests the presence of at least one adult woman. The large number of school supplies suggests a child might be present, but the lack of child's clothing and toys such as those found in the Atchison box make this assumption less viable. When the archaeological evidence is compared with the historical documentation, the items in the box are less of a mystery.

The two dresses were probably the Campbell sisters' school uniforms. The girls' ages for the time period would be considered adult. The abundance of school supplies is explained by the fact that the girls were traveling from boarding school.

The two Chinese or oriental boxes are significant in this artifact set. There is no evidence that the Campbell sisters were traveling with anyone, and there are no other items in the collection to suggest the presence of an individual of Chinese origin. It was, however, trendy in the nineteenth century for upper middle class and wealthy individuals to collect oriental decorative objects.

The collection of oriental objects by wealthy Europeans was well developed by the sixteenth century. By the eighteenth and nineteenth centuries, the European market for original art as well as copies of oriental objects was well established. This fascination with Eastern materials was called *chinoiserie* and included objects of Chinese, Japanese, Far Eastern, and eastern Egyptian origin. By the late eighteenth century, Far Eastern countries established trade houses solely for the purpose of exporting goods to Europe and then to the United States. Items that were collected included furniture, textiles, paintings, and ceramics; architecture was also copied (Honour, 1961; Impey, 1977). The presence of two chinoiserie boxes suggests that the Campbell sisters had a means above the average for the time.

Chapter 6

Bertrand MSC-128

Bertrand box MSC-128 was excavated between August 24 and August 30, 1969, from the midships cargo section, starboard side. There are no measurements available for this box. The box pieces were discarded with few records taken. The box was marked:

UNW

With painted scrawl on the other side of this face:

S_ _ IO_ _

On the opposite side of the box:

1 _ _

ROBT. CAM(B)_ _ _ _

_ _ ES _ O

PL _ _ _ AD

6.1. ROBERT CAMPBELL AND COMPANY

This box was probably being shipped to Robert Campbell and Company. Robert Campbell was a successful fur trader in the Rocky Mountain–Upper Missouri region during the 1820s and 1830s. Campbell provided financial support for several fur trading expeditions that competed with the American Fur Company. By 1845, he had established several outfitting houses serving Indian country traders. Later he became a respected businessman in the Rocky Mountain region and

71

established a dry goods and Indian goods store on Main Street in St. Louis (Sunder, 1965). Several times, the *Bertrand* carried goods to Campbell's supply houses in the Montana Territory. Campbell was heavily involved with supplying Indian annuities and handling furs and camp supplies for several groups. It is not improbable that boxes were to be shipped to Fort Benton in Campbell's charge.

It was originally assumed that this box was going to a Campbell supply house as general merchandise; but items in the box are more personal in nature, and most of the items were well used before being shipped on the *Bertrand*. A more probable suggestion is that the box was being shipped to a Campbell supply house to be picked up later by its owner. In the upper river country, both mail and packages were commonly shipped this way (Settle, 1971).

6.2. BOX MSC-128: ARTIFACTS

6.2.1. Personal Utilization

6.2.1.1. Clothing and Footwear. *6.2.1.1a. Children's Socks* (Cat. #3171 and 3493). There were six wool children's socks with alternating horizontal 1/4-inch-wide black and maroon stripes in the box (Figure 6.1). Only the leg and heel portions of the socks survived; the toes and cuffs are gone. There were also several black socknet pieces and ten black pieces 2 inches wide that may have been sock cuffs associated with the sock pieces.

6.2.1.1b. Silk Ribbons (Cat. #3170). This assemblage includes two groups of silk ribbons. There are sixteen gray-green ribbon pieces that are 1 1/8 inches wide and five 2-inch-wide black-bronze ribbon fragments. The pieces have stitch-

Figure 6.1. Three pairs of striped wool socks (Cat. #3171 and 3493) in the box labeled J. A. Campbell. Photograph courtesy of DeSoto National Wildlife Refuge, U. S. Fish and Wildlife Service, Missouri Valley, Iowa.

ing holes along one side that may indicate that the ribbons were once sewn on a garment.

6.2.1.1c. Ceramic Buttons (Cat. #784). Seven white ceramic buttons 1/4 inch in diameter and 3/32 inch thick were in this box. They each have three small holes set in a circular front cavity 1/8 inch in diameter. The remaining front surface slants to a flat edge that is 1/32 inch thick. The button backs are convex with rough (processor) surfaces around the holes. This style of button was commonly sewn on cotton shirts or calico blouses if for ladies (Brown, 1942).

6.2.1.2.   Adornment.   *6.2.1.2a.* Fifty-one loose *Beads* were found in this box (Figure 6.2). They represent a variety of materials, sizes, and colors. As with

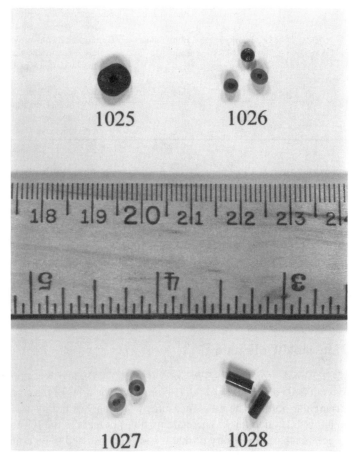

Figure 6.2. Loose beads found in this box. Cat. #1025 is a particular mystery. Although cataloged as a flat metal bead or disk by the museum, it is not typical.

Table 6.1. *Bertrand* Box MSC-128: Beads

Catalog number	Number	Material	Color	Diameter × thickness	Description
1024	27	Glass	Silver/ black	6mm–7mm × 10mm–7mm	Blown glass of light weight and thin walled. Circular in cross-section, oval in plan view. Fine parallel striations running from end to end on outer surface. Silver with black paint.
1025	01	Brass	Brass	6mm × 9mm × 2mm thick	Circular disk with wide oblong shape and oval 2mm-long hole in center. Edges are flat and at right angles to face.
1026	11	Glass	Brown-gray	3mm × 2mm	Flat and circular with rounded edges. All are opaque.
1027	07	Glass	Gray/ black	3mm–5mm × 3mm	Circular with convex sides and flat ends. Translucent gray to gray-white with black paint on surface.
1028	05	Glass	Black	3mm × 7mm	Circular tubular beads, similar to #1019 but larger. Black opaque with iridescent patina. Some are green-blue, green, or red-yellow.

the two previous boxes, the beads could not be associated with any particular artifact or artifacts. Table 6.1 contains a description of the beads.

6.2.1.3. Health and Hygiene. *6.2.1.3a. Brushes* (Cat. #4043). The remains of two hairbrushes were found in the box. The bristles are gone, but the wooden heads and handles remain in good condition. Both have oval heads that narrow into an hourglass neck with a lozenge-shaped handle. The bottom bristle surface is flat and rough. The top side is smooth and slightly rounded. Both brushes show evidence of being painted a soft cream color. The brushes measure 8 1/4 inches in total length.

6.2.2. Household Utilization

6.2.2.1. Ritual. *6.2.2.1a. Felt Cross* (Cat. #3725). The box contained a black cross cut from a thin piece of felt (Figure 6.3). The arms of the cross are cut to form triangular points. The cross measures 1 9/16 inches tall by 1 1/4 inches wide; the felt is 1/16 inch thick. There are no holes or tears in the felt to suggest that the piece was part of a rosary or that it had been fastened to a garment.

6.2.2.2. Linens. *6.2.2.2a. Bolt of Cloth* (Cat. #3492). A 27-inch-wide bolt

Figure 6.3. A small, delicate, felt cross (Cat. #3725) in the J. A. Campbell box. Photograph courtesy of DeSoto National Wildlife Refuge, U. S. Fish and Wildlife Service, Missouri Valley, Iowa.

of red wool flannel was found in the box. The fabric was very deteriorated when found and has since been discarded.

6.3. CONCLUSION

The variety of items in this box suggests that its contents are personal in nature. The large number of personal items and the few household items suggest that perhaps the box belonged to an adult woman. However, a number of seemingly relevant items such as clothing are missing from this box. Like the Atchison box, it contains no cooking items or ceramics. The lack of many items, the sparseness of items, and the packing label suggest the box was being sent to an individual already in the upper territories and not someone traveling on the steamboat. The items in the box resemble items that may have been left behind, deemed nonessential for the initial journey.

Chapter 7

Bertrand FSC-234

Bertrand FSC-234 was a barrel that was 28 inches tall with a 16 1/2-inch diameter. It was excavated between August 18 and August 23, 1969 (Figure 7.1). The barrel was removed from the forward cargo spaces on the starboard side.

7.1. WILLIAM WHEATLEY: FRONTIER COBBLER?

There is no positive identification for the owner of *Bertrand* Box FSC-234, but based on the items found in it, the box has been commonly been referred to as the "cobbler's box." Unlike the previous boxes, there was no name or identifiable label associated with this packing crate. Other than the assumption that the owner was a working man, it was thought that nothing more would ever be known of the individual who used these items. In 1997, however, Peter Binkley of Ontario, Canada, contacted officials at the *Bertrand* Museum about William Wheatley, a relative, who was a passenger on the *Bertrand* when it sank in 1865.

William Wheatley (Figure 7.2) grew up in Northumberland, Pennsylvania, where he learned the finer arts of cobbling from his father, John Wright Wheatley. Young William worked in his father's shoe shop through the 1840s, but he did not actively pursue a career as a cobbler. In the 1850s, he moved first to Georgia and then to Missouri where he was sometimes a secretary and bookkeeper and later a farmer. It seems that William never forgot his cobbling skills, however. While he was in Missouri, according to his papers, he purchased cobbling supplies and may have been repairing shoes for his family and others on the side while farming. In 1860, William returned to Pennsylvania to work again in his father's shoe shop. "Something else," however, always seemed to call William to parts unknown. In 1865, William loaded a sawmill on-board the *Bertrand* and headed to the gold mines in Montana Territory to seek his fortune. Presumably, William

77

Figure 7.1. A barrel similar to FSC-234 being excavated from the *Bertrand* hull by two members of the field crew. Photograph courtesy of DeSoto National Wildlife Refuge, U. S. Fish and Wildlife Service, Missouri Valley, Iowa.

took along his cobbling tools just in case this venture, like the previous farming venture, was not profitable (Binkley, 1998).

7.2. FSC-234 ARTIFACTS

7.2.1. Occupational Utilization

7.2.1.1. Tools.   *7.2.1.1a. Leather Working Tools* (Cat. #3949) This catalog number contains seven different leather-working tools. All were found wrapped in a large piece of finely tanned, dark carriage upholstery leather. One tool is a *parallel ruler* constructed of two thin rectangular pieces of ebony (Figure 7.3). When closed, the pieces fit edge to edge and form a parallelogram in cross-section. The ruler arms measure 5 15/16 inches in length, and 11/16 inch in width and are 3/32 inch thick. Brass figure eight hinges measuring 2 1/8 inches long, 3/8 inch

Figure 7.2. An etching of William Wheatly, a *Bertrand* passenger and trained cobbler. We will probably never be able to positively identify the cobbling supplies found in the Bertrand collection with Wheatley, but he is a good possiblity. Illustration courtesy of the Robert W. Binkley Collection, London, Ontario.

wide, and 1/16 inch thick allow the ruler to open and close.

There was also a *Steel Gimlet* in the bundle. The gimlet has an elongated, elliptical-shaped handle dished slightly in the center top and bottom with a rectangular hole through the center for the drill shaft. The gimlet handle measures 1 15/16 inches in length and is 5/16 inch in diameter. The shaft is 6 inches in length and 1/8 inch in diameter; the spirals compose 2 1/4 inches of the shaft length and are 5/16 inch in diameter.

A *Wooden awl or tool handle* with an oval shape having two flat ends (Figure 7.3) was among the tools. One end of the handle has a conical metal face cut into quarters, through the center of which awl points are pressed and held. The

Figure 7.3. Several tools (Cat. #3949) were found in the cobbler's barrel, including this parallell ruler, a tool handle, and a shoulder stick. Photograph courtesy of DeSoto National Wildlife Refuge, U. S. Fish and Wildlife Service, Missouri Valley, Iowa.

metal tip is no longer in a working condition. The handle measures 3 13/16 inches in length and 5/16 inch in diameter.

Toolholders evolved from the common changeable-point-type cobbler's awls to their modern form in the 1860s. The cobbler's changeable awl was similar to the one described above. The wood on the handle end was heavily scored to allow a tool tip to be pushed between the metal X and held fast. The first adjustable versions were more solid and required a chuck wrench to adjust the metal collar holding the tool head. In 1867, Stanley versions offered a hand-tightened chuck, which survives in the modern tool (Barlow, 1991).

Two pieces of rectangular *cork* were found among the tools. Both pieces measure 8 inches by 2 7/8 inches by 1/8 inch. The purpose of the cork is unknown.

Another piece is a *celluloid or rubber form*. Presently, the piece is missing from the collection. The only reference is a drawing made when the piece entered the lab. There were no exact measurements, and the piece has not been positively identified. It had a diameter approximately the size of a silver dollar, with a flat bottom. The piece had a domed top, divided vertically from the base to form equal segments. Its outer surface had a hard rubber texture. The piece was cast from a mold as there was evidence of a swirling flaw on the top center. It was described as buttermilk in color.

A *Shoulder Stick*, used for finishing the outer edges of heels and soles (Figure 7.3) was also among the tools. The stick was rubbed along the leather and had a polishing effect on the surface (Saguto, 1995). Shoulder sticks came in a variety of styles, straight, J, round, and oval (Timmons & Sons, 1820). This piece is a straight shoulder stick measuring 7 13/16 inches by 1 inch by 3/4 inch.

7.2.1.1b. Folding Rule (Cat. #883). One half of a brass and wood folding rule was found in the barrel. Originally, the ruler consisted of two strips of wood 3/8 inch wide and 3/16 inch thick (Figure 7.4). Each edge is covered with a strip of brass 1/16 inch thick, which gives the ruler a total width of 1/2 inch. The ruler has a circular brass hinge between the two arms and is marked in inches 1 through 12 on one arm, and 13 through 24 on the other arm. Additional marked units included 1/2-inch and 1/4-inch increments on one side and 1/10-inch and 1/12-inch increments on the other side.

The carpenter's folding rule was used since the seventeenth century. It was a

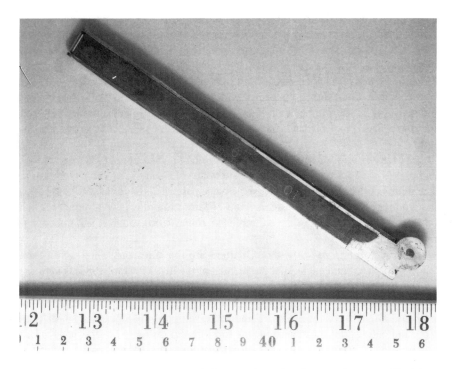

Figure 7.4. Half of a carpenter's folding rule (Cat. #883) was found among the pieces of leather in the cobbler's barrel. Photograph courtesy of DeSoto National Wildlife Refuge, U. S. Fish and Wildlife Service, Missouri Valley, Iowa.

mass-produced item by the mid-nineteenth century. The rule was generally scaled in inches, halves, quarters, and eighths. Factory models were hinged, first in two and later in four brass-tipped, boxwood sections (Mercer, 1960).

7.2.1.2. Trade Supplies. *7.2.1.2a. Shoe Repair Pieces* (Cat. # 3992, 5306, and 5308). The barrel contained multiple pieces of leather used in shoe manufacture and repair. A taxonomic structure has not been applied to shoe materials in the past. For clarity in this study, the collection of shoe leather was divided into nineteen different classes of leather parts.

Class 1 soling leather. There are twenty-five heavy pieces of leather ranging in thickness from 1/8 inch to 3/8 inch in the barrel. The pieces are of various sizes and shapes. Most are roughly cut, and several have tracing outlines. Pieces range in size from 6 3/4 inches by 19 1/4 inches (1/8 inch thick) to 3 1/2 inches by 7 inches (3/8 inch thick).

Class 2 scrap leather. There are 110 pieces of scrap leather in various sizes, shapes, and thicknesses. Many pieces were originally shoe or boot parts being reused for repairs. Many have patches cut from them; most are well worn.

Class 3 farmer's bundles. A farmer's bundle is a rolled packet of leather scraps used for all types of leather repairs. The bundles are usually tied with a thin leather thong. They were purchased in mercantile and supply houses throughout the nineteenth century (Saguto, 1995). Most of these bundles contain medium-sized, shovel-shaped pieces 1/16 inch thick, most measuring 16 3/4 inches by 9 ½ inches. Each shovel-shaped piece was tightly rolled and tied with a leather thong. Many of the smaller individual rolls have smaller pieces inside; each roll was then placed in a farmer's bundle. There are eighteen bundles in this collection.

Class 4 vamps. A vamp is the front section of a shoe upper covering the toes and part of the instep (Swann, 1982). There are 118 rough-cut vamps varying in size in this collection, but with the same basic pattern and thickness. Most vamps in this collection are for children's shoes. Many examples have a number inked on their grain sides. There are examples of round-toed, square-toed, and wing-tipped vamps.

Class 5 hexagonal quarters. Quarters are the sides of a shoe joining the vamp at the front and each other at the back of the heel (Swann, 1982). There are 151 hexagonal quarters of fairly uniform shape and thickness, although the size range varied in this set. Each quarter is cut in a rough pentagonal shape. One edge is always slightly concave to accommodate a vamp. Many pieces are small, possibly indicating that they were meant for children's shoes. Several have inked numbers on the grain sides, which may correspond with similar numbers on leather in other classes. There are both new and used quarters. Several have eyelets, and a few are lined.

Class 6 backstays. There are five bottle-shaped backstays, strips of leather that cover the back seams, with bulging bases that tapered to long, slender necks (Swann, 1982). The necks widen slightly at the tops. They are single stitched along all sides with the grain to the inside.

Class 7 shoe tongues. Shoe tongues are flaps of leather or cloth under shoelaces or buckles (Swann, 1982). There were fourteen examples shaped like isosceles triangles with square tops in the barrel. Seven measure 2 1/4 inches by 6 inches, two measure 1 1/2 inches by 4 3/8 inches, and one measures 1 3/8 inches by 5 1/2 inches.

Class 8 heel welt. Heel welts are thin strips of leather stitched along the seam between the insole and upper to strengthen a potentially weak place in a shoe (Swann, 1982). There is one horseshoe-shaped example.

Class 9 arch welts. Arch welts are pieces of leather sewn between the upper and insole at the arch. There are two examples with a trapezoidal cross-section.

Class 10 heels. The heel is the built-up part of a shoe or boot that supports the rear of the foot (Swann, 1982). Shoe heels were often made of several pieces of leather to give the heel height. The eight leather heels found in the barrel are approximately the same shape but in various stages of completion.

Class 11 boot uppers. Uppers are leather parts of a shoe or boot above the sole, normally consisting of a vamp, quarters, and lining (Swann, 1982). This class contains four boot uppers. All of the uppers have a liner or extender that is whipstitched 3/4 inch from their tops.

Class 12 boot backs from uppers. There are sixteen boot backs from worn boot uppers in the artifact set. Each has a full length liner whipstitched   the top line and then sewn into the side seams.

Class 13 top line extenders. The barrel contained thirty-four top line extenders of various sizes. All are rectangular and have a single row of stitching holes along their top and bottom edges.

Class 14 boot pull tabs. There are twenty-one rectangular boot pull tabs in the artifact set. As the tab width became smaller or larger, the length varied accordingly. Each rectangular tab is doubled over and stitched by two single rows of stitches to the boot backs.

Class 15 boot counters. Counters are outside reinforcement for quarters. There are five rectangular pieces of stiff, heavy leather folded gently in the center to a U shape in the barrel.

Class 16 back extenders. There are seven triangular pieces or "horns" that originally would have been sewn on the back of a top line and up the side seams of taller shoes. They have a doming front top line, thus making a gentle merge between the front and the back of the shoe.

Class 17 seam welts. There are twenty-five narrow strips of leather that would have been sewn into seams for reinforcement (Swann, 1982).

Class 18 top liners. There were ten top liners for women's shoes in the barrel. They are 3/8-inch- to 3/4 inch-wide leather strips folded over and sewn to shoe top lines (Swann, 1982). Two of the top liners have scalloped edges; and two are plain and quite wide.

Class 19 counter seam cover. There was one small rectangular piece 1 **3/8** inches by 2 3/16 inches that was once stitched over a boot counter and side seam at the sole on a boot interior. There is a line of stitching on both sides and sole pegging holes are present on both sole edges.

7.2.1.3. Products. *7.2.1.3a.* One pair of *complete boots and one shoe ready for soling* (Cat. #2958) are part of this artifact set. The boots are in ten pieces each (Figure 7.5). The soles have a single layer outsole that tapers into a now separate single layer leather half-sole. The soles measure 10 inches by 3 1/2 inches and were held in place with a single row of stitching (no longer present) 1/4 inch from all edges. The straight heels are six layered and slightly tapering toward the back. The heels are held in place with a row of square nails 3/16 inch from the side and back of the heel. A second row of larger nails was inside the first row. The heels are worn down, exhibiting much wear. The insole still displays heel and toe impressions and is perspiration stained.

All the boot pieces were deliberately separated before they were packed in the barrel. Perhaps the cobbler planned to use the parts in other shoes or was simply going to replace the worn pieces and re-sew the boots. One shoe ready for soling is in this collection of leather pieces. The shoe is composed of a wing-

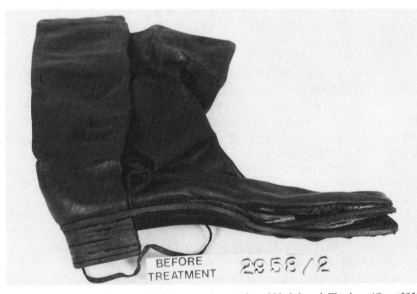

Figure 7.5. There were few completed boots or shoes in the cobbler's barrel. This boot (Cat. #2958) was one of the few examples. Photograph courtesy of DeSoto National Wildlife Refuge, U. S. Fish and Wildlife Service, Missouri Valley, Iowa.

tipped vamp, a backstay, and hexagonal quarters. All the stitching is missing, and no numbers appear on any of the pieces.

7.2.1.3b. Catalog #5308 contains one *lady's shoe.* The shoe has five-sided quarters with nine brass eyelets. Only the eyelet row is leather lined. The rest of the quarter is lined with cloth that did not survive, but some fabric remnants are present. There are two additional eyelets in a short slit cut into the vamp. The heel is five layered and fastened to a single layer sole with one row of wood pegs. The sole is decorated with an acute-angled outline of chain link stamping.

7.2.1.3c. Riding Boots (Cat. #4069). The collection also contains one well-worn pair of men's boots. The boots have a manufacturer's mark, "(CAL)IN'S," stamped offcenter on both heel faces. The boots were manufactured on crooked lasts; that is, there is a right and a left boot. The boots have a seven-layer, straight leather heel, which tapers slightly from the sole inward on three sides. The heel breast is straight. The remains of seven or eight square iron pegs used to attach the heel to the sole are visible.

The boots have a rounded toe and measure 19 inches in overall height. They have a sole length of 9 7/8 inches and a maximum width of 3 inches and a heel height (including sole) of 1 1/4 inches. The boots are well worn but were still in good condition at the time the vessel sank.

7.2.1.3d. Seven Dress Boots and Fragments (Cat. #2958). This catalog number includes seven finished dress boots along with thirty-nine parts and fragments. There are no manufacturer's marks on the boots. The boots were made on crooked lasts; there are three lefts and four rights. The boots all have square toes and were McKay stitched and pegged. McKay-sewn shoes were introduced in the 1860s. The McKay sewing machine imitated the sewing of the "channel pump": a thread passed completely through the sole, upper, and insole (Peterkin and Saguto, 1989). These boots are sewn with the grain side on the boot interiors. All appear to be new and ready for sale.

7.2.1.3e. Leather Belt (Cat. #5307). The barrel contained a cut and stitched leather belt with no manufacturer's marks. The belt consists of a single strip of black leather 36 5/8 inches by 1 1/4 inches wide that tapers at both the tongue and buckle ends. The tongue end contains eleven circular holes with the first eight holes being 1/2 inch apart and the last three holes 7/8 inch apart. The tongue end was 3/4 inch wide and begins to taper at the ninth hole. The belt appears to have been cut off, as the rounded end had a half-hole in its tip.

The buckle end tapered inward to a 7/8-inch minimum width and tapered back out to be 1 inch wide. At the narrowest point on the belt, an oval slot is cut for the buckle tongue. A buckle would have been stitched into the fold. The belt is decorated with a thin, impressed line stamped down both sides. The belt is in good condition but shows considerable signs of wear.

7.2.1.3f. Leather Billfold (Cat. #2671). This billfold consists of a rectangular piece of fine leather folded into fourths (Figure 7.6). One end of the rectangle

Figure 7.6. Among the many pieces of leather in this barrel was a well-used leather billfold (Cat. #2671), probably being used as scrap leather. Photograph courtesy of DeSoto National Wildlife Refuge, U. S. Fish and Wildlife Service, Missouri Valley, Iowa.

is narrower and slightly convex to form the billfold flap. The second folded section serves as the front of the billfold and is highly decorated. It has two small vertical slits ½ inch long and 1 1/8 inches wide. A narrow leather keeper would be inserted through the slits. Stitching along the sides and bottom of the front section holds a rectangular pocket 1/4 inch narrower than the front, to the back of the front section. Sewn into the same stitching at the sides are two small flaps, one to each side, with a 5/8-inch gap at the center and placed in front of the pocket, grain side out. Each flap has a 1/8-inch hole about 3/8 inch from the gap edge. This once held a string or button that secured the two flaps together.

The billfold is in good condition. It measures 7 3/4 inches (total open length with fourth section as pocket), 3 1/4 inches closed length, 6 3/8 inches wide, 5 3/4 inches length of strap, and 1 1/4 inches width of strap.

7.2.1.3g. Leather Bible Cover (Cat. #3986). A thin leather bible cover was found in the Cobbler's barrel. The cover is rectangular, measuring 7 inches by 5 1/8 inches. A 130-degree angle is cut from each corner to allow the cover to fold over a book without bulging at the corners. The cover is divided into three decorative units consisting of a front, binding, and back.

7.2.1.3h. Book Covers and Binding (Cat. #5309). Two leather book covers and one binding were also found among the scrap leather in the barrel. No manufacturer's marks are present. Each cover consists of a leather rectangle with an inked design stamped into the flesh side. The book covers are identical except for size; one measures 15 3/8 inches by 13 1/4 inches, the other 19 1/4 inches by 14 inches. All the corners are angled inward toward the sides. The rate of the angle is not uniform but does allow the folded corners to lie completely flat. The narrower ends of the covers fold over the hard backing of a book. The long sides of the cover end flush with the top and bottom edges of the book (it does not overlap). These edges are covered by a folded, narrow strip of lightweight leather adorned with gilt stenciling. The bottom (or top) two corners of this strip are cut at a diagonal to facilitate smooth folding. Each cover once had one of these strips on both the top and bottom book edges.

A volume number (?), either a *6* or *9* in this case, is on the binding. Folds indicate that these were once complete books. Only the leather covers, however, and one binding are now present. The book binding reinforcement strips, three more bindings, and the paper are now missing.

7.3. CONCLUSION

The items in this barrel are not completely typical for the cobbler's craft. The tanned hides, scrap leather, farmer's bundles, shoe and boot pieces, and completed or nearly completed shoes represent examples of supplies owned by most cobblers in the nineteenth century. It is, however, uncommon for cobblers to practice leather trades other than shoe making or repair. It is therefore, unlikely that this cobbler made the book covers and bindings or the belt for sale. These pieces of leather were probably being used as scrap leather for shoe repair (Saguto, 1995).

The tools in this barrel are not typical, either. The only cobbler's tool in the barrel is the shoulder stick. The shoulder stick provides a definitive clue that this barrel did belong to a cobbler and not to a farmer or merchant repairing leather. The tool was used only in finishing shoes. There are several important tools used in shoe manufacture that were not found in the barrel. The absence of shoe hammers, lasts, pincers, and other primary tools suggests that the items in the barrel were "extras." The cobbler probably kept his tools with him while on the vessel. The tools were the implements of his trade; the items in the barrel were far less important and easier to replace.

Although there is no way to positively identify William Wheatley as the owner of this barrel, he is a feasible possibility. What we do know is that although Wheatley was a trained cobbler, he practiced his trade only sporadically. His letters he wrote to his wife from his 1865 journey on board the *Bertrand* mentioned the attempted salvage of the *Bertrand* and the recovery of his sawmill. He did not mention the loss of his cobbling tools or supplies. He did note that he lost a valuable opportunity because he did not manage to make it to the goldfields of Montana with his mill before the snow set in (Binkley, 1998; Wheatley, 1865).

Chapter 8

Arabia Carpenter's Box

One of the more intriguing boxes in *Arabia*'s hold apparently belonged to a carpenter. This was the only box in the *Arabia* collection used for this study because the items in this box could be positively associated with one another. The *Arabia* had other boxes associated with passengers, but because no archaeological field notes were kept, few items could be positively associated throughout the collection. The carpenter's box (Figure 8.1) contents were identified from photographs taken in the field as the box was opened (this was the only box in the hold that was not filled with mud when opened). The tools from this box were reassociated in the collection by using salvage photographs and by interviewing members of the salvage party, particularly members of the Hawley family and museum staff who all helped to put the appropriate items back in the box.

Many tools, however, were in the *Arabia*'s cargo, and during conservation, storage, and display, some tools associated with this box were mixed with those from the regular cargo. Often, tools from the general cargo were undistinguishable from tools in this box. As a result, many of the items shown in field photos of this box could no longer be positively identified in the collection. Tools that were worn or well used, those with personal initials stamped or stippled on them, and those that were one-of-a-kind items in the collection were assumed to be those tools noted in the photographs and therefore treated as personal. The following collection is, therefore, as complete as possible at this time. The museum is making every effort to place associated items in their proper context. Notable omissions are discussed at the end of this chapter.

8.1. CARPENTER' BOX ARTIFACTS

8.1.1. Occupational Utilization

8.1.1.1. Tools. *8.1.1.1a. Carpenter's Whetstone* (Cat. #A2129P). A very well-used sandstone whetstone was found in the box (Figure 8.2). Whetstones

89

Figure 8.1. The carpenter's box being opened in the field before disassembly for conservation. Illustration by David Hawley, *Arabia* Steamboat Museum.

were also known as Turkey stones. By 1800, most fine-grade whetstones sold in the United States were quarried, made, and sold by Christian Schneeberger of Moselem Church, Berks County, Pennsylvania. According to local tradition, he carried his whetstones fifty-eight miles by foot to be sold in Philadelphia; they eventually were sold across the United States (Mercer, 1960).

This stone was cemented in a hollowed wooden block or box, which measures 10 inches by 2 7/8 inches by 3/4 inch. The box is handmade to hold a precut stone. The stone measures 8 inches by 2 inches by 1 1/2inches and shows extensive wear or use.

8.1.1.1b. Draw Knife (Cat. #A2127P). The carpenter's box contained a draw knife with a steel blade that measures 16 inches in length. The blade is beveled

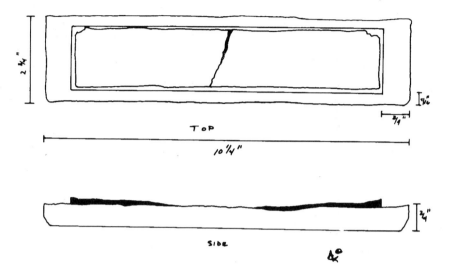

Figure 8.2. A sandstone whetstone found in the *Arabia*'s carpenter box. The whetstone (Cat. #A2129P) was well worn.

and straight with a slightly rounded front surface (Figure 8.3). The blade is 1 1/4 inches wide in the center and 7/16 inch wide where it joins two wooden handles.

Draw knives were pulled with both hands to thin the sides of shingles held by a shaving horse or to round off tool handles, wagon spokes, or ladder staves (Mercer, 1960). To use, the blade is held almost flat to the work surface and pulled toward the carpenter. For a deeper cut, the blade angle is increased. Throughout the country, draw knives were commonly made by small, local edge-tool companies, village blacksmiths, and farmers on their own forges from wrought iron stock or worn-out files (Kebabian, 1978).

The front surface of the blade of this draw knife has the initials J V or (U) K stippled into its surface. Also evident are the remnants of a manufacturer's mark stamped on the lower front surface of the blade: " _ _ _ C A M." The manufacturer has not been identified. In the nineteenth century, this style of draw knife was specifically a carpenter's draw knife because of the straight nature of the blade and the blade's width. Non-carpenter-specific draw knives, coach makers, and concave or hollow-ground draw knives often had rounded or concave blades rather than straight blades (Russell and Erwin Manufacturing Company, 1865).

8.1.1.1c. Sticking Knife (Cat. #A2065P). There was a steel and wood sticking knife in the carpenter's box. The blade is spear shaped and measures 4 ½ inches in length and 1 inch in width. The manufacturer's mark on the blade is "J. RUSSELL & Co. GREEN RIVER WORKS." The knife has a rectangular cocoawood handle, 4 1/8 inches by 3/4 inch. The handle is attached to the blade's tang

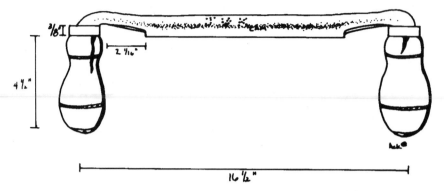

Figure 8.3. Draw knives were a common tool in any nineteenth century carpenter's chest. This draw knife (Cat. #A2127P) has the owner's initials stimpled into the blade.

with two brass pins that run through each face of the handle. There are two notches cut into either edge of the handle so that the handle could be rope or leather wrapped. The wooden handle displays impressions of some type of wrapping or cording. The initials "I K" are carved into the spine of the knife handle.

In the early nineteenth century, most mountain men's store-bought knives came from England, but in 1834 John Russell began manufacturing butcher and carving knives on the Green River at Greenfield, Massachusetts. Russell's knives were shipped west to companies such as Pierre Chouteau, Jr., & Co., where they were purchased by hunters, trappers, and Native Americans. It is estimated that between 1840 and 1860 five thousand dozen were purchased in the West for between $1.50 and $3.50 a dozen. The knives were well made and beveled on only one edge for skinning. The two most common blade lengths shipped west were the 6-inch butcher knife and the 8-inch carving knife. The term "Green River" became a standard part of mountaineer vocabulary. Journals commonly referred to a successful hunt or fight when a knife was thrust up to the "Green River" (H. Peterson, 1958).

8.1.1.1d. Sawmill Dogs (Cat. #A2162P and A2163P). Two wrought iron staple-shaped sawmill dogs were found in the box (Figure 8.4). The larger one is 13 inches by 3 1/4 inches by 9/16 inch thick. The smaller one measures 7 7/16 inches by 3 1/4 inches by 7/16 inch thick. Neither has a manufacturer's mark.

Sawmill dogs came in a variety of shapes and sizes. Most varieties were readily available and used throughout the nineteenth century. Sawmill dogs resembled heavy iron staples and were used to hold logs or balks in place by placing a heavy log across blocks or crosspieces placed at right angles to the log being hewn. One spur of the dog was driven into the underplaced crosspiece, and the other at an upward tilt into the log side. The dog prevented the log from rolling from side to side. They were employed at sawmills or over saw pits and

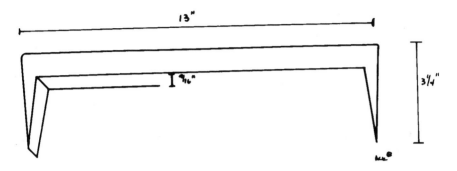

Figure 8.4. Two sawmill dogs were found in the carpenter's box. This is the larger sawmill dog (Cat. #A2162P).

were also used by carpenters for log hewing when logs were not heavy enough to lie still under their own weight (Mercer, 1960).

8.1.1.1e. Screw Arm Plow (Cat. #2160P). The box also contained one box-wood and iron screw arm plow with screw stops, stop plate, and eight irons (Figure 8.5). The assembled mechanism measures 10 inches in overall height and is 8 1/2 inches wide.

Screw arm plows were used to cut narrow tongues and grooves in door panels. Adjusting the screws and stop plates allowed the carpenter to vary the depth of the groove (Pollak and Pollak, 1983; Russell and Erwin, 1865).

8.1.1.1f. Carpenter's Wrench (Cat. #A2165P). There was an oak and iron adjustable carpenter's wrench in the box. The total length of the tool is 12 1/2 inches, with a handle length of 5 1/2 inches. The handle is attached to the wrench head by means of an iron screw shaft. The wrench head is 3 inches by 1 7/8 inches. There are no manufacturer's marks present, but the design matches one noted as "Taft's Pattern," L. & A. G. Coe's patent, advertised in the *Russell and Erwin American Hardware Catalog of 1865*. There are two initials stippled into one side of the wrench head, "J (K)."

The first metal wedge jaw on a shifting-type spanner or "monkey wrench" appeared between 1790–1835, but provided only a small amount of adjustment in the wrench head. In 1835, Solyman Merrick of Springfield, Massachusetts, patented the first sleeve or screw adjusting feature. This was further improved in 1841 when two brothers, L. & A. G. Coe, replaced Merrick's wrap handle with a knurled-rosette nut on a shaft parallel with the handle. The new design allowed the wrench to be adjusted with the same hand that held the wrench. By 1860, Coe's patent wrenches were in worldwide distribution, and many new patent modifications were beginning (Barlow, 1991).

8.1.1.1g. Lever Saw Set (Cat. #A2166P). Also in the box was a wood and steel lever saw set, of the Stillman patent design. The tool has a total length of 6 1/

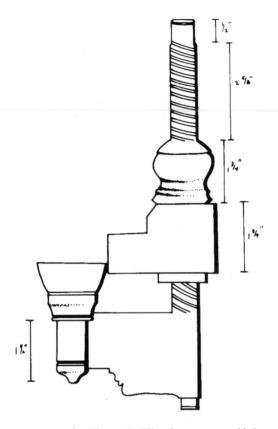

Figure 8.5. A screw arm plow (Cat. #A2160P) and accompanying blades were among
the carpenter's tools.

2 inches and a lathed oak handle. The faint remains of a manufacturer's mark are
present on the neck of the steel tool head, but are unreadable. The letter "J" is
stamped on the back of the steel neck above another stamped letter, possibly an
"O."

   Saw sets were used to align or set saw blades. It was the "set" or outward
splaying of the teeth that kept the blade from binding or freezing up. Saw sets in
the nineteenth century appeared in three basic designs: hammer-struck saw sets,
wrests with wooden handles, such as #A2166P, and plier types. All served to
ensure a uniform tooth pitch on cross-cut and rip saws (Barlow, 1991).

   8.1.1.1h. Chisels (Cat. #A2161P, A2172P, A2169P, A2170P, A2167P,
A2168P). Several forms of chisels were positively identified in the carpenter's
box. The most prominent chisel types are forming or firmer chisels and paring

chisels. Forming chisels or firmers are the heaviest tool of their class. The head has a socket in the larger, heavy models used by carpenters and a tang when used by joiners. The socketed chisel has a conical socket above the blade to receive a handle with a rounded taper on its lower end that fits into the socket. Tanged chisels stopped above the blade in a shank with an elongated spur that is inserted into a handle. Both models are, however, used interchangeably (Kebabian, 1978).

Artifact #A2169P is a large forming chisel 17 inches in total length, with a 10 3/4-inch handle length, and a blade of 6 inches by 1 7/8 inches. The manufacturer's mark on the chisel blade reads, _ HAYWOOD. It has a pinewood handle that may not have been original as it is too big for the socket.

Paring chisels are lighter duty tools than forming chisels. These chisels are used for shaping and preparing long planed surfaces, especially in the direction of the grain of the wood. Paring chisels are generally pushed with the hand or shoulder. They have the smallest cutting edge angle, no more than 15 degrees (Blackburn, 1974). The only difference between forming and paring chisels is the manner in which they were used. Both could have straight or beveled edges, and they are manufactured in the same way (Mercer, 1960).

Artifact #A2161P is either a paring chisel or a flat sweep gouge (see below) with a blade measuring 9 inches by 2 inches by 1/8 inch with a socket handle 4 3/4 inches in length. The back of the blade has a slight curve, but is not beveled. Portions of a manufacture's mark are present:

T. H. _ _ T
CAST S(T)(E)(E)(L)
(T) A R K (A) _ _ _

Artifact #A2170P is a paring chisel with no visible manufacturer's marks. It has a blade measuring 6 1/2 inches by 1 3/8 inches with a pine socket handle 7 1/4 inches long. The handle has an elegant figure-eight shape and was turned on a lathe.

Artifact #A2172P is long and narrow with a beveled edge. The blade measures 8 3/4 inches by 1 inch, and the handle is 8 7/8 inches in length. It is the only example of a bevel-edge paring chisel in the box. There are faint impressions of a manufacture's mark visible:

W _ _ N R
_ _ _ T R T _ _ _

As with the forming and paring chisels, mortise chisels vary greatly in form and size. There were three basic styles of mortise chisels produced in the nineteenth century. The common short-handled joiner's mortise chisel had a straight and almost square-ended blade. This type of chisel came in several varieties. Catalog #A2167P may be a London-pattern sash mortise, a thinner and finer lined version of the joiner's mortise. There were also swan- or goosenecked mortises; a lock-style mortise that resembled a pry bar; and the twibil, a straight-bladed tool with a right angle socket handle (Barlow, 1991). The latter two styles were not found in the carpenter's box. All three styles were produced in several variations and used primarily for soft wood mortising where no preliminary boring was required. Most mortising chisels were socket handled; they were generally pounded with a mallet, and the socket withstood the force better than a tang (Mercer, 1960).

Artifact #A2168P is a joiner's mortise chisel 11 1/4 inches in overall length, 6 1/4 inches in handle length, 5 inches in blade length, and 3/8 inch in blade width. This chisel seems little used; the blade angles are still sharp and well defined. A manufacturer's mark stamped into the steel neck of the tool reads: W _ C R _ _ _ _ F.

Because of the fine lines of this tool, catalog #A2167P may be a London-pattern sash mortise chisel. It has no manufacturer's marks and measures 10 1/2 inches in total length, 5 1/2 inches in handle length, 5 inches in blade length, with a 1/4-inch blade width. The artifact is well worn; sharp angles of the blade are visible only under close scrutiny. The blade is beveled on one side and flat on the other.

8.1.1.1i. Gouges. Constructed in a fashion identical to chisels, gouges also had several uses and forms and were produced with both socket and tang handles, in a variety of sizes. Gouge blades form an arc in cross-section, which produces a rounded cut. They are constructed in three type of curvatures: full sweep, middle sweep, and flat sweep, to produce a deep, medium, or shallow concave cut (Kebabian, 1978). Gouges were one of many tool types in the salvage photo of this box, but were not positively identified in the collection. Because of the slightly curved nature of its cutting edge, artifact #A2172P may be a shallow gouge rather than a paring chisel.

8.1.1.1j. Open-handed Compass Saw (Cat. #A2171P). A pine handled and steel bladed compass saw was in the box. The narrow steel blade is attached to the saw arm with two brass pins arranged side by side. The saw measures 19 1/2 inches in total length, the blade is 13 3/4 inches long by 3/4 inch wide, with a handle 5 1/2 inches across at its widest point.

A keyhole or compass saw has un-set teeth with an extra heavy blade for strength while being narrow and straight for cutting circular kerfs, or key and latch holes, in doors. This saw type is called a keyhole saw when it is mounted on a straight handle and a compass saw when mounted on a modeled handle grasp like #A2171P. Compass saws are also referred to as fret saws or lock saws, depending on use (Mercer, 1960).

8.1.2. Child Utilization

8.1.2.1. Toys. *8.1.2.1a. Frozen Charlotte Doll* (Cat. #A2134P) A 3 inch tall porcelain doll (Figure 8.6) with outstretched arms was found in the bottom of the carpenter's box. The doll's delicate facial features are painted in black, the lines of her bonnet in pink. The doll was wrapped without clothing in the toe of an old wool sock that was carefully placed in the corner of the box (Hawley, 1998). The doll is a Frozen Charlotte Doll (Borger, 1983).

Popular in the late nineteenth century, Frozen Charlotte dolls came in a variety of sizes and styles. The name was derived from a popular folk ballad "Fair Charlotte," credited to William Lorenzo Carter. Carter was a blind minstrel who composed the verses in 1833 while in Vermont. Legend suggests his ballad was based on the true tale of a young woman who passed away on a New Year's Eve

Figure 8.6. The Frozen Charolette doll (Cat. #A2134P) found in the bottom of the carpenter's box. Illustration by David Hawley, *Arabia* Steamboat Museum.

carriage ride. The young woman froze to death on her way to a dance with her young love. The minstrel's ballad was said to have inspired the production of the little dolls (Freeman, 1962). The porcelain dolls were produced from 1850 through 1914 in Germany. They were either white- or pink-toned porcelain or black china (Borger, 1983).

8.2. CONCLUSION

The box itself and several other items appearing in the photograph remain to be considered. The box holding the tools was rectangular in shape, approximately 4 feet by 3 feet. Exact dimensions of the box are not available. Few records were kept during salvage, and the box is now frozen in a block of ice awaiting conservation. The box has a wooden tray (Figure 8.7) with a central handle that separated the tools. The tray has a three-dimensional parallelogram shape. Its base measures 24 1/4 inches by 12 1/4 inches and has a 13 4/3-inch flared lip; the overall depth of the tray is 4 inches. The total height of the handle is 6 inches. The tray fits neatly into the larger tool box. Initials were found on the outside of the box but were not recorded in the field before freezing. The mystery of the correlation between the initials on the box and the initials noted on some of the artifacts awaits the box's conservation. The museum staff did note that this box was

Figure 8.7. The toolbox tray displayed with carpenter's tools from the general collection. Illustration by David Hawley, *Arabia* Steamboat Museum.

the only one in the collection not filled with mud when opened; presumably an indication that the carpenter was a fine craftsman (D. Hawley, 1995). The box top is constructed with a complex pattern of joints to display the quality of the carpenter's work. This type of toolbox, a joiner's box, was common in the nineteenth century (Allen, 1992).

The box also contained several gun parts: ramrod guides, trigger guard, trigger, wood screws for a gun, pins, and percussion cap hammer. There are no measurements or other information on these items.

Strangely, there are no rules, mallets, hammers, plumb bobs, drills, screwdrivers, augers, or levels noted in the box photo, but the photo was taken when the box was first opened. There are no photos of the box as it was unpacked or with the tray removed. All the items mentioned above are present, however, in the *Arabia* collection; some may have come from the carpenter's box. A large number and variety of carpenters' planes appear in the photo. Although none could be directly linked to this box, there are several different types of carpenter's bench planes in the museum collection.

The *Arabia*'s carpenter box represents a fine example of a working nineteenth century craftsman's toolbox. The quality of the box and tools suggests a craftsman dependent on his craft for his livelihood. Most tools in the box are well worn, and some may have had handles or parts replaced, which is indicative of much use.

Chapter 9

Quantitative Analysis

9.1. STATISTICAL METHODOLOGY

The purpose of submitting the artifact assemblage to a quantitative analysis was to suggest a means for cross-checking observed phenomena in the archaeological record. The main goal of the statistical study was to better understand interrelations between gender and socioeconomic class by studying material culture.

The statistical package used to perform the artifact analysis was *SPSS* (SPSS Inc., 1990). *SPSS* operates on a mainframe system and is widely used by universities and companies with mainframe networks with DOS, Windows, or APPLE/Macintosh compatible systems.

Statistical analysis used in this study included means tables, frequency distributions, and logistic regression. The *mean*, or arithmetic mean, is the most widely used statistical application. The *mean* estimates central tendency; it expresses the average or center of gravity of a set of variants. A *variable* is a measurable quantity, represented by a symbol, which is free to assume more than one value. A *variate* is an individual measurement of a variable (Thomas, 1986).

In SPSS, the means application displays the mean standard deviation (*standard deviation* is the square root of variance or the average dispersion of the values about the mean) and group counts for a dependent variable in groups defined by one or more independent variables (*independent variables* are the possible causes on the dependent variables, the possible effects, contained in the same data set). This relation can be expressed by means tables displaying requested univariant statistics for the population as a whole and for each value of the first independent variable defined by the table (Jarausch and Hardy 1991; SPSS Inc., 1990:457; Thomas, 1986).

Frequency distribution presents the values and counts of a variable. Frequency distributions allow the researcher to better visualize trends and distributions in the data (Thomas, 1986). *Logistic regression* is a technique by which values on a dichotomous dependent variable are "predicted" by a set of independent variables (SPSS Inc., 1990). Logistic regression allows a dependent variable such as gender to be compared with independent variables such as age and personal. The statistical application measures how the variable "age" affects the variable "gender" and then assesses how the variable "personal" is affected by "age" and how the combined influence of "age" and "personal" affects "gender." In short, logistic regression allows researchers to examine the effects of one variable influencing another measured at the dichotomous level. The resulting analysis explains how independent variables in a data set (a collection of information *about* people or a specific culture; in this case, the data set is the collection of individual artifacts being submitted to quantitative analysis) influence one another and how they affect, inconcert, the dichotomous measure (Thomas, 1986).

9.2. VARIABLES AND VALUE LABELS

The unit of analysis for this project was the individual artifact in each artifact assemblage. An individual artifact is referred to as a "case." *Variables* are distinctive features of each case, while attributes of each variable are called *values* (Jarausch and Hardy, 1991). Each artifact was measured based on fourteen variable questions (Table 9.1).

Table 9.1. Variables and Value Labels

Variable	Value
Gender	Female, male, or no sex (referring to items that are not sex specific).
Age	Adult items, child items, or no age (referring to items that are not age specific).
Clothing	Outer garments (hats, coats, gloves, etc.), dresses (including skirts and blouses), male-specified clothing (trousers and shirts), shoes, buttons, and beads.
Adornment	Yes or no. Every item is subjected to this variable. For example, beads would answer yes, buttons, no.
Household	Yes or no. Is the item household or not?
Occupational	Tools, supplies, or products.
Child use	Toys, educational, or miscellaneous.
Sewing	Yes or no, is the artifact a sewing item or not?
Personal	Yes or no, is the artifact personal or not?
Manufacture mode	Was the artifact homemade or manufactured?
Maker's mark	If manufactured, was a maker's mark present or not?
Luxury item	Yes or no, is the artifact a luxury item or not? An artifact is defined as a luxury item if it exceeds the documented norm for that particular type of item. For example, silk clothing was labeled luxury because in the nineteenth century silk was an expensive, uncommon item. Typical emigrant clothing was made of cotton, linen, or wool, all more economical fabrics.

Frequently, the determination of how each item fit within a variable was subjective. Little historical documentation about specific breakdowns of material culture use exists. For example, were nineteenth century women the only members of society who cooked or sewed? Generally yes, but in certain circumstances no. Men often cooked in the Montana mining camps, military camps, or locations where women were not present. The only feasible way to deal with these problems was to assign values based on a combination of archaeological site information and available historical information about that site, while remaining consistent when assigning values in variable questions. As an example, there were many beads in some of the boxes. The beads were evaluated in the gender (female), clothing, and adornment variables. Assessment of the value for gender was based on the individual box and historical context. Emigrant men typically did not use beads as clothing adornment, but period photographs clearly demonstrate that emigrant women often adorned their finer clothing with beads.

Beads, along with buttons, hooks, and eyes were not, however, assigned to the sewing variable. This was my choice. There was no way of determining whether beads, buttons, hooks, or eyes came from a single garment or multiple garments, or if they were placed in the packing boxes as sewing notions. Because of differential preservation of cotton and linen thread and fabrics, there were many loose buttons and beads in some of the boxes. It is reasonable to assume at least some of these items were sewn with cotton or linen thread, possibly onto cotton or linen garments that did not survive.

Cotton was a staple clothing fabric in the nineteenth century West because it was relatively inexpensive and readily available. Cotton garments were almost certainly packed in some of the boxes. Buttons, beads, hooks, and eyes could not be evaluated as sewing notions, nor should they be evaluated as intact artifacts; they are embellishments of an artifact that no longer exists. For these reasons, they were evaluated with the clothing variable.

This method of evaluating artifacts is viable only if the researcher is consistent in evaluating like artifacts, if the assumptions are based on valid historical references, and if each choice is carefully documented and tested. Table 9.2 provides specifications on artifact placement in variables.

9.3. ANALYSIS

Variable distribution across the five sample surveys and in individual boxes was determined through frequency analysis (Table 9.3). Frequencies were run to determine the number of cases (n) in each box. There were 1,685 individual artifacts in the sample. Only 180 cases made up the statistical sample size because there were only 180 catalog numbers representing the five boxes. There were many multiple, similar artifacts associated with a single catalog number. For ex-

Table 9.2. Notes on Artifact Placement in Variables and Values

Gender: Items considered as gender specific included clothing, beads, ribbons, parasols, glass buttons (based on photographic research), perfume, hat pins, tools, dolls, and glass heart. Items that were not labeled gender specific included toys such as blocks, marbles, and tin toys, educational items, generic buttons, household items such as linens, carpets, medicinal items, and illumination devices.

Adornment: Items labeled as adornment included beads, ribbons, lace, and hat pins.

Household: Household items included decorative items (glass heart, clock), books, ritual items (bibles, felt cross), illumination devices, linens, carpets, medicinal items, jewelry box, and seeds.

Sewing: Sewing items included straight pins, bobbins, and spools.

Personal: Items labeled as personal included clothing items, ritual items, school slate (the owner carved her name in it), hat pins, glass heart, parasols, perfume, hairbrushes, doll. Items not labeled personal included toys, tools, household items such as carpets, lamps, linens, and educational items.

Age: Age-specific items included clothing, medicinal items, toys, educational items, and tools.

ample, buttons and beads were cataloged according to type in each box; a single catalog number might have 35, 100, or 300 beads assigned to that number. Therefore, one bead of a given type in each box stood as a case number.

Seventy-eight cases (43.4%) of the sample were in the Atchison box, 56 cases (31.1%) in the Campbell sisters' box, and 13 cases (7.2%) in the Robert Campbell box. The cobbler's box contained 12 cases (6.7%) of the sample, while the carpenter's box contained 17 cases (9.4%) of the total sample size. Table 9.4. illustrates mean figures in each of the artifact boxes.

Significant figures (any probability smaller than alpha, determined for this study to be between 0.000 and 0.050, is called statistically significant) across the entire sample included: 13.3 percent of the items were male and 30.6 percent

Table 9.3. Frequencies across Sample (n = 180)

Gender	Male = 13.3%, female = 30.6%, not sex related = 53.9%
Age	Adult = 25.6%, child = 10.8%, no age = 62.2%
Clothing	Outer = 6.1%, dress = 4.4%, male clothing = 0.6%, shoes = 1.7%, buttons = 22.2%, beads = 10.6%, total clothing = 45.6%
Adornment	Yes = 13.3%, no = 83.3%
Household	Total household = 26.7%
Occupational	Tool = 10.0%, supplies = 3.9%, product = 1.1%, total occupational = 15.0%
Toys	Total = 9.4%
Educational	Total = 5.0%
Sewing	Total = 10.0%
Personal	Yes = 17.8%, no = 80.0%
Manufacture	Manufactured = 58.9%, homemade = 3.3%, unknown = 35.6%'s
Maker's mark	Yes = 3.3%, no = 90.6%
Luxury item	Yes = 6.7%, no = 91.1%

female, while 53.9 percent were not gender specific. Adult items made up 25.6 percent of the total sample, 15.0 percent were occupational, 17.8 percent were personal, and 6.7 percent were luxury items. Most items in the sample generally fell well within the "other" or "no" category. This suggested that most items were not variable specific or that current parameters for determining values in each variable are not yet refined enough for specific identification across the sample.

Table 9.4. suggests there are significant relation between gender and items carried with passengers on the steamboats. Historical information is available on the Atchison and Campbell families. This information showed that these boxes were associated with women and children; it also provided information about where they came from and their economic status. Archaeological information demonstrated that the cobbler and carpenter boxes were largely occupational in nature and probably belonged to men. The combined statistics from the four marked boxes supplied the basis for general hypotheses about the Robert Campbell or unknown box.

Table 9.4. Means Tables in Boxes

Variable	Atchison $n = 78$	Campbell $n = 56$	Unknown $n = 13$	Cobbler $n = 12$	Carpenter $n = 17$
Gender
Male	2.6%	-0-	-0-	41.6%	94.1%
Female	29.4%	42.8%	53.8%	-0-	5.8%
Age
Adult	14.1%	19.6%	7.6%	58.3%	94.1%
Child	15.3%	8.9%	-0-	-0-	5.8%
No age	70.5%	71.4%	92.3%	41.6%	-0-
Clothing	57.6%	50.0%	61.5%	8.3%	-0-
Adornment
Yes	14.4%	12.5%	46.1%	-0-	-0-
Household
Total	57.6%	35.5%	38.4%	-0-	5.8%
Occupational
Total	-0-	-0-	-0-	100.0%	88.2%
Toys	14.1%	8.9%	-0-	-0-	5.8%
Educational	-0-	14.2%	7.6%	-0-	-0-
Sewing	12.8%	10.7%	15.3%	-0-	-0-
Personal	15.3%	30.3%	15.3%	-0-	5.8%
Manufacture
Manufactured	67.9%	46.4%	53.8%	41.6%	88.2%
Homemade	5.1%	1.7%	7.6%	-0-	-0-
Maker's mark	1.2%	1.7%	-0-	-0-	36.3%
Luxury	7.6%	10.7%	-0-	-0-	-0-

Note: Percentages throughout the variable column are based on the total number of artifacts in each box sample that are representative of each artifact category. For example, 7.6% of the total number of items in the Atchison box are luxury items.

For example, both the Atchison box and the Campbell box contained mostly feminine items. The cobbler and carpenter boxes had a significant percentage of typically male-specific occupational items. The items found in the unknown box suggested that it was associated with at least one woman. The age percentage, although low, suggests an adult owner when compared with the high household percentage of 38.4 percent. The cobbler and carpenter boxes contained predominantly adult, male, and occupational-based items, while the Atchison, Campbell, and unknown boxes displayed a significant percentage of adult and female items, as well as items that were not age specific. Examples of items not considered age specific include buttons, perfume bottles, beads, lamp chimneys, and so on. These are all items that could be used by either adults or children. There is no logical way of assigning specific ownership of such items. Clothing was associated in the 50 percent or higher range in the feminine boxes.

At first glance, it appears that 8.3 percent of the items in the cobbler's box were also clothing. This figure, however, is an anomaly due to cross-correlation. For example, one item in the cobbler's box was a leather belt. Belts were classified as outer garments in the clothing variable. The belt in this artifact assemblage, however, also fell in the occupational variable as supplies. Cobblers in the nineteenth century generally did not produce leather objects other than shoes (Saguto, 1995). The belt was well used, and the buckle was missing, suggesting that the belt was probably being used as scrap leather.

Other items of consequence in Table 9.4. include occupational items solely associated with male boxes and sewing and personal items associated with female boxes. The presence of toys in the Atchison box suggested at least one child was represented by the box contents. It was also notable that there were no luxury items associated with occupational boxes, while the Atchison and Campbell boxes had some luxury or wealth dependent items.

Several general conclusions can be made based on information in Table 9.4. The Atchison box represented at least one adult, probably female, traveling with at least one child. The moderate percentage of luxury items suggests the owners were upper middle class. Lillian Schlissel (1982) asserted that the majority of emigrants migrating overland between 1840 and 1870 were made up of "peasant proprietors." These families had owned land before and would own land again. They were dependent on the land for livelihood and subsistence and represented a moderate or median class structure.

Statistically, the Campbell box seemed associated with at least one adult female. The clothing percentage was comparable to the Atchison box, as were household items. This box displayed high percentages of personal items in comparison with the Atchison box. The higher percentage of luxury items combined with the Atchison box may also suggest a higher socioeconomic standing.

When comparing the Robert Campbell (or unknown) box with the Atchison and Campbell boxes, the data suggest that it was associated with at least one

Table 9.5. Logistic Regression "Luxury" with "Personal" (n = 176)

Variable	Significance	R*	Exp(B)**
"Personal"	0.0000	0.4155	2.9109

*Compares the overall similarity of two ordinal (or values with an unknown measure) rankings (Thomas, 1986).
**Measures the percentage of statistical probability.

female. The clothing percentage was similar to the other feminine boxes as was the household percentage, which suggests that the box owner was an adult. This box suggests a female owner of lower social class based on the absence of luxury items.

The male-associated boxes presented no surprises from the original hypotheses. Items were dependent on the owner's occupational, trade, and nothing in these boxes was classified as luxurious. This suggests that these men traveled west with items needed to practice their trade, probably their only monetary means.

9.4. LOGISTIC REGRESSION ANALYSIS

Several questions raised about interrelations between variables were answered by using logistic regression analysis. When "luxury" was regressed with "personal" as the independent variable, there was a 190 percent greater probability that "personal" items were "luxury" items (Table 9.5). When gender was regressed with "age" and "personal," there was a 80 percent greater chance that adult items were female and an 1,100 percent greater chance that "personal" items were female (Table 9.6).

These results support assumptions made in Table 9.4. Personal and luxury items were gender specific, and both were dependent on age. There was no explanation of the discrepancy between personal and luxury items in the unknown box except that the sample number was small. The discrepancy would probably disappear with a larger sample.

Table 9.6. Logistic Regression "Gender" with "Age" and
"Personal" (n = 79)

Variable	Significance	R*	Exp(B)**
"Age"	0.0000	–0.4012	0.2076
"Personal"	0.0009	0.3063	12.5736

*Compares the overall similarity of two ordinal (or values with an unknown measure) rankings (Thomas, 1986).
**Measures the percentage of statistical probability.

9.5. CONCLUSION

The statistical analysis supported most of the archaeological hypotheses about the individuals who owned the boxes made before statistics were applied. The Atchison box was represented by an adult woman and at least one child; the Campbell box contained largely feminine and adult artifacts. The unknown or Robert Campbell box displayed characteristics of an adult female, while both the cobbler and carpenter boxes were almost exclusively occupationally based. Both interpretations are supported by historical information available on some boxes.

The Atchison box belonged to the John S. Atchison family. Mary (24), Charles (5), and Emma (4) were on board the *Bertrand* (*Montana Post,* 1865). John Atchison preceded his family to Montana where he eventually became involved with several banks and was the owner of the Atchinson Trading Post, which supplied the mining camps. The Campbell box belonged to Annie (19) and Fannie (16) Campbell, two daughters of James B. and Sarah Campbell, who moved from St. Louis to Montana in 1862. The young women remained in St. Louis where they attended a Catholic boarding school until they completed their education. These circumstances may explain the high frequency of educational items in their belongings. They were on their way to Montana when the *Bertrand* sank. As founding citizens of the territory, their family was involved with ranching, and politics and owned or had stock in several supply posts in Montana (Petsche, 1974). Historical information, therefore, supports the archaeological and statistical hypothesis that the Campbell and Atchison families were of moderate means and that individuals reflected in the boxes were women and children.

The methods used in this study are replicable if strict consistency is maintained. This analysis can be applied to a larger sample and will provide an opportunity for making general assumptions about the western population as a whole. The difficulties about artifact classification encountered in this sample can be overcome by carefully establishing parameters regarding artifact definitions.

Chapter 10

Conclusions

The goal of studying the material culture of nineteenth century passengers traveling west on board the steamboats *Arabia* and *Bertrand* was to gain information about the gender and socioeconomic background of the passengers who used the nation's inland river system as a primary mechanism for migration. This goal was accomplished by means of an analysis that included historical research, archaeological observations, and quantitative statistical analysis. This combined research methodology has produced information against which the research hypotheses can be tested. The result is some general assumptions about emigrant use of steamboat travel.

10.1. FINDINGS

10.1.1. Hypothesis A

Single men and family groups used steamboats as a mechanism for western travel, whereas single or individual women did not make the journey unaccompanied. The sample used in this study suggested that single men, represented by the cobbler and carpenter, did use steamboat travel as a mechanism for westward movement, as did family units represented by the Atchisons and the Campbell sisters. The Robert Campbell box probably does not represent an individual traveling on board the *Bertrand*; rather, it may represent a package sent to an individual already in the territory.

Single men traveling on the Missouri River are well documented. Brazier, Upham, Granville, and Moss all mention the presence of single men and family groups in their narratives, although the presence of families does not seem as prevalent in the journals as that of single men. There are few instances where single women are reported traveling on steamboats; in most of these cases, the

109

women were referred to as "actresses," implying their association with saloons or makeshift theaters (Brazier, 1953).

The trend of single or unaccompanied women rarely traveling west by steamboat is also typical of documentation for the overland journey. Schlissel (1982) reported that only two of the sixty-eight journals in her study belonged to single women making the journey. One was a widow looking to start over, and the other was a young woman going to Oregon to become a teacher. The new teacher often mentioned in her journal being isolated from the other women in the train because she was traveling alone.

10.1.2. Hypothesis B

Family groups have a greater frequency of household goods, personal items, female and child items, and luxury items than do single males. Quantitative analysis of the study sample demonstrated the viability of Hypothesis B. Statistical analysis suggested that the relationship between women or family groups corresponds to the presence of children and the high frequency of personal, luxury, and household items. The statistical ratio of household and personal items present in boxes associated with women versus male-only boxes was almost 5 to 1. The difference in the amount of luxury items was even greater. Logistic regression analysis demonstrated that there is a viable relation between gender and whether an artifact was both a personal item and a luxury item.

10.1.3. Hypothesis C

Archaeologically and statistically observed data suggested that Hypothesis C, *single men have a higher frequency of occupational-based items associated with their boxes and fewer personal and household items,* is also correct. The lack of household goods and the low frequency of personal items in this sample supported Blee's (1991) contention that single men were far more mobile than were family units. The two examples in this study represent men who probably depended solely on their trade for their livelihood.

10.1.4. Hypothesis D

Children are more likely to be associated with groups that include a definite female presence rather than with just men. The *Arabia* and *Bertrand* examples in the study support this claim. The two men did not appear to have children traveling with them on the steamboats. The carpenter, may, however, have had a child who was left behind, as represented by the Frozen Charlotte doll. This is just one explanation for the presence of the doll. Children represented in the Atchison box journeyed with their mother. No historical references were found indicating that children traveling on the Missouri River did so without a woman present.

10.1.5. Hypothesis E

A statistical method can be devised to demonstrate gender and socioeconomic differences across an artifact population. The primary statistical method used in this study, logistic regression, makes possible general assumptions about artifact use based on statistical inference. The method demonstrated that, if an artifact was used by women, there was a statistically significant probability that the artifact was also a personal and a luxury item. The same was viable for male-specific artifacts. Tools in this example were male specific and not personal or luxury items. Statistical analysis also demonstrated a significant relation between gender and household items, clothing items, adornment, sewing items, and occupational use of artifacts.

This statistical method could not, however, confirm wealth or luxury for a given artifact. The method could only suggest wealth across a comparative sample. An indicator of wealth is irrelevant in a single sample; it only gains relevance as a cultural indicator when compared with measures of wealth in other samples. The variable "luxury" was the most difficult variable in the sample to define. There are no accepted archaeological standards for wealth attributes for artifacts. Archaeologists can evaluate wealth only in terms of a culture or society, in this case steamboat passengers, applicable to the study group. When compared with other boxes in the study, the Campbell sisters displayed a higher ratio of "wealth" than did the Atchisons. Both, however, were considerably more wealthy than the cobbler or carpenter. An archaeological and statistical measure of wealth should be used sparingly and with caution.

10.2. CONCLUSION AND RECOMMENDATIONS

Historically, the people who traveled west onboard steamboats were thought to have been limited to the wealthy and to fur trappers or traders. The wealthy were believed to have traveled to the territories as "well-to-do" cabin passengers, whereas the trappers or tradesmen lounged on the vessel's deck. A survey of steamboat passengers in popular history would have demonstrated two distinct classes. Research using personal journals as well as archaeological evidence examined in this study, however, does not suggest these traditional assumptions are viable.

It is not known exactly how many emigrants used steamboats for westward travel. Certainly, more people crossed the continent overland. However, most emigrant journals that mention steamboats, either as a mechanism for travel or as a sight seen along the way, noted the presence of a few passengers. There probably were some passengers who traveled exclusively as deck passengers, and deck passage was the preferred practice of the American Fur Company trappers. These men, however, were familiar with traveling and living in the open. When on the river, they traveled in fairly large groups and enjoyed one another's merriment (Jackson, 1985). This practice may have been the exception rather than the rule in the upper Missouri mountain trade.

All five boxes used in this study were preserved because they were packed in the holds of the steamboats. Typically, passengers traveling on deck kept their possessions with them on the deck. Hold space was reserved for goods being transported to supply houses and for the cabin passengers who paid more for their passage. The fact that all these study boxes were found in the hold suggests that individuals represented by these boxes traveled as cabin passengers. This is not surprising for the Campbells or Atchisons; but tradesmen, according to popular belief, should not have been able to afford cabin passage. Perhaps the answer to this question lies in the fact that what has been accepted for the upper Missouri River as fact is really the product of popular western "dime" novels.

A careful examination of Missouri River steamboat travel journals shows that they rarely mention deck passengers. Journals imply that the number of passengers was few and that owing to the lengthy journey, the passengers had an opportunity to get to know one another. The journal edited by Brazier (1953) mentions passengers sitting at dining room tables playing cards or tiddledywinks to pass the time. The passengers would work together with the crew to help free the boat from snags or sandbars, and the men on board the vessel would hunt and gather berries during wood stops. These activities suggest a homogeneous population of travelers rather than strict division by class. Regardless of wealth (presumably some passengers were more wealthy than others), all steamboats that were not full or crowded may have had only cabin passengers. This may help explain why cobbler and carpenter boxes were in the holds of two steamers that were lost almost a decade apart.

This study has suggested some possibilities about the variety of individuals who traveled west via the upper Missouri River. It should be noted, however, that the study examined only five examples. Although the *Arabia* and *Bertrand* are the only steamboats salvaged from this area, the results and conclusions of this study should be carefully examined in a larger population. The statistical methods used to examine steamboat passengers should be applied to other historic sites. For example, logistic regression can be used on a large sample of sites with known associations. Organized family units such as homesteads or homes in frontier communities can be compared with male-only households in mining camps and homesteads or frontier community tradesmen. Examining the statistical applications from this example on a larger database will help to verify the validity of logistic regression as a means for evaluating artifact use. Presumably these boxes represent only a portion of the personal belongings of the passengers. Other items that were more important, or used repeatedly, would have been with the passengers in their cabins and are not therefore represented in the collection. A more comprehensive investigation of the statistical application may find several important differences.

Both the *Arabia* and the *Bertrand* offer many other possibilities for archaeological investigation. Both vessels should be considered unique and, therefore, historically significant. In these two collections is a wealth of information about American emigrant travel, based not only on the items lost by passengers but also on the items being shipped to emigrants who had already settled on the upper Missouri River. The mining and settler stores provide information about the economic success of the region, the types of items available for everyday life, and items that were needed. The material culture represented by these two vessels provides a glimpse into the experiences and everyday life of our not so recent past.

Appendix A

Bertrand Box 74 Artifacts (Atchison Family)

Catalog number	Artifact description	Catalog number	Artifact description
62	Fabric scraps	877	Buttons, brass (2)
63	Knitted wool cap	881	Straight pins, brass (2)
66	Silk shawl	899	Box (to blocks)
67	Boy's trousers	900	Box pieces
68	Strip of black silk	901	Veneer strips
69	Wool scraps	982	Whistle
72	Alphabet blocks	922	Buttons, textile (6)
107	Blocks: school	974	Leather boot extender
330	Blocks (alphabet)	1017	Beads, glass (132)
331	Blocks (alphabet)	1018	Beads, glass (23)
332	Blocks (alphabet)	1019	Beads, glass (75)
333	Blocks (alphabet)	1020	Beads, glass (12)
334	Blocks (alphabet)	1021	Beads, glass (10)
335	Blocks (alphabet)	1022	Beads, glass (4)
449	Pony cart (toy)	1023	Beads, glass (4)
507	Nails	1646	Lamp chimneys (4)
508	Nails	1647	Lamp chimneys (8)
509	Nails	1789	Plantation Bitters
581	Steel strap and nails	2870	Rug runner
704	Umbrella tip	2924	Dress fragments (plaid)
715	Wool yarn	2925	Bodice and skirt fragments
803	Button, wood (1)		(brown)
874	Hooks and eyes, brass	3158	Wool fragments
876	Hook (fastener), brass	3159	Ribbons (silk and velvet)

(continued)

Catalog number	Artifact description	Catalog number	Artifact description
3160	Fur wrap	5255	Straight pins, steel (2)
3166	Beads	5287	Crochet fragment
3294	Umbrella covering	5292	Buttons, ceramic (36)
3295	Tablecloth/ fabric bolt	5293	Button, ceramic (1)
3296	Woman's jacket/ smock	5294	Button, ceramic (1)
3297	Cloth fragments	5295	Button, ceramic (1)
3298	Boy's frock coat	5296	Button, ceramic (1)
3763	Buttons, white china (13)	5297	Button, ceramic (1)
3764	Hooks (fasteners), brass (2)	5298	Button, ceramic and brass (1)
3766	Buttons, china (2)	5302	Buttons, glass and brass (10)
3767	Button, china (1)	5339	Buttons, brass (25)
4063	Parasol and parts	5340	Brass shoe eyelets (13)
4130	Beads, glass seed (325)	5343	Buttons, textile (2)
4415	Lady's boot	5344	Buttons, textile (21)
4888	White glass lamp part	5349	Beadwork fragments
4889	Unidentified white glass	5351	Beads, glass (103)
4891	Assorted clock parts	5352	Cloves (3)
4761	Leather fragments	5353	Shoestring tips
4762	Metal fragments	5354	Straight pins, brass (2)
4765	Corks	5355	Straight pins, brass (2)
4890	Clock face fragments	5356	Straight pins, brass (3)
4973	Cloth fragments	5358	Hooks and eyes, iron (7)
5216	Button, ceramic (1)	5359	Hooks and eyes, brass (4)
5244	Buttons, textile (2)	5360	Straight pin, brass (1)
5249	Buttons, glass (9)	5361	Straight pins, brass (2)
5254	Straight pins, steel (60)	5362	Straight pin, brass (1)

Note: Catalog numbers 4888, 4889 (white glass fragments) and 4891, 4890 (clock pieces) were assigned accession and catalog numbers, but there were no records of these items in the collection.

Appendix B

Bertrand EPC- 8 Artifacts (Campbell Sisters)

Catalog number	Artifact description	Catalog number	Artifact description
87	Pair of shoes	485	Book cover
142	Black laquer box	700	Nails from black laquer box
144	Book back binding "MUSIC"	704	Umbrella handle? tip
146	Bible cover	707	Drawer nob
145	Reed mat	710	Toiletry vial and cork (1)
147	Bottom tray (associated with jewelry box)	711	Toiletry vials and corks (2)
		712	Toiletry vials and corks (17)
148	Jewelry box	714	Toiletry vial and cork (1)
149	Metal strips and loose fasteners from jewelry box	725	Hat pins, brass (2)
		738	Artist pastels (sticks)
150	Blackboard	741	Leather packet
152	Braid, thread, ribbon	744	Hinges from black laquer box
153	Tacks, jewelry box (20)	745	Hinges from jewlery box
159	Black net lace fragments	746	Lock from black laquer box
353	Buttons, white china (66)	747	Lock from jewlery box
354	Buttons, turquoise (22)	875	Wood fragments from jewelry box
436	Peach pits		
454	Wood fragments from jewelry box top tray	906	Laquer fragments from black Chinese box
482	Book back binding "HERBARIUM"	933	Buttons, textile (21)
		948	Button, ceramic (1)
483	Book back binding	991	Glass fragments
484	Book back binding "MITCHELL'S SCHOOL GEOGRAPHY"	997	Nail fragments from jewelry box
		998	Screws from jewelry box

(continued)

117

Catalog number	Artifact description	Catalog number	Artifact description
999	Nails from black Chinese box	2917	Bow (blue, associated with school
1041	Bead, glass (1)		uniform)
1042	Beads, glass (39)	2918	Cape (black, silk)
1043	Beads, glass (27)	2919	Buttons, silk (19)
1161	Watermelon seeds	2920	Buttons, silk (6)
1197	Cape, silk	2921	Button (1)
1206	Straight pins, brass (2)	2922	Hooks and eyes, brass (36)
1211	Wood fragments	2923	Straight pins, brass (65)
1222	Nails from black Chinese box	2965	Dress/coat, silk
1223	Screws from black Chinese box	3339	Fringe, thread, yarn
1843	World map	3698	Child's gloves (3)
2846	Dress (2 school uniform)	3720	Buttons, wood (2)
2906	Sock fragments	3915	Chinese box (green)
2910	Buttons (19)	4033	Glass heart
2911	Beads, glass (64)	4203	Buttons, glass (1)
2912	Mitt, girl's	4204	Button, glass (1)
2913	Cloth (wool, redfloral on beige	4295	Nail
	background)	4308	Eye (fastener) (1)
2914	Tassels (2 associated with	4678	Leather (miscellaneous pieces)
	2913)	4689	Spool of elastic (fragments)
2915	Wrist warmer (knitted)	4690	Corset stays
2916	Material (petit point pieces)	4763	Picture frame and glass

Note: Peach pits, picture frames, and six pairs of ladies' shoes were associated with this box but are missing catalog numbers.

Appendix C

Bertrand MSC-128 Artifacts (Robert Campbell)

Catalog number	Artifact description	Catalog number	Artifact description
784	Buttons, ceramic (7)	4043	Brush backs (2)
1024	Beads, glass (27)	4648	Feathers from duster, missing
1025	Perforated disk (bead?) (1)	4669	Straw, missing
1026	Beads, glass (11)	4670	Painted wood, missing
1027	Beads, glass (7)	4754	Book cover bindings, missing
1028	Beads, glass (5)	5381	Wood strips
3170	Ribbon fragments, silk	5406	Miscellaneous leather, missing
3171	Sock fragments (6)	—	Wooden spools
3492	Wool flannel fragments	—	Wooden spools
3493	Striped sock fragments	—	Metal bobbins
3725	Felt cross		

Note: Two sets of box fragments (accession # 2055, 2952) were discarded in 1972; they probably made up the original container.This box also contained two sets of wooden spools (accession # 2930, 2935) and a set of metal bobbins (accession # 2930).These items were never given catalog numbers and cannot be located, although they were recorded in the box notes.These items were considered important for the computer analysis and were included.

Appendix D

Bertrand FSC-234 Artifacts (Cobbler's Barrel)

Catalog number	Artifact description
883	Folding rule section
2671	Billfold, leather
2958	Dress boots
3949	Leather working tools (7)
3986	Leather bible cover
3992	Shoe repair parts
4069	Riding boots
5306	Farmer's bundles, shoes, leather repair parts
5307	Belt, leather
5308	Scrap leather and shoe repair items
5309	Book covers and binding
—	Cobbler's tool case

Note: In 1972, several uncataloged box fragments and barrel staves were discarded. There was no information available on the size of the box, but the barrel measured 16 ½ inches in diameter by 28 inches long. Field notes indicated the above items were packed in the barrel. There was also an uncataloged cobbler's tool case discarded in 1972. No information was available on this item either. All these items were included in the computer analysis.

Appendix E

Bertrand Cargo
(Total Artifact Collection)

Artifact	Count
Personal utilization	
Clothing and footwear	
Belt	1
Billfolds	1 complete, 2 incomplete
Necklace clasps	11 complete, 1 incomplete
Parasols	2 incomplete
Pocketknives	33 complete, 28 incomplete
Coats, children's	1
Coats, ladies'	4
Coats, men's, caped	61
Coats, men's, dusters	5
Coats, men's, frock	17
Men's slickers and leggings	13 slickers, 12 leggings
Mens suit coats	125
Mens suit and trousers	2
Gloves	3
Handkerchiefs	22
Hats, ladies'	22
Hats, men's, beaver	36
Hats, men's, felt	192 complete, 106+ incomplete
Mufflers and scarves	6
Shawls	6
Shirts	80+
Stockings	125+
Sweaters	45+

(*continued*)

Artifact	Count
Ties	6 complete, 7 incomplete
Trousers	103
Vests	24
Boots	616
Boots, children's	78
Boots, ladies'	62
Boots, men's, buffalo	116 complete, 132+ incomplete
Boots, men's, dress	358
Boots, men's, hobnail	714
Boots, men's, riding	26
Shoes, children's	726
Shoes, ladies'	513
Shoes, men's	234
Shoes, laces	288
Slippers	2

Household utilization

Armaments

Howitzer cases	2
Howitzer shot	55
Howitzer sabots	86 complete, 2 incomplete
Howitzer primers	29 complete, 28 incomplete
Miscellaneous howitzer parts	250+
Maynard	123 complete, 12 incomplete
Percussion caps	62 boxes containing a total of 7,320 caps
Shot balls	780
Shot bars	221
Shot molds	2 complete, 1 incomplete
Flasks and pouches	29 complete, 31 incomplete
Gun worms	13 complete, 3 incomplete

Books and stationery

Almanacs	13 incomplete
Book covers	16 complete, 59 incomplete
Clipboards	11 pieces
Letter clips	5
Paper spindle	1
Rubber bands	1 mass
Ink	115 bottles
Pencils	7 complete, 97 pieces
Pens	20 complete, 90 incomplete

Furnishings, culinary, linens, lighting devices, and the like

Blankets	Several incomplete
Chamber sets (basins, pitchers, pots)	2 basins, 9 pitchers, 2 pots

Artifact	Count
Dusters	2 complete
Scrub brushes	40 incomplete
Soap	8 cases
Clocks	1 complete, 3 incomplete
Floor coverings	3
Fireplace shovels and tongs	13 each
Stove parts	8
Kitchen knives	95
Butter churns	9 incomplete
Coffee grinders	15, plus 310 parts
Coffee pots	5
Colanders	3 complete, 5 incomplete
Corkscrews	31
Cups	78 complete, 42 incomplete
Dredge box	1
Mixing bowls	2
Pots and pans	19 complete, 8 incomplete
Cake pans	2, complete, 4 incomplete
Frying pans	48
Griddles	2
Kettles	2
Teakettles	5
Waffle irons	2
Indigo laundry dye	1 case
Irons	2
Washboards	66
Candles	12,371
Candleholders	51
Candle molds	8
Lamp bases	151
Lamp brackets	19
Lamp burners	300
Lamp chimneys	296
Lamp fonts	138
Lamp frames	16
Lamp reflectors	5
Smoke bells	8
Matches	12 cases
Mirrors	1 case
Picture frames	2
Bowls	17 complete, + many parts
Butter dish	1 incomplete
Cups and saucers	8 cups, 8 saucers
Gravy boats	1 incomplete

(*continued*)

Artifact	Count
Ladles	1
Pitchers	4
Plates	48 complete, 23+ incomplete
Platters	12 complete, 8 incomplete
Tureens	1
Forks	66
Knives	69
Tablespoons	34
Teaspoons	100
Candy dishes	3
Compotes	20 incomplete
Condiment bottles	14 complete, 6 incomplete
Goblets	18 complete, 23 incomplete
Mugs	2
Salt Cellars	5
Tumblers	71 complete, 13 incomplete
Caster set with tray	1
Shot glasses	110 complete, 43 incomplete
Groceries	
Animal remains	1,693 miscellaneous bones
Meat	10 cases
Tallow	1 sack
Cream of tarter	2 cases
Saleratus	1 case
Yeast powder	5 cans, 1,193 incomplete cans
Coffee	1 case
Essence of coffee beverage	3 cans, 42+ incomplete cans
Lemonade	57 cans, 293 vials, 10 cases
Lemon syrup	22 bottles
Candy	22 cases
Chow chow	1 case
Cloves	1 bag
Horseradish	65 bottles
Ketchup	63 bottles
Western spice mills	29 bottles
London club sauce	61 bottles
Mustard	45 bottles, 7 incomplete cans
Nutmeg	2 cans
Pepper	10 complete bottles, 16+ incomplete
Pimento	1 case
Spice Mills Pepper Sauce	16 bottles
Spice Mills St. Louis Sauce	65 bottles
Spice Mills Western Sauce	120 bottles
Superior Bird Sauce	44 bottles

Artifact	Count
Worcester Sauce	31 bottles
Fish remains	1 case of bones (3 lbs.), codfish, and mackerel
Oysters	77 cans
Sardines	35 cans, 5 cases
Fruits, assorted cans	1 case, 23 incomplete cans
Fruits, berry	1 case
Brandied cherries	14 bottles
Brandied peaches	11 bottles
Cranberries	1 case
Currants	2 bags
Gooseberries	1 case
Grapes	1 bag
Peaches	91 cans, 10 cases
Pineapple	1 case of cans
Raisins	+ sacks
Strawberries	17 cans, 4 cases
Tamarinds	10 bottles, 1 case
Almonds	8 bags
Hazelnuts	3 bags
Peanuts	4 bags
Pecans	3 bags
Jelly	138 bottles, 4 cases
Marmalade	1 case
Butter	2 jars, 4 chunks
Lard	2 complete containers, 13 incomplete
Olive Oil	35 bottles
Honey	311 bottles
Sugar	In kegs and barrels
Syrup	In kegs and barrels
Mixed vegetables	10 bottles
Peppers	3 bottles
Pickles	260 bottles
Tomatoes	2 bottles, 2 cases
Ale	73+ bottles
Brandy	1 case
Champagne	230 large bottles, 702 small bottles
Schnapps	63 bottles
Whiskey cocktail	64 bottles
Wine	19 bottle, 2 Demijohns
Health and hygiene	
Combs	365 complete, 65 incomplete
Hairpins	6 complete, 4 incomplete

(*continued*)

Artifact	Count
Medicinal	
Apothecary bottles	1 case
Essence of ginger	132
Drake's Plantation Bitters	67 complete, 18 incomplete
Hostetter's bottles	7 large, 593 small
Bottle corks	254
Kelly's bottles	102
Kintzing bottles	10
Schroeder's bar measure	1
Schroeder's spice	233 bottles
Schroeder's stomach	90 bottles
Prescription bottles	19
Cod liver oil	2 complete, 18 incomplete in pails, tins, and cases
Sewing	
Cloth, bolts of	9+
Cotton print pieces	1,697 pieces—use unknown
Buckles, grips, and guides	82 complete, 28+ incomplete
Suspenders	106 complete, 45+ incomplete
Buttons—varied types	8,532
Hooks and eyes	2,085 hooks, 1,901 eyes
Needles	115
Pins	12 + two 2 lb. masses
Scissors	14 complete, 10 incomplete
Thimbles	118
Thread, spools	44
Beads	4,377
Braid	57
Tobacco	
Cigars	18 complete cases, 43 incomplete cases
Match safes	31
Pipes—bits	2
Pipes—bowls	358
Pipes—stems	23
Tobacco	3 cases, 17 bags, 5 jars

Architectural utilization

Building and hardware supplies	
Hook fasteners	103
Nails and spikes	327 complete, 74 incomplete
Kegs	1 incomplete
Nuts, bolts and washers	19 complete sets, 3 incomplete
Screws	540 (11 bags, 2 boxes, 1 can)

Artifact	Count
Tacks	424 (2 bags—10 lbs. 11 oz. each)
Curtain fixtures	17
Furniture hardware	46
Hinges and parts	982 complete, 21 incomplete
Locks and latches	207 (22 sets) complete, 34+ (24 sets) incomplete
Doorknobs and parts	73 pairs, 1 single complete, 72 incomplete
Keyhole covers and plates	102 complete, 7+ incomplete
Keys	42
Padlocks	4 with keys, 5 without keys
Miscellaneous lock parts	39
Shutter screws	24
Bricks	164 complete, 323 pieces
Paint, white lead	24 kegs
Tar paper	2 bags
Window frames	8
Window glass	60 cases (most broken)
Buckets and parts	28 complete, 190+ incomplete or parts
Chain	1 case (102.5 feet)
Grease cans	13 complete, 11 incomplete
Grease, cases of	3 cases (27 cans total)
Oil cans	1
Spigots	27 complete, 4 incomplete
Tubs and parts	3 complete, 11 incomplete

Transportation utilization

Wagon springs	4

Occupational utilization

Agriculture and husbandry

Plows and parts	3 incomplete plows, 142+ parts
Forks and parts	25 complete forks, 113 incomplete forks, 101 parts
Grain cradle parts	135 complete, 51 incomplete
Hoes	3 complete, 15 incomplete
Scale	1
Scythes parts	36
Cowbells	12
Sleigh bells	2 complete, 5 incomplete
Harness	361 complete, 7 incomplete
Spur straps	23
Whips	17 complete, 32+ incomplete
Slave shackles	17

(*continued*)

Artifact	Count
Blacksmith equipment	
Anvils	1 complete, 1 incomplete
Bellows and parts	1 complete, 16 incomplete
Miscellaneous	11
Nails	662 (1 bag, 1 box - 42 lbs, 1 case - 26 lbs)
Rasps	30
Stock, dies, and tap set	1 (8 pieces)
Tongs	5
Leather working	
Leather	6 rolls (639 Pieces)
Polish brushes	72
Shoe blacking	5 cases
Tools	2 complete, 6 incomplete
Mining equipment	
Blasting fuses	6 bags
Mercury flasks	9
Mortars and pestles	4
Picks	103
Powder	24 kegs
Shovels	185 complete, 613 incomplete
Tools	
Axes, heads, and handles	4 assembled, 239 handles, 120 heads
Brace and bits	62 complete, 14 incomplete
Carpenter's squares	2 incomplete
Chisels	24 complete, 6+ incomplete
Clamp and vises	9 complete, 7 incomplete
Draw knives	4
Files—various types	672 complete, 36 incomplete
Froe	1
Gimlets	11 complete, 25+ incomplete
Grindstone hardware	15+
Grindstones	5
Hammers	12 complete, 14 heads
Hatchets	5 complete, 3 incomplete
Levels	12 complete, 1 incomplete
Mallets	5
Measuring dividers	1
Measuring pans	3
Rulers	1 complete, 2 incomplete
Scales	1 complete, 3 incomplete
Tape measures	2
Nail puller	1

Artifact	Count
Planes	17 complete, 4 incomplete
Saws and parts	7 complete, 603 incomplete or parts
Screwdrivers	2
Trowels	2 complete, 2 incomplete
Wedges	104
Whetstones	163 complete, 3 incomplete
Wrenches	4 complete, 4 incomplete

Note: This cargo listing is a synopsis of material from the *Bertrand* Museum database modified to fit my artifact scheme.

Appendix F

Arabia Carpenter's Box Artifacts

Catalog number	Artifact description
A2065P	Sticking knife
A2127P	Draw knife
A2129P	Whetstone
A2134P	Frozen Charlotte doll, ceramic
A2160P	Screw arm
A2161P	2" paring chisel
A2162P	Large sawmill dog
A2163P	Small sawmill dog
A2165P	Carpenter's wrench
A2166P	Lever saw set
A2167P	1/4" London-pattern sash mortise chisel
A2168P	3/8" mortise chisel
A2169P	1 7/8" forming chisel
A2170P	1 3/8" paring chisel
A2171P	Hand-held saw
A2172P	1" bevel-edge paring chisel or gouge
—	Miscellaneous pistol parts

Appendix G

Arabia Cargo
(Total Artifact Collection)

Artifact	Count
Personal utilization	
Clothing and footwear	
Mitten	16
Trousers, men's	9
Scarf	9
Shawl	1
Shirt	58
Sock	86
Underwear, long	35
Vest	10
Sweater, woman's	1
Coat	103, wool and beaver
Hat	247, wool and beaver
Bolt	60, wool, beaver, silk
Belt	72
Leather boots and shoes	5,000
Shoes, rubber	252
Purse	25
Adornment	
Earring	13 pairs
Brooch	41
Ring	10 gold plate, 6 gold
Bonnet Stick Pin	102

(*continued*)

Artifact	Count
Toiletries	
Hairbrush	51
Jar, cosmetic	24 ironstone, 11 glass
Toothbrush	45
Hairpin	6,000 steel, 13 rubber
Eyeglasses	24
Tinted eye protector	24
Mirror, hand held	42
Lotion, coconut	18
Lotion, unscented	32
Perfume	23
Perfume vial	4
Straight razor	50
Chamber pot	1
Shaving brush	36
Comb, tuck	132

Child utilization

Toys	
Charolette doll	1
Toy rickshaw	1
Marbles	7
Doll arms and legs	80
Doll shoe	1
Sea shell	2

Household utilization

Armaments	
Percussion boot pistol	14
Ram rod	14
Bullet mold	14
Flintlock trade gun	48
Percussion double barrel shotgun	2
Percussion single barrel shotgun	1
Percussion single barrel rifle	1
Ball shot, lead	500,000
Powder flask	31
Powder horn	9
Percussion cap	1,000
Books and stationery	
Inkwell	163
Slate board	50

Artifact	Count
Pencil, slate	1,000
Writing pen	220
Nib	2,000
Pencil, lead	506
Ink, writing	11 bottles
Book cover	25

Furnishings, culinary, linens, lighting devices, and the like

Blanket	3
Can, tin	230
Can with lid and spout	1
Canning jar lid	14
Cylinder, tin	5
Fuel can with folding lid	1
Tea canister (empty)	1
Square tin	1
Spice box	7
Pail with lid and handle	11
Pail with locking lid	2
Coffee tin	1
Oval tin box	5
Oil can	4
Round, flat tin	4
Canister	10
Scroll bottle	96
Bucket	74
Washtub	20
Canning jar	18
Whiskey jug	6
Butcher knife	188
Fighting knife	3
Table knife	616
Fork	676
Spoon	665
Bread pan	2
Bowl with strainer	5
Coffee grinder bottoms	19
Baking pan	50
Coffee pot	27
Cookie cutter	3
Cake pan	12
Fluted muffin tin	5
Fluted pie pan	2
Funnel	4

(*continued*)

Artifact	Count
Ladle	1
Nutmeg grinder	1
Pie pan	3
Pan with handle	2
Round lid	17
Strainer	1
Shaker	13
Scoop with handle	9
Tea kettle	2
Pan with pouring lip	1
Wash basin with 3 feet	6
Pat with swing handle	10
Skillet	13
Griddle	5
Pot, 3 footed	2
Meat grinder	1
Grain grinder	4
Kettle with lid	2
Deep skillet	1
Stove	1
Stove base	12
Coffee mill wrench	25
Pot with flared rim	1
Pot with straight sides	1
Stove foot	26
Ladle, coconut	12
Coffee grinder	42
Rolling pin	2
Coconut dipper	15
Caster set with shaker top	24
Salt dip	18
Drinking glass, small	5
Syrup jug	19
Candy dish	1
Shot glass	30
Cruet with stopper	4
Davenport, Frieberg,	Ironstone—2 bowls, 2 bowls with lids, 2 pitchers, 14 plates, 14 sauce dishes, 9 saucers
Davenport, White	Ironstone—1 bowl, 1 pitcher, 11 plates, 8 saucers
Davenport, Cypress	Ironstone—2 washbowls, 3 pitchers
Davenport, Queensware	Ironstone—17 basins
Davenport, White	Ironstone—9 saucers, 4 pitchers

Artifact	Count
Davenport, Shell-edge blue	Ironstone—26 platters, 11 bowls, 69 plate
Unmarked, Shell-edge blue	Ironstone—11 rectangular casseroles
J. Wedgewood	Ironstone—2 platters, 2 casseroles and 4 lids, 52 plates, 18 dishes
C. Meigh & Son	Ironstone—2 pitchers, 6 bowls, 2 casseroles
T. Goodfellow	Ironstone—8 saucers, 5 cups, 1 bowl
Unmarked, White	Ironstone—54 bowls, 88 plates, 27 cups, 11 containers with lids, 2 pitchers, 1 lid
J. Heath	Ironstone—2 pitchers
Edwards & Hall, Felsphar	China—9 plates
J & R Booth	China—1 platter
J. Edwards, Dale Hall, Felsphar	China—11 bowls, 1 teapot, 1 sugar bowl, 2 pitchers, 2 shell-shaped dishes, 4 oval platters, 4 oval vegetable dishes
Gold-rimmed dishes	China—2 dinner plates, 11 pie plates, 10 sauce dishes, 11 saucers, 1 sugar bowl, 1 teapot
Imperial French	China—2 saucers
Real Ironstone	China—2 relish dishes
Pankhurst & Co. ironstone	China—1 bowl
Unmarked floral tea set	China—1 teapot, 5 saucers, 20 cups
Unmarked brown	Ceramic—2 pitchers
[___]NET & BRO. PITTSBURGH	Ceramic—5 yellow ware bowls
Unmarked yellow ware	Ceramic—1 bowl
Syrup jug	1
Serving tray	13 cast iron
Tin cup with handle	12
J & J Water Dale Hall Pottery	1 Lonoport raised-relief pitcher, porcelain
Brass tray	12
Spigot	43
Dust pan with no handle	1
Lacquered tray	12
Washboard	4
Cuspidor	1
Statuette	2
Hemp rug	1
Clothespin	418
Mirror and frame	29
Wall candle holder	1
Lamp, top	2
Lantern top with hanging ring	2
Lantern	6
Candle mold	6

(*continued*)

Artifact	Count
Candlestick holder	24
Whale oil lamp	67
Match containers with matches	179
Candle	3,168
Lamp	2
Lantern with glass globe	4
Soap	5 kegs
Clothes boiler top	1
Shoe polish	21
Sad iron	23
Clothes boiler	2
Clothes boiler bottom	8
Jaw harp	48
Umbrella	72
Pocket knife	328

Groceries

Gin	13 bottles
Wine	1 bottle
Cider champagne	13 bottle
Cognac	77 bottles
Sherry	2 bottles
Western Mills Spice Sauce	20 bottles
Large pickle	23 bottles
Small pickle	6 bottles
Pickle relish	6 bottles
Ketchup	12 bottles
Apples	5 bottles
Gooseberries	9 bottles
Rhubarb	2 bottles
Cherries	36 bottles
Currants	8 bottles
Blackberries	2 bottles
Peppercorn	1 bottle, 10 lbs. boxed
Ale	1 keg
Spiced pigs' feet	2 kegs
Butter	10 kegs
Cheese	10 kegs
Lard	8 kegs
Mackerel	2 kegs
Sardines	48 cans
Oysters	24 cans
Grapes	5 lbs.
Fish	5 lbs.
Cloves	10 lbs.

Artifact	Count
Coffee	15 lbs.
Nuts and seeds	12 lbs.
Ox	1
Pig	2

Indian trade goods

Bead	5,000,000 glass, silver, brass
American vermillion	6 boxes

Medicinal

Pine tar	6 kegs
Barrell's Indian Lineament	3
Genuine Essence	1
Dr. D. Jaynes Expectorant Philada	1
Mexican Mustange Lineament	8
Nerve and Bone Lineament	11
Maguire Druggist St. Louis Mo.	9
Castor oil	24
Pills in round tin	9
Lancet with 3 blades	5
Lice comb	56
Old Dr. J. Townsend's Bitters	1
Dr. J. Hostetter's Stomach Bitters	11
Leg bottle	11
Test-tube–shaped clear bottles	90 with a variety of colored liquids
Cylinder-shaped clear bottle	14

Sewing

Suspender pull	57
Buckle	111
Hook and eye	1,250
Eyelet, shoe	100
Button	34,939
Needle	5,000
Scissors	100
Thimble	469
Straight pin	10,000
Bias tape, wool	32
Rickrack, wool	9
Empty spool	500
Yarn, wool	26 skeins, 5 balls
Embroidery floss, silk	28
Thread, silk	28
Thread twist, silk	65

(*continued*)

Artifact	Count
Tobacco	
Tobacco chew	200
Cigar	7,000
Cigar box	500
Chewing tobacco	3 kegs
Pipe tobacco	100
Pipe stem	100
Pipe bowl	100

Architectural utilization

Building and hardware supplies	
Paint can with paint	2
Various parts to door latch	700
Door handle	377
Door lock	338
Door lock hardware	180
Shutter screw	40
Gate lock	2
Door latch	8
Rope fastener	27
Staple	14
Door knob plate	203
Rope guides	27
Key, bit (steel)	366
Key, bit (brass)	248
Hinge	314
Bolt	85
Nail	1,000,000
Wood screw	10,000
Coffin screw	60
Tumbler padlock	81
Screw pulley	36
Padlock (brass)	1
Latch plate	2
Keyhole cover	19
Door lock	12
Cupboard catch	41
Curtain rod cap	18
Keyhole plate	1 brass, 45 brass and steel
Square lock	19
Dead bolt	8
Doorknob	1 ceramic and steel, 10 porcelain and brass, 186 ceramic and steel, 78 ceramic
Nut, square	40

Artifact	Count
Window pane	700
Prefabricated house	2
Lumber, building	10 tons
Coat hook	239
Bootscraper	9 iron, 1 steel
Bed caster	27
Bootjack	6
Steelyard scale	11
Lightning rod bracket	13
Curtain rod holder	18
Sash pulley	28
Bunghole gate valve	3
Animal trap	9
Bed spring	20
Curtain rod	24
Lead bar	1,040
Lightning rod insulator	14
Rope	1,000 feet
Chain	30
Hide	300 hides

Transportation utilization

Wagon wheel	6
Wagon axle	2
Double tree	1
Wagon tongue	1

Occupational utilization

Agriculture and husbandry

Bell	17
Cow bell	1
Curry comb	120
Riding whip	36
Bridle ornament	4
Bridle, ring harness	27
Bridle, rosette	5
Stirrup	18
Spur	19
Bridle	24
Bull whip	24 leather, 12 rubber
Saddle	5
Rein	24
Bit	11

(*continued*)

Artifact	Count
Printing equipment	
Glue pot	2
Printers' type	250,000
Printer block	1
Sawmill equipment	
Sawmill gear	6
Shaft	1
Lumber mill cog	2
Sawmill mill bearing	6
Sawmill blade, round	2
Sawmill blade, straight	6
Caster for moving logs	8
Belting	2
Tools	
Auger handle	19
Ax handle	76
Ax head	235
Freight carrier	1
Tool box	1
Shovel handle	8
Scribe	12
Yardstick	3
Folding ruler	3
Hand ax	9
Saw handle	63
Saw brace	15
Pick handle	26
Hand maul	1
Wood screw	2
Wood vice	3
Wood nut	3
Shoe form	2
Mallet	1
Carpenter plane	50
Paint brush	10
Level	10
Hatchet with hammer	11
Hatchet with claw	2
Chisel with handle	22
Eye auger with handle	5
Leather punch	3
T-auger	21
Saw set	15

Artifact	Count
Block and tackle	2
Screwdriver	5
Hammer	1
Square trowel	3
Triangular trowel	4
Draw knife	25
File	324
Hand saw and blade	111
Spoke shave	2
Snatch block	2
Shovel	20
Wrench	96
Block plane blade	8
Engine drain valve wrench	1
Barrel lifting tong	6
Cargo hook	6
Fireplace shovel	34
Fireplace tong	34
Bed key	19
Boiler tool	7
Needle nose pliers	3
Horseshoe pliers	1
Carpenter adze	1
Poll adze	1
Gutter adze	1
Shipbuilder adze	1
Divider	12
Compass	2
Grub mattock	12
Fro	1
Pick	24
Hammer head	3
Gouge	9
Combination 5-hole wrench	30
Three-hole wrench	6
Crosscut saw	17
Chisel	35
Square	49
Swedge	16
Broad ax	9
Gimlet	89
Keyhole saw	27
Drill bit	119

(*continued*)

Artifact	Count
Pitch fork	3
Screw wrench	12
Tap and die set	12
Sharpening stone	169
Tape measure	6
Ladle with pouring edge	1

Note: This cargo listing is a synopsis of material from G. Hawley (1998), modified to fit my artifact scheme.

Appendix H

Steamboats on the Missouri River

The material used in the compilation of this appendix has come from printed sources, private manuscripts, historical society collections, and both public and private archives. Published sources include Brazier (1953), Cassler (1999), Chappell (1905), Chittenden (1897 and 1903), Corbin (1998), Granville (1867), D. Hawley (1995), G. Hawley (1998), Hunter (1949), Jackson (1985), Lass (1962), Lytle and Holdcamper (1975), McDonald (1927), Moss (1963), Overholser (1987), W. J. Peterson (1945), Petsche (1974), Upham (1865), Vyzralek (1970), and Ways (1983).

A. B. Chambers, a side-wheel packet built in Cincinnati, Ohio, in 1855. 225' × 33', rated at 417 tons, with two engines (22' × 6') and five boilers (24' × 38'), which allowed a working pressure of 151 lbs. Named for the editor of the *Missouri Republican* newspaper. Captain Jim Gormley originally built the vessel for the Missouri River trade. Snagged and sank on her first trip up the Missouri above Atchison, Kansas, in March 1856. The vessel was raised and sold. During the winter of 1858–59, she operated on the Mississippi River with Samuel Clemens (Mark Twain) as pilot. Was snagged and lost in the Missouri River just above the mouth on September 24, 1860, and was a total loss. This vessel is also referred to as A. B. CHAMBERS No. 2.

A. C. Bird, a stern-wheel packet built in Grafton, Illinois, in 1875. 144.4' × 26.6' × 4.1' and rated at 132 tons, with two engines (16' × 5') and three boilers (22' × 38'), which allowed a working pressure of 164 lbs. The vessel was owned by John and George Burruss at the time of loss, with Captain George Burress serving as master. The vessel was sunk by a snag near Kansas City, Missouri, on October 15, 1880, becoming a total loss.

A. C. Goddin, a side-wheel packet built in Madison, Indiana, in 1856. The vessel was rated at 351 tons. Ran the Glasgow trade and was sunk by a snag on April 20, 1857, on the lower Missouri River. Captain John LaBarge was master at the time of the loss. The boat and cargo were a total loss. The vessel was valued at $20,000.

A. M. Phillips, a 175-ton vessel built in 1836. Very little is known about this vessel. She was reported as snagged on the lower Missouri River in Missouri on September 11, 1841.

Abeona, a stern-wheel packet built in Paducah, Kentucky, in 1864. 158' × 35' × 5.6' and 206 tons. The steamer was at the Fort Benton, Montana Territory levee in 1867. The vessel burned on March 7, 1872.

Abner O'Neal, a stern-wheel packet built in Freedom, Pennsylvania, in 1884. 160' × 28' × 3.8', rated at 197 tons. Originally designed and built by John M. Sweeney of Wheeling for the Wheeling–Seubenville trade. Captain George O'Neal commanded the boat until she was sold to the Missouri River Transportation Company in 1890. When she was sold her name was changed to CHASKE, but the name was not approved by customs and therefore never used. Captain R. A. Talbott was in command when the boat snagged in North Dakota on July 17, 1892, while carrying wheat to Bismarck from points above for the Mandan Roller Mill Co. Some of the cargo was salvaged, but the boat and approximately 1,600 sacks of grain were a total loss. The wreck reportedly reappeared in the 1950s during a period of low water.

Abraham, see LEXINGTON

Ad Hine, a 94-ton vessel built in 1874. She a long career despite the fact that so little is known about her. The boat foundered on August 9, 1928, at Musick Ferry, Missouri.

Ad Hine, see NUGGET

Admiral, a side-wheel packet built in McKeesport, Pennsylvania. 169' × 26' with two engines (20' × 5.5'), three boilers (24' × 38"), which allowed a working pressure of 130 lbs. Operated out of St. Paul in 1854 and then ran principally on the Missouri River (St. Louis to Council Bluffs trade). On the Missouri River, the boat was owned and commanded by Captain William Barker. The boat sank in shallow water at Weston, Missouri, in October 1858 but was raised. The vessel finally burned and was lost at Columbus, Kentucky, on April 5, 1862.

Adriatic, a stern-wheel packet built in Shousetown, Pennsylvania, in 1854. The vessel was 200' × 45' × 6.5' and is reported to be one of the largest stern-wheelers of her time. The vessel was unusual in that she actually had two stern-wheels, each handled by two engines. She was one of only four multiple engine/wheel vessels (also the ALAM, AUNT LEE, J.S. PRINGLE, and the CHALLENGE). She ran on the Missouri River with Captain Charles Stone as master and was part of Porter's Red River expedition in 1864. The boat sank at the head of Palmyra Bend in the Missouri River on March 28, 1865. The vessel was raised and later dismantled.

Aggie, a stern-wheel packet built in Manchester, Ohio, in 1875. 92.4' × 20.4' × 3'. The boat originally ran the Evansville–Owensboro trade daily in 1875. She was sold to Azro Powell of Uniontown, Kentucky, in 1876 with no cash involved. The steamer was traded for a 250-acre farm on Mississippi Bend. The boat was then sold onto the Missouri River where she was reported to run in connection with the railroad at Portland. She was noted on the Osage River in 1880 and 1881 and then sank at Kansas City in 1885 from unknown causes.

Agnes, a stern-wheel packet built in Cincinnati, Ohio, in 1864. 160' × 33' × 5' and rated 236 tons. The boat was originally named the FLORENCE MILLER No. 3 but was impressed into service on December 7, 1864, and made the U. S. tinclad #52 ORIOLE. The boat was sold on October 14, 1865, and renamed AGNES. She was logged in at Fort Benton in 1866 and 1867 but was then snagged and lost on March 3, 1869.

Alert, 66 tons and possibly a ferryboat. Not much is known about this vessel. She foundered at Musick Ferry, Missouri, on August 9, 1928.

Alert, a side-wheel packet built in 1835. The boat struck a snag and sank near Herman, Missouri, in 1840 and became a total loss. The location of the wreck was later referred to as Alert Bend.

Alex Majors, a side-wheel packet built in St. Louis, Missouri, in 1857. 371 tons with two engines and boilers that allowed a working pressure of 100 psi. The boat was originally built for the U.S. government and originally named MINK because she was painted brown. Later the boat was painted white and the name changed to ALEX MAJORS. The newly painted and named boat operated at St. Joseph, Missouri, in connection with the Hannibal and St. Joseph Railroad to Omaha. The steamer was struck by a tornado on March 15, 1862, which blew the boat from her moorings in St. Joseph. The damage was slight. The boat had another accident in 1866 when she took a sheer and hit the shore head on and sank at Brunswick, Missouri. The steamer was raised and repaired and ultimately destroyed in the great steamboat fire at St. Louis on April 7, 1866.

Algoma, a side-wheel packet in the Missouri River trade. The boat sank when she was destroyed on rocks near Lexington, Missouri, in 1849. Most of the cargo was saved.

Alice, a side-wheel packet. The boat was owned by Captain Joseph Kinney who named the boat for his daughter. The steamer struck a snag and sank near Frankfort, Missouri, on September 12, 1874. The boat was raised, repaired, and returned to service on the Missouri River.

Alice Blair, a stern-wheel packet built in Osceloa, Missouri, in 1890. 130' × 25' × 4', with two engines (10' x4') and one boiler (20' × 56'), which allowed a working pressure of 129 lbs. The boat was owned by R. D. Blair and operated with Captain Henry M. Dodds as master on the upper Osage River. The steamer was snagged at Early Point, Missouri, on October 13, 1890; the boat was raised and then sold to T. L. Smith Sr. who took her to Texas and ran her on the Brazos River between East Columbia and Velasco. The boat sank shortly after arriving at Columbia but was raised and returned to service.

Alice Grey, a stern-wheel freight steamer built at Tuscumbia, Missouri, in 1871. 96 tons with two engines (10" × 3') with one boiler (18' × 42"), which allowed a working pressure of 137 lbs. The boat operated in the Missouri River trade and was owned by A. A. Hibbard and others. The boat was destroyed by a boiler explosion a few miles below Rochport, Missouri, on December 16, 1875.

Alice, see BRIGHT LIGHT

Alice No. 1, a side-wheel packet built in Elizabeth, Pennsylvania, in 1848. 232 tons. Operated mainly on the lower Missouri River. The boat burned at St. Louis, Missouri, on May 17, 1849.

Alma, a stern-wheel packet built in Belle Vernon, Pennsylvania, in 1855. 220' × 36' × 5' and rated at 311 tons. This boat was built for the Missouri River trade by Charles P. Chouteau. The steamer was dismantled in 1861.

Alone, see GOVERNOR SHARKEY

Amanda, a side-wheel packet built at Metropolis, Illinois, and St. Louis, Missouri, in 1865. 140 tons with two engines (16' × 5') with three boilers (22' × 38"). In 1867, the boat was sold to operate in the St. Joseph–Omaha trade on the Missouri River. The boat burned in Iowa while running light from Omaha to Sioux City on November 3, 1867.

Amaranth, a stern-wheel packet built in Warsaw, Illinois, in 1864. 156' × 29' × 4.5', rated at 160 tons. Owned by the Eagle Packet Co. mainly running the St. Louis–Illinois River trade. During cotton season, she often ran New Orleans-Red River. The boat was lost on the Missouri River near Doniphan, Missouri, on November 17, 1867, after returning from Fort Benton. Captain William Bell was the pilot on watch at the time of the sinking, and most of the cargo was saved.

Amazon, a side-wheel packet built in Jeffersonville, Indiana, in 1847. 250' × 32'. 257 tons with two engines (20" × 6') and three boilers (28' × 40"), which allowed a working pressure of 155 lbs. Originally built and owned by Captain H. Hazlett of St. Louis, who sold her to Menard Chouteau shortly before she struck a snag and sank in 1856 on the lower Missouri River.

Amelia, a side-wheel packet built in St. Louis, Missouri, in 1846. Rated at 151 tons. The boat was named for Miss Amelia Cordell of Glasgow, Missouri. The boat often participated in the mountain trade and is reported to have carried Native Americans back to their home after they visited Washington, D.C. The boat was at Fort Union in 1849 and was snagged and lost in Missouri on December 11, 1849.

Amelia Poe, a stern-wheel packet built in Georgetown and Pittsburgh, Pennsylvania, in 1865. 165' × 27' × 4.5' and rated at 321 tons. Owned by Captain Thomas Poe of Georgetown, Pennsylvania, and named for his wife. The boat made trips to Fort Benton in 1866 and in 1867. She passed Fort Buford on May 20, 1868, loaded with a quartz mill for the Montana mines. Three days later, the boat struck a snag at Little Porcupine Creek near Oswego, Montana Territory. Much of the cargo was salvaged and taken to Helena, Montana, by the insurance underwriters. The quartz mill was stowed on shore and as late as 1927 was reported to still be there. Captain Thomas Townsend was master at the time of loss. Several St. Louis speculators bought the rights to the AMELIA POE wreck from the insurance company and attempted to salvage the vessel but were driven off by Indians and returned home empty-handed. The steamer HIRAM WOOD helped salvage the engines and remaining freight.

Andrew S. Bennett, a stern-wheel ferryboat built at Sioux City, Iowa, in 1880. 115' × 30 × 3.5', rated at 78 tons, with two engines (11.5' × 4.5') and two boilers (22' × 38"), which allowed a working pressure of 140 lbs. Captain Grant Marsh built the vessel for ferry service at Sioux City and hired another captain to manage it. The ferry was named for Captain Andrew S. Bennett of the Fifth Infantry, who was killed in a battle with the Bannock Indians at Clark's Ford, Montana. Originally the steamer was built with cogwheel machinery from the wrecked steamer HIRAM WOOD No.2; this was later replaced with the machinery from the steamers M. LIVINGSTON and the Dr. BURLEIGH. The ferry was sunk by ice while lying at winter quarters at Sioux City, Iowa, during the winter of 1888–1889. The boat was raised, repaired, and sold to D. Ayers and later dismantled.

Andrew S. Bennett, a side-wheel steamer built in 1835. The boat was owned by the American Fur Company and named for the captain of the first steamboat YELLOW STONE. The vessel was lost from unknown causes in 1840.

Anna Lee, sunk on the Missouri River in Missouri in 1881. This may be the boat referred to as the ANNIE LEE (below).

Annie Cade, a center-wheel ferry built in Leavenworth, Kansas, in 1879. 127' × 32' × 4.5' and rated at 178 tons, with one engine (20.5' × 5.5') and two boilers (16' × 42"), which allowed a working pressure of 119 lbs. The ferry was owned by William A. Cade, and Captain Thomas Cade served as master. The boat was sunk by ice while lying in winter quarters at Harlem, Missouri on January 28, 1887. She was raised and taken to Kansas City where she was sunk by ice again on February 8, 1887. The boat was once again raised, repaired, and returned to service. She was dismantled in 1907.

Annie Lee, a stern-wheel packet built in Boonville, Missouri, in 1876. Rated at 42 tons, with two engines (8' × 2') and one boiler (15' × 42"), which allowed a working pressure of 110 lbs. The boat was owned by Horace Kingsley. Captain John L. Farris often served as pilot. The steamer struck a snag in the vicinity of Boonville, or Griffths Landing, Missouri, on November 11, 1881.

Annie Lewis, a center-wheelferry boat built in Glasgow, Missouri, in 1879. 93.4' × 27' × 4.2', rated at 81 tons with one engine (15.5" × 5') and one boiler (18' ×

46"), which allowed a working pressure of 113 lbs. The ferry was destroyed by fire at Kansas City, Missouri, on September 4, 1891.

Antelope, see TRAPPER

Antelope, a side-wheel packet built in Metropolis, Illinois, and St. Louis, Missouri, in 1866. 180' × 32', rated at 400 tons. The steamer was owned by Captain William R. Massie, and she typically operated on the Missouri River and was logged in at Fort Benton in 1867. The boat burned above Yankton, South Dakota, on April 12, 1869. Two passengers were killed, and several others were burned.

Anthony Wayne, a side-wheel packet built in Wheeling, Virginia, in 1846. The hull was built by Dunlevy and McNaughton and the engines by Hobbs and Taylor. The boat was rated at 146 tons and typically operated in the Galena–St. Louis trade. The vessel was snagged and lost near Independence, Missouri, on the Missouri River, on March 25, 1851.

Arabia, a side-wheel packet built in Brownsville, Pennsylvania, in 1853. 181' × 31' × 5.5', rated at 222 tons. Captain John Shaw had her on the Missouri and then sold the boat to Captain William Terrill. The boat reportedly brought military supplies for General Harney's Sioux Expedition to Fort Pierre in 1855. The boat struck a snag and was lost on the Missouri 1.5 miles below Parkville, Missouri, on August 10, 1856. The boat was reported to have been carrying a large cargo of whiskey, and over many years numerous attempts were made to salvage her. The boat was actually filled with settler stores headed for the Council Bluffs area. The boat was salvaged by River Salvage, Inc., of Kansas City, Missouri, in 1989. Portions of the vessel's hull and all of the cargo are on display at the *Arabia* Steamboat Museum in Kansas City.

Arabian, a stern-wheel packet built in Brownsville, Pennsylvania, in 1866. 145' × 30' × 4.5' and rated at 305 tons. The boat first ran Pittsburgh-Cincinnati in the summer of 1866. The boat was sold for the Missouri River trade in January 1867. Captain Ben Johnson was the new owner. He first ran her from St. Louis to the Tennessee River and then out to the Missouri. The boat was snagged and lost in Kansas on the Missouri River on May 4, 1868.

Arethusa, a stern-wheel towboat built in Gasconade, Missouri, in 1894. 91' × 18.4' × 4.8', rated at 45 tons. The boat was owned by the U. S. government with Captain Jesse B. Neff serving as pilot. With a barge in tow, the steamer struck a bridge at St. Joseph, Missouri, and sank on September 14, 1914. The paddle wheel and some of the machinery were salvaged.

Ariel, a stern-wheel packet, built at Lexington, Missouri, in 1897. 84.6' × 21' × 3.8' and rated at 53 tons, with two engines (9" × 3') and one boiler (18' × 42"), which allowed a working pressure of 134 lbs. The boat was owned by the Lexington Coal and Transportation Company. During the winter of 1897–1898, the boat was caught on the bank by a rapidly rising river at Lexington, Missouri, and was a total loss.

Armanda, a stern-wheel packet built in Brownsville, Pennsylvania, in 1863. The boat was rated at 381 tons. She was lost on the Missouri River on November 16,1867.

Asa Wilgus, a side-wheel packet built in Louisville, Kentucky, in 1857. 210' × 36' × 6' and rated at 412 tons. The boat was owned by R. R. Hopkins, A. C. Hopkins, and Henery Thronbrough. Captain R. R. Hopkins was master, with William R. Massie serving as pilot and George G. Keith as steerman. The boat was snagged and lost near Weston, Missouri, on September 3, 1860. Until 1903, the rudder post of the boat was visible at low water along with a diving bell used in an early salvage attempt. "Steamboat Bill" Heckman eventually bought the wreck. He sold it for junk in St. Louis, where he lost money on the deal.

Assiniboine, a side-wheel packet built in Cincinnati, Ohio, in 1833 for the American Fur Company. The boat was rated at 149 tons with a single engine. The vessel landed at Fort Union in 1833, and in 1834 the boat was stranded near Fort Union because of low water and was forced to winter on the upper river. On the way back downriver in 1835, the boat was left aground on the Missouri in North Dakota when the river began falling rapidly. The boat was soon left high and dry. A flatboat was ordered built on which the cargo, from the mouth of the Yellowstone River, could be floated down the river. Before the cargo was removed, the boat caught fire from a stovepipe in the cabin and with her cargo was a total loss on June 1, 1835. Prince Maximilian of Weid, who traveled on the *Assiniboine* from 1833–1835, lamented the loss of a stag skin and other specimens from the Missouri River area when the vessel burned.

Astoria, a side-wheel steamer built in 1836. The boat was reported at 148 tons and was an early fur company boat. It struck a snag and was lost near the Blue River in Missouri in 1840.

Atlanta, a stern-wheel towboat owned by the U. S. government. The boat was 91' × 18' and was sunk by ice at Missouri City, Missouri, on January 26, 1910.

Atlas, a vessel rated at 135 tons. Little is known about this boat, which was built in 1844. She was snagged and lost on March 8, 1847, in Missouri.

Augustus McDowell (also noted as A. MCDOWELL), a side-wheel packet built in St. Louis, Missouri, in,1860. The boat was rated at 451 tons. This steamer played an active role in the Civil War. She was one of three steamboats sent up the river to Jefferson City a day or two before the capture of Camp Jackson (May 10, 1861), loaded with gunpowder for Confederate forces. Just before the evacuation of the capital (June 13, 1861), the three steamboats were run across the river to Cedar City where they were abandoned by their officers. They were captured by General Blair on the evening of the 15th. The boat was eventually burned in St. Louis on October 27, 1862.

Australia, a side-wheel packet built in Brownsville, Pennsylvania, at the John S. Pringle yard. The cabin was finished by Hopkins & Co. in 1853. 182' × 31' × 7.5' and rated at 289 tons. The vessel's engines were 20s (6.5' with 26" diameter wheels and 8' buckets). The steamer ran Pittsburgh-St. Louis-New Orleans her first season and was snagged at Hat Island on the Mississippi River that first season. The boat was raised and snagged again on June 10, 1855, while carrying military supplies to Fort Pierre. In the Pacific Railroad Packet Line on the Missouri River by 1856. The boat burned in St. Louis on April 1, 1859.

Avalanche, a stern-wheel vessel rated at 148 tons and built in 1837. The boat was lost on the Missouri River in 1840.

B. F. Weaver, a stern-wheel packet built in Galena, Illinois, in 1872. 89' × 21.8' × 4'. The boat was part of the Yellowstone Expedition in 1878 and was used to scout ahead and to locate fuel and supplies. Apparently, the steamer was in continual trouble and finally was left moored at Fort Pierre. On the return trip back downriver, she was tied alongside the TIDAL WAVE and towed back. The steamer reportedly ended up as a rafter on the upper Mississippi and was popularly know as the B. F. LOSER.

Baby Rose, a stern-wheel packet built in Fort Benton, Montana, in 1909. 71' × 18'. The boat was owned by Charles Crepeau of Fort Benton who planned to use the boat to supply homesteaders in the area with lumber, hardware, groceries, etc. The boat's first trip was on July 4, 1909, but proved a disaster when it was discovered the boat lacked the power to shove her barge. The venture failed, and the vessel was cut down by ice at Fort Benton. The vessel was then abandoned. What remains of the hull of the steamer can often be seen at low water off the Fort Benton levee.

Bachelor (also noted as BATCHELOR) a stern-wheel (also reported as a side-wheel) packet. The boat was lost by snag near Fort Pierre in South Dakota in November 1869. This boat is often confused with the F. Y. BACHELOR.

Banner State, a side-wheel packet built in Brownsville, Pennsylvania, in 1851. The boat was rated at 254 tons, with two engines (20" × 6') and three boilers (24' × 38"), which allowed a working pressure of 165 lbs. The boat was first owned in Pittsburgh and operated on the Mississippi River. In 1852, the boat struck a snag, which caused considerable damage. In 1855, the steamer was sold to Captain Josh B. Holland, Captain Joesh S. Nanson, and others for the Missouri River. The boat was snagged and lost on April 11, 1855, in Missouri.

Bartram, a mountain boat that sank above Omaha in 1864. It is probable that this entry is not reliable. I believe this entry really refers to the BERTRAND, which sank above Omaha in 1865.

Bedford, a side-wheel packet built in 1839 with only a single engine. The boat ran the St. Louis–St. Joseph trade. The boat was snagged and lost on April 25, 1840, near the mouth of the Missouri River. The boat reportedly sank in only a few minutes all the way to her hurricane deck. Several passengers were lost.

Belle Golding, a stern-wheel packet built in New Albany, Indiana, in 1852. 200' × 36' × 6.5', rated at 207 tons. The boat was snagged and lost on the Missouri River on June 14, 1855.

Belle of Jefferson, a stern-wheel vessel, possibly a ferry. The boat sank when a boiler exploded near Jefferson City, Missouri, on July 3, 1874. The steamer was raised, repaired, and equipped with a new boiler. The boat struck a snag and sank in Missouri on July 13, 1875, becoming a total loss.

Belle of Lexington, a center-wheel ferryboat built in New Albany, Indiana, in 1866. 120' × 30', rated at 124 tons. She apparently ran out of Lexington, Missouri, on the Missouri River and was owned by the Lexington Ferry, Coal & Railroad Transportation Company.

Belle of Peoria (also noted as BELLE PEORIA), a side-wheel packet built in Monongahela, Pennsylvania, in 1859. 180' × 32', rated at 238 tons, with two engines (15' × 6') and two boilers (28' × 44"), which allowed a working pressure of 131 lbs. The boat ran St. Louis-Poeria as an independent boat. It burned at Sharp's Landing on the Illinois River on March 11, 1860. The steamer was rebuilt and in 1862 was in U.S. service taking supplies to the Cumberland River. On the Illinois again in 1863 and in the spring of 1864 made trips to Fort Benton. The steamer was part of General Sully's 1864 Yellowstone expedition. The boat ran on a sandbar near Acrow's Trading Post, 5 miles above the mouth of the Cheyenne River, in October 1864 and had to lay there all winter. That season, the empty boat was wrecked by the ice in the spring of 1865. Local settlers found the pilothouse on the prairie near the river that summer and named the place Peoria Bottoms.

Bellemont, a ferryboat built in 1861. Captain Walker served as master. The ferry sank opposite Charles Street in St. Joseph, Missouri, in 1861.

Ben Johnson, a side-wheel packet built in Metropolis, Illinois, and completed in St. Louis, Missouri, in 1866. This was a big boat rated at 525 tons; her engines were 22's-8 ft, with three boilers. The steamer was owned by Captain Ben Johnson and ran on the Missouri River. In 1866, the boat carried a U.S. peace commission to Fort Sully to treat with the Sioux . The boat made a Fort Benton trip in 1867 and snagged several miles below Brownville, Nebraska, in 1868. The boat was raised only to be burned in the steamboat fire at St. Louis on March 29, 1869.

Ben West, a side-wheel packet built in Brownsville, Pennsylvania, in 1849. The vessel was rated at 241 tons, with two engines (17.5" × 6') and three boilers (24' × 38"), which allowed a working pressure of 160 lbs. The steamer usually ran in the Pittsburgh–St. Louis trade, but in 1855 she was participating in the St. Louis–St. Paul trade. On August 10, 1855, while headed up the Missouri River with lumber consigned to Lexington, Missouri, the steamer was fatally snagged near Washington, Missouri.

Bennett, a side-wheel wrecking boat. In 1852 the boat was on her way to raise the steamer DACOTAH, which had sunk at Peru cutoff in Nebraska when the wrecker hit a snag and sank near the mouth of the Kaw River.

Benton, a stern-wheel packet built in McKeesport, Pennsylvania, in 1864. 197' ×

33' × 5' and rated at 246 tons. This boat was originally named the INTREPID. The steamer was part of General Sully's 1864 Yellowstone expedition and was logged in at Fort Benton that same year. It came to Fort Benton again in 1865 and in 1867. The boat snagged and sank on May 19, 1869.

Benton No. 2, a stern-wheel packet built in Pittsburgh, Pennsylvania in 1875. 197' × 33' × 5' and rated at 394 tons. The engines were built by James Rees (15's -5 ft, with three boilers, each 38" by 24' with two flues). When new, the vessel drew only 18" light . The boat was built for T. C. Power & Bros., and I. G. Baker & Company of Fort Benton for Missouri River service and was the first boat to carry the famed "Block P" insignia. This boat had a very long and successful career, making a total of 44 trips to Fort Benton. The BENTON participated heavily in the Indian wars of the late 1870s including the Sitting Bull and Nez Percé campaigns. It is estimated that the BENTON made more trips and carried more freight than any other boat serving Fort Benton. The boat was often referred to as "Old Reliable," and in July of 1887, her last time out of Fort Benton, the boat carried 1,000 bags of wool and 350 bales of pelts. The boat was sold in 1889 to James P. Boland and T. B. Sims. The boat struck a snag and was lost near Washington, Missouri, on September 15, 1889. The steamer was sunk and raised three more times on the lower Missouri before she was finally wrecked while heading downriver on July 18, 1897. The vessel got stuck waiting for the drawbridge at Sioux City and backed into submerged piling. The incident knocked a hole in her hull; the boat floated down under the still unopened drawbridge, which tore off the boat's upper works, and was wrecked.

Benton No. 3, a stern-wheel packet. Sank in Missouri in 1895.

Bertha, a stern-wheel packet built in Belle Veron, Pennsylvania, in 1863. 180' × 28' and rated at 218 tons, with two engines (15" × 5') and three boilers (22' × 38"), which allowed a working pressure of 134 lbs. The vessel was primarily a freight boat that ran trips on the Missouri River. The boat hit a pier of the St. Joseph, Missouri, bridge on June 24, 1872, and was lost. She was owned by C. S. Ebaugh at the time.

Bertrand, a stern-wheel packet built in Wheeling, West Virginia, in 1864. 161' × 32' × 5' and rated at 251 tons. The hull was built by Dunlevy & Company, and the engines by A.J Sweeney. The boat's machinery came from the steamer A. J. SWEENEY. The boat was owned by the Montana–Idaho Transportation Company, owned largely by John J. Roe and John G. Copelin. On April 1, 1865 , the boat was snagged and sank above Omaha at Portage La Force. Part of the deck cargo was recovered. There was a large quantity of quicksilver (mercury) consigned to Virginia City abroad. As a result, several attempts were made over the years to locate the wreck and recover her. The wreck was located in February 1968 by two Omaha salvagers, Jessie Pursell and Sam Corbino, 25 miles above Omaha on DeSoto National Wildlife Refuge. The vessel remained the property of the federal government and is now on public display at the *Bertrand* Steamboat Museum at DeSoto National Wildlife Refuge in Missouri Valley, Iowa.

Big Hatchie, a side-wheel packet built in Pittsburgh, Pennsylvania, in 1844. Rated at 195 tons. The boat's boiler exploded on July 25, 1845, near Herman, Missouri, and killed 35 people. The boat, however, survived and was turned over to the U.S. War Department in 1846. There is a 3-foot column in the Protestant Cemetery at Hermann, Missouri, dedicated to the memory of those who were lost.

Big Horn No. 1, an American Fur Company boat that was lost in 1841 on the upper river.

Big Horn No. 2, a stern-wheel packet built in New Albany, Indiana in 1865. 154' × 33' × 4.5', rated at 312 tons. The boat landed at Fort Berthold in 1865 and to Fort Benton in 1866 and 1867. She burned and sank April 10, 1873.

Bighorn No. 4, a stern-wheel packet built in Pittsburgh and California, Pennsylvania, in 1879. 178' × 31', rated at 293 tons. The boat was owned by S. B. Coulson, D. W. Martta, Josephus Todd, Nicholas Buison, and W. S. Evans. The material used in building Fort Custer went up on this boat. She was snagged and lost on the Missouri in Montana, on May 8, 1883. Captain John A. William was master at the time of loss.

Birdie Brent, a ferryboat rated at 152 tons built in 1866. She sank from unknown causes on November 21, 1887, in Missouri.

Bishop, a small stern-wheeler that operated in the Missouri River trade. The boat was swamped by a heavy current when coming out of the Old River in Missouri and was lost on July 15, 1867. Andy Gouff, the mate, was reported killed.

Bismarck, a stern-wheel packet built in Pittsburgh, Pennsylvania, in 1878. 194' × 33' × 4.5'. Used on the upper Missouri River by Isaac P. Baker and the Benton Transportation Company. The boat was later sold to A. S. Bryan and others for use on the lower Missouri. She snagged at Lower Bonhomme Island in 1887 and was raised. The boat was fatally lost on October 23, 1891, in Missouri while Ed Anderson was the pilot on watch. The roof bell went to the belfry of a church in Washington, Missouri.

Black Hawk, a side-wheel packet built in New Albany, Indiana, in 1859. The boat was rated at 211 tons and had two engines (21" × 6') with three boilers (26' × 44"), which allowed a working pressure of 144 lbs. It was originally built for Captain Silas Haight for the Fort Madison-Rock Island trade. In 1860–1861, she ran St. Louis–Memphis and then went to the Missouri River. The boat was snagged at the mouth of Bee Creek, 2 miles below Weston, Missouri, but was raised. In a confiscation procedure, the U. S. government took the boat at Port Hudson, Mississippi, on November 3, 1863. The boat was finally destroyed by fire at New Orleans on May 28, 1864.

Black Hills, a stern-wheel packet built in California and Pittsburgh, Pennsylva-

nia, in 1877. 190' × 32' × 4'. The boat operated in T. C. Power & Bros. Block P
Line in the Fort Benton trade. She first arrived at Fort Benton in 1882. In 1883,
the boat became the first at Fort Benton to be electrically lit. The steamer spent
the winter of 1884 at Bismark where she was cut down by ice on March 28,
1884.

Bluff City, a side-wheel packet built in Paducah, Kentucky, and completed in St.
Louis, Missouri, in 1853. 186' × 33' × 7'. The boat was built for the St. Louis–
Council Bluffs trade. She burned in St. Louis on July 27, 1853.

Boonslick, a boat named for the Boonslick settlement, the first Anglo-American
settlement on the Missouri River opposite what is now Boonsville, Missouri.
The boat collided with the MISSISSIPPI BELLE in St. Louis on November 24,
1834.

Boonville, a side-wheel packet with a single engine built for the Missouri River
trade in 1835. The boat was snagged on the Missouri on November 19, 1837,
en route to Fort Leavenworth with corn. The boat and cargo were a total loss

Boreas No. 1, a side-wheel packet built in Pittsburgh, Pennsylvania, in 1841. The
boat was rated at 157 tons. It was originally built for Captain Thomas M. Fithian
and George Barnard who ran her in the St. Louis–Keokuk trade. Later, the boat
ran on the Missouri River. She burned in the big wharf fire at St. Louis with
twenty-three other steamers on May 17, 1849.

Boreas No. 2, a side-wheel packet built in Elizabeth, Pennsylvania, in 1847 for
the lower river trade and rated at 264 tons. The boat had double engines and
was built by Thomas M. Fithian and George Barnard. The boat reportedly burned
at Hermann, Missouri, in 1846 while bound downstream. The vessel had a
large amount of Mexican bullion and silver dollars on board, which were sto-
len. The boat was set on fire to cover up the theft.

Bowling Green, a side-wheel packet built in Cincinnati, Ohio, in 1839. 125' × 33',
rated at 148 tons. The boat hit a rock at the head of Osage Chute, Missouri, on
December 12, 1842, and was lost. At the time of loss, the boat was owned by
John J. Roe and others of St. Louis. The engines were salvaged. In the low
water of 1927, remains of the wreck were visible.

Bridgeport, a stern-wheel packet built in Bridgeport, Alabama, in 1865 . The boat
was rated at 184 tons and was built by the U.S. Quartermaster Corps for Tennessee River service. On April 24, 1866, she was sold to private owners who
operated it on the Missouri River. The boat was snagged and lost in Nebraska
with a load of government supplies on June 1, 1868. Captain T. L. Chappelle
was master at the time of loss.

Bright Light, a stern-wheel packet built in Pittsburgh, Pennsylvania, in 1878. Originally, the boat was named the ALICE. The boat sank on the falls at Louisville
but was raised, sold, and renamed BRIGHT LIGHT. In 1883, Captain David H.
Silver and Captain William Thompson owned and operated the boat on the
Missouri River. On June 30, 1883, the steamer hit the railroad bridge at

Boonville, Missouri. The disabled boat floated downriver and lodged on Boone Island. The boat was left high and dry through the fall, and later the machinery was removed and the hull refloated. Captain Henry Leyhe used the hull as a barge in St. Louis.

Bright Star, a center-wheel ferry built in New Albany, Indiana, in 1864. The boat was rated at 85 tons, with one engine (16" × 5') and three boilers (16' × 36"), which allowed a working pressure of 125 lbs. The ferry was owned by Frederick Blackman and others of Missouri. The vessel was cut down by running ice at Washington, Missouri, on February 6, 1873. She was raised and repaired, but ultimately the ferry was dismantled and the hull used as a barge.

Brunette, a side-wheel packet built in Jeffersonville, Indiana, at the Howard boatyard in 1852. 180' × 29' × 6', rated at 228 tons. The boat was built for Charles Barger and designed for operation on the Missouri River. It burned at Bloody Island, St. Louis, on October 15, 1859.

Burkesville, see O.K.

Butte, a stern-wheel packet built in Sewickley and Pittsburgh by the Sewickley boatyard in 1879. The boat was built for T. C. Power & Brothers Block P Line of steamboats for operation on the upper river. The boat made a total of twenty five trips to Montana. She burned and was lost near Old Fort Peck, Montana, on August 1, 1883.

C. C. Carroll (also the CHARLES C. CARROLL), a stern-wheel packet built in Pittsburgh, Pennsylvania, in 1875. 222' × 36' × 5.5', rated at 571 tons. The boat was originally called the JOHN L. RHOADS. She was owned by the Missouri River Transportation Company. The boat snagged and was lost in Missouri on September 15, 1886.

C. H. Green (also the CHARLES H. GREEN), this vessel was reported lost in Missouri in 1840.

C. R. Suter, a side-wheel snagboat built in Pittsburgh, Pennsylvania, in 1888. 187' × 52' × 7'. The boat was owned by the Missouri River Commission and was equipped with compound oscillating engines, with piston rods that were directly connected to the crank. The boat was rebuilt and renamed the MISSOURI. The boat burned at Gasconade, Missouri on July 29, 1928. The dredge KAPPA disposed of her in 1929.

C. W. Sombart, a side-wheel packet built in Jeffersonville, Indiana, in 1858. The boat was rated at 411 tons with two engines (22" × 7') and three boilers (24' × 42"), which allowed a working pressure of 125 lbs. The steamer was owned by A. L. Shortridge and Company with Henry McPherson serving as master. The boat sank near the Saline River on June 27, 1859.

Calypso, a side-wheel packet built in Wellsville, Ohio, in 1863. 193' × 30' × 5'. The boat's engines were 18s equipped with two boilers. The boat operated on the Missouri River with Captain Burton serving as master. The steamer was lost in an ice breakup at St. Louis on December 16, 1865.

Camden, a side-wheel packet that operated in the Missouri River trade. The boat struck a snag in 1839 in Missouri.

Car of Commerce, a side-wheel, single-engine packet that operated in the lower Missouri River trade. The boat was rated at 250 tons. She was sunk by a snag on a trip from Chariton to St. Louis on May 8, 1832. Most of the cargo and part of the boat's furniture were saved.

Carrie, a stern-wheel ferryboat built in Rulo, Nebraska, in 1869. The ferry had two engines (8" × 2') and one boiler (14' × 40"), which allowed a working pressure of 90 lbs. She was owned by Frank Lajoys and L. Wiscamp. The boat was laid up because she failed to pass inspection. She was caught on the bank by a falling river and became a total loss.

Carrie, a stern-wheel packet built in Vanport, Pennsylvania, in 1863. 159' × 30' × 4'. Her engines were 14s equipped with two boilers . The boat was owned By Captain William J. Kountz and others, with Captain D. M. Brady serving as master. The steamer ran St. Louis-New Orleans and the Missouri River. The boat was snagged and lost while headed upbound with government supplies from St. Louis to Fort Benton when it was lost in Nebraska on April 14, 1868.

Carrie V. Kountz, stern-wheel packet built in Pittsburgh, Pennsylvania, in 1869. 187' × 40' × 4.5', with Hartupee compound engines. The boat burned at St. Louis on March 29, 1869.

Carrier, a side-wheel packet built in Jeffersonville, Indiana, at the Howard boatyard in 1855. 215' × 33'. The boat had a double stern with stern posts 10" apart. The boat was built specifically for running the Missouri River. She was snagged the first time at the head of Penn's Bend on the Missouri on October 12, 1858. She was finally lost in Missouri on September 12, 1861.

Carroll, a stern-wheel packet built in Pittsburgh, Pennsylvania, in 1875. 185.7' × 31' × 6'. This boat departed from the Pittsburgh boatyard direct for Fort Benton, Montana, in March 1875. The steamer was named for Matthew Carroll of the Fort Benton firm of Carroll & Steel. All told the boat made nine trips to Montana points. She burned on April 16, 1877, near Fort Randall, South Dakota.

Carroll No. 1, a stern-wheel packet built for the mountain trade in 1840. She was snagged and lost near the Grand River in 1840.

Castalia, a stern-wheel packet built in Sioux City, Iowa, in 1892. 110' × 26.2' × 3.7', rated at 90 tons, with two engines (10" × 4') and one boiler (20' × 42''), which allowed a working pressure of 160 lbs. The boat was owned by by B. S. Holmes and others. The steamer struck a hidden piling below the Sioux City bridge on November 7, 1897, and sank. She was raised and repaired and then sold to Woods Brothers Construction Company.

Cataract, a side-wheel packet built in Brownsville, Pennsylvania, in 1851. The boat was rated at 282 tons. The steamer was owned by Captain E. W. Gould and C. S. Rodgers, both of St. Louis, for the Illinois River. She ran in the Pacific Railroad Packet Line (Lighting Line) from St. Louis- Jefferson City-Kansas

City in 1856. In 1857, her mud drum exploded, killing five passengers and ten crew. The boat was dismantled in 1859.

Centralia, a stern-wheel packet built in Wheeling, West Virginia, in 1864. The boat was rated at 239 tons. The boat was logged in at the Fort Benton levee in 1867. She was snagged and lost on the Missouri River on May 27, 1868.

Chain, a side-wheel packet built for the American Fur Company. The boat's name is a form of "Cheyenne." The vessel struck a snag and sank while downbound in Missouri on October 12, 1836. The cargo was lost, but the engines were salvaged.

Challenge, a 229-ton vessel built in 1854. She struck a snag in the Missouri River above St. Louis on February 25, 1860.

Champ Clark, a stern-wheel towboat built in Mudd's Landing, Illinois, in 1912. She was originally a towboat used by Rust & Swift. They sold the boat to Rocheport Ferry & Transportation Company; then the Hermann Ferry Packet Company bought the boat and had her lengthened as a packet for use on the Missouri River. The boat was finally dismantled at Hermann, Missouri.

Champion, a side-wheel packet built in Cincinnatio, Ohio, in 1858. She was rated at 676 tons with two engines (20" × 6') and three boilers (26' × 42"), which allowed a working pressure of 137 lbs. The boat sank in Missouri in 1863 or 1864:

Chariton, a side-wheel packet 160' × 25' that operated on the Missouri River. She was equipped with a single engine and ran the St. Louis–Liberty–Independence route. She sank and was repaired four times before she was fatally lost on October 12, 1837, in lower Missouri.

Charleston, a 94-ton Missouri River steamer built in 1887. She was stranded on the Missouri on February 10, 1906.

Chas. H. Durfee, a stern-wheel packet built in Pittsburgh, Pennsylvania, in 1869. 178' × 35' × 5' and rated at 398 tons. This boat got her machinery from the steamer BENTON. She typically ran the New Orleans-Red River with Captain Joseph H. Aiken as master. The boat burned at the New Orleans levee on March 21, 1870, and was then rebuilt. She was finally lost on December 18, 1878, on the Missouri River.

Chaske, see ABNER O'NEAL

Chippewa, a stern-wheel packet built in Belle Vernon, Pennsylvania, in 1857. 160' × 30' and rated at 175 tons. The boat was owned by the American Fur Company. The boat traveled to St. Paul and operated on the Mississippi in 1858–1859. The CHIPPEWA was the first boat ever to reach Fort Benton, Montana, in 1860. It caught fire and then exploded on the Missouri River in Montana on June 23, 1861.

Chippewa Falls, a stern-wheel packet built in Monogahela, Pennsylvania, in 1857. 120' × 24' × 3.5', rated at 93 tons. The boat was one of the boats used by General Sully. She made numerous trips with supplies to Fort Randall and Fort

Union. She was one of the first boats to navigate the Yellowstone River. It was dismantled in 1868.

City of Dardenella, a towboat owned by A. W. Farney, general contractor of North Kansas City. The boat sank on the Missouri River and was a total loss.

City of Fort Benton, a dredge boat built in 1885. She burned in August 1892 near Eagle Creek in Montana.

City of Keithsburg, a 184-ton steamer that was reported snagged and lost on November 25, 1872, above St. Louis.

City of Plattsmouth (also VIENNA), a stern-wheel packet built in Plattsmouth, Nebraska, in 1879. 89.6' × 24' × 2.3', rated at 73 tons. The boat was owned by E. Schleff and others. After a year or so of operation, she was renamed VIENNA. She was snagged and lost below New Haven, Missouri, on December 10, 1889.

Clara, a side-wheel packet built in Elizabeth, Pennsylvania, in 1851. The boat was rated at 248 tons. She was up the Missouri to Fort Pierre in 1855 and to Fort William (Fort Mortimer) in 1856. She was lost in ice at St. Louis on February 26, 1857.

Clara, a side-wheel packet built in Cincinnati, Ohio, in 1864. 225' × 34', with two engines (20" × 6.5') and three boilers (20' × 42"), which allowed a working pressure of 140 lbs. The boat was part of the Star Line Packet Company running from St. Louis to Kansas City. It was snagged and lost on May 24, 1870, in Missouri. Captain William L. Heckman reportedly bought the cabin from the wreck and built a two-story house at Bluffton, Missouri, with the wreckage.

Clark H. Green, a center-wheel ferryboat. The boat snagged and sank while carrying cargo of flour for the Glasgow Milling Company from Glasgow to Leavenworth on January 28, 1858.

Clay Dixon, a stern-wheel ferry rated at 20 tons. The ferry was built in Decatur, Nebraska, in 1883. The boat was lost while lying at winter quarters at Vermillion, South Dakota, on March 22, 1884.

Clermont No. 2, a side-wheel packet built at Cincinnati, Ohio, in 1845. The boat was rated at 132 tons. It was to Fort William on the Missouri River in 1846 and was lost December 9, 1851.

Clinch (also GALLATIN), a stern-wheel packet built in Kingston, Tennessee, in 1864. The vessel was rated at 131 tons. The boat was built for use as a transport during the Civil War by the U. S. Quartermaster Corps. The vessel was sold into private hands on April 10, 1866, and renamed the GALLATIN. In 1866, she was logged in at Fort Benton, and in 1867 she steamed 40 miles beyond Fort Benton to the Great Falls. The boat was snagged and lost on April 16, 1868.

Col. A. B. Chambers No. 1, a side-wheel steamer named after the editor of the *Missouri Republican.* She typically ran the St. Louis–St. Joseph route. She was snagged near Atchison, Kansas, in 1856. Much of the vessel was salvaged.

Col. McLeod (also COL. MACCLOUD), a stern-wheel packet built in Cincinnati, Ohio, in 1878. 160' × 26' and rated at 171 tons. This boat was built specifically to run freight at low water from Cow Island to Fort Benton when the larger packets could not get through. She was owned by I. G. Baker & Company of Fort Benton, Montana. The boat was smashed on November 18, 1879, when the steamer BUTTE slipped off her ways at Bismarck. The boat was totally destroyed.

Coleman, a steamer that was reported lost in an explosion in Missouri in 1882.

Colona, a boat lost in 1858, operated on the Kansas River.

Colonel Gus Lynn (also noted as COLONEL GUS LINN), a stern-wheel packet built in California, Pennsylvania, in 1859. 132' × 25.7' × 2.8' and rated at 83 tons. The boat was first owned by C. P. Bud of St. Louis. She was commanded by Captain B. F. Beasley. The boat was snagged and lost in Iowa in April 1860.

Colonel Kinsman, see GRAY CLOUD

Columbia No. 1, a lower Missouri River boat built in 1847. She sank near the mouth of the Missouri in 1849.

Columbia No. 2, a side-wheel packet built in Monongahela, Pennsylvania, in 1864. The boat was rated at 350 tons. Initially she ran Pittsburgh-St. Louis, charted to the Keokuk Packet Company. The boat was impressed to U. S. service during the winter of 1864. The boat was on the Cumberland River in 1865 and in July 1866 was running between St. Joseph and Omaha. The boat was sold in 1868 to Captain Joseph Throckmorton who ran the boat to Fort Benton and made several trips on the Illinois River. The boat was lost in ice at St. Louis on February 24, 1872.

Columbian, a side-wheel packet built in New Haven and St. Louis, Missouri, in 1865. 237' × 36' × 6', with two engines (22" × 7') and three boilers (26" × 44"), which allowed a working pressure of 131 lbs. The boat was owned by the St. Louis & Omaha Packet Company and was the largest hull ever built at New Haven. The hull was made of locally procured burr oak and leaked badly. Later, the boat ran St. Louis–Atchison. The steamer was snagged and lost on June 23, 1870, en route from Omaha to St. Louis.

Columbiana, a stern-wheel packet built at Wellsville, Ohio, in 1843. The boat was rated at 124 tons and made trips from Pittsburgh–Zanesville in 1843. She was reported sunk at Lexington Bar on the Missouri River on September 25, 1845. The boat was sold to the U.S. government in 1847.

Commander, a steam towboat rated at approximately 200 tons. The boat was owned by James Ostander of Louisville, Kentucky. She sank on April 3, 1929, while upbound with a tow of barges for the U.G.I. Company. She struck a rock a few miles below Boonville, Missouri, on April 3, 1929. The wreck was sold to J. W. Mencke of Paducah, Kentucky, who was to remove her.

Commerce, a side-wheel packet in the Missouri River trade in 1855. She was lost in Missouri on its maiden voyage on the river in 1855.

Commodore, a stern-wheel packet built in New Haven, Missouri, in 1890. 97' × 23.2' × 3.2'. The boat was owned by D. N. Burress and others of Miami, Missouri. She was sunk by ice while lying at winter quarters one half mile above Miami on February 24, 1903.

Companion, a 89-ton steamer built in 1831. She was snagged and lost in Missouri in 1835.

Conquest, see J. M. RICHTMAN

Convoy No.2 (also IDA FULTON), a stern-wheel packet built in Cincinnati, Ohio, in 1863. 145' × 26' × 4.5' and rated at 143 tons. The boat was owned by the U. S. Quartermaster Corps in 1864. She was sold on January 29, 1867, into private hands and renamed the IDA FULTON. The steamer came to Fort Benton in 1867 and was dismantled in 1884.

Coosada (also NEW HAVEN), a stern-wheel packet (originally a ferry) built in Grafton, Illinois, in 1882. 136' × 24' × 3' (originally 94' × 24' as a ferry), with two engines (10" × 3.5') and two boilers (14' × 38"), which allowed a working pressure of 130 lbs. The boat was originally named NEW HAVEN and owned by the New Haven Missouri Ferry Company. She sank on February 25, 1885, while at winter quarters in New Haven. The wreck was raised and in 1888 was lengthened to 136' and acquired a cabin and two stacks. In 1892, the U. S. Engineers, Mobile, bought the steamer at New Orleans and changed its name to COOSADA for use on the Alabama River. She was sold to Captain John Baker of Mobile in 1906 and resumed her original name. The boat was finally snagged and lost downbound from Demopolis to Mobile on the Tombigbee River in January 1910.

Cora No.1, a side-wheel packet built in Rock Island, Illinois, in 1846. 140' × 24' × 5', rated at 144 tons. This boat had a single engine with a stiff shaft and an 18" cylinder with two boilers. The hull was built by Captain Joseph Throckmorton and the engines came from St. Louis. Captain Throckmorton, ran the boat on the upper Mississippi. The boat was bought by Frank Dozier and others in 1848 for the Missouri River. The boat snagged in Howard's Bend above St. Charles on April 17, 1851. She was raised and was fatally snagged and lost in Iowa with the loss of 15 lives on May 5, 1851.

Cora No. 2, a stern-wheel packet built in Cincinnati, Ohio, in 1864. The boat was rated at 215 tons, and had two engines (15" × 5') and two boilers (24' × 40"), which allowed a working pressure of 144 lbs. The boat was owned by Captain Joe Kinney of Boonville, Missouri and was named for his daughter. The boat was snagged and lost on May 1, 1865, near Omaha. When being salvaged, the crew could still see the wreck of the BERTRAND, which had sunk a few days earlier.

Cora No.3, a side-wheel packet built in St. Louis, Missouri, in 1865. The boat was rated at 395 tons. The steamer was owned by Captain Joe Kinney of Boonville, Missouri. The machinery was from the prior CORA. She was logged in at Fort Benton in 1866. The boat was snagged and lost on August 13, 1869, on an island in the Mississippi now known as Cora Island.

Cornelia, a steamer built in 1860. She was lost in ice above St. Louis in the mid-1860s.

Cornelia No. 2, a side-wheel packet built in 1865, ran in the Omaha trade. C. K. Baker served as her master. The boat burned at New Orleans in 1870.

Corvette, a side-wheel packet approximately 180 feet long, built in 1842, which operated in the Missouri River trade. The boat sank to her skylights in Missouri in 1842. There was a partial salvage of some of the furniture.

Cumberland Valley, a side-wheel packet built in Smithland, Kentucky, in 1842. The boat was rated at 176 tons. She ran Cincinnati-Nashville with Captain David Gren. Then the boat went to the upper Mississippi and finally to the Missouri River where she was snagged and lost on October 22, 1849.

Cutter, a stern-wheel packet built in Anoka, Minnesota, in 1863. The boat was a small steamer rated at only 92 tons. In 1864, enroute for La Crosse, Wisconsin, the boat was stopped by General Sully's command near Fort Randall. The boat traveled to the mouth of the Marias River in Montana in 1864 and to Fort Benton in 1865. She was snagged and lost in October 1869.

D. A Crawford, a steamer lost on the Missouri River in Missouri.

D. A. January (also NED TRACY), a side-wheel packet built in Cincinnati, Ohio, in 1857. 225' × 34', rated at 440 tons. She ran St. Louis-St. Joseph on the Missouri River with Captain Patrick Gore. The boat was impressed during the Civil War from 1862–1864. She was sold to the U. S. Quartermaster Corps on June 1, 1864, for use as a hospital boat. The steamer was sold on March 14, 1865 into private hands and renamed NED TRACY. The boat was logged in at Fort Benton in 1866 and was snagged and lost in Illinois on December 18, 1867.

D. H. Morton, a side-wheel packet built in Cincinnati in 1856. The boat was rated at 173 tons. In 1857 the boat carried military stores and property from old Fort Pierre to Fort Randall. She burned on March 11, 1859, while carrying supplies for the military on the Arkansas River.

Dacotah, a stern-wheel packet built in California and Pittsburgh, Pennsylvania, in 1879. 252' × 48' × 5.5', rated at 956 tons; its engines were 18s equipped with four boilers. The boat was one of the Coulson Line of steamers. Her maiden voyage was from Pittsburgh to Fort Benton in 1879, arriving with 550 tons of freight. All told, the boat traveled to Fort Benton seven times and held several freight records during her tenure on the river. She struck the Kansas City bridge on August 15, 1889. The boat was eventually sold to Captain Hunter Ben Jenkins and others. The steamer was snagged at Providence, Missouri, on September 17, 1884. She was raised and in 1889 was sold to New Orleans where Captain William T. Boardman ran the boat on the Red River. After a long and distinguished career, the boat was dismantled at Jeffersonville, Indiana, in 1893.

Captain Lud Keefer of Pittsburgh bought the hull. He used part of the hull as a wharf boat at Manchester, Ohio, and the other half became the hull for the excursion barge KEEFER, used at Pittsburgh. The boat's machinery and portions of the superstructure went into building the IMPERIAL.

Dacotah, a side-wheel packet built in Freedom, Pennsylvania, in 1857. The boat was rated at 90 tons. She was owned by the St. Louis & Hannibal Railroad at St. Joseph, Missouri. The boat was struck by a tornado at St. Joseph on March 15, 1862, with the loss of four lives.

Dakota, a steamer built in Breckinridge, Minnesota, in 1872. The boat was rated at 117 tons. She was destroyed by fire on the Missouri River on August 9, 1879.

Dakotah, a side-wheel packet estimated at 300 tons. She operated on the Missouri River and was snagged on the river in Nebraska in 1851.

Dallas, a small stern-wheel packet in the Missouri River trade. She stuck a snag and was lost in Nebraska in the 1870s.

Damsel, a stern-wheel packet built in Wellsville, Ohio, in 1864. The boat was rated at191 tons. She originally ran on the upper Mississippi. She was bought by Dan Rice, a circus owner, to convey a circus across the country. The troupe was up the Missouri River in mid-July 1878. When the pilot Charles Davis was landing the boat at Decatur, Nebraska, the vessel struck a snag and was lost. The circus was not on board at the time of the loss. Mr. Rice presented the town of Decatur with the boat's bell.

Dan B. Hulbert, a side-wheel packet built in Warsaw, Missouri, in 1881. 62.6' × 11' × 2.4', the boat was rated at 12 tons, with two engines (6" × 19") and one boiler (11.75' × 40"), which allowed a working pressure of 115 lbs. The boat was owned by John Radmacher, and Captain Jackson W. Hardin served as pilot. She was sunk by ice while lying in winter quarters at Osage City, Missouri, on February 13, 1866. The steamer was raised and repaired.

Dan Converse, a stern-wheel packet built in McKeesport, Kansas, at the Coursin yard in 1852. 142' × 27' × 4.10'. In 1852, she operated in the Pittsburgh–Zanesville trade. The boat was snagged and lost in Missouri on November 15, 1858.

Dart, a side-wheel packet built for the Missouri River trade in 1835 and reported at 113 tons. The boat had a single engine and was partially owned and commanded by Captain John Cleveland. The boat was lost on rocks in Missouri in 1838.

David Tatum, a large side-wheel packet built for the lower Missouri River trade in 1860. She sank near the mouth of the Gasconade, but was raised. Governor Reeder came up on this boat on May 5, 1856.

David Watts, a stern-wheel packet built in Paducah, Kentucky, in 1864. 158' × 35' × 5.6', rated at 293 tons. The boat was advertised from Pittsburgh for Virginia City, Hancock City, Deer Lodge, and all points in the Idaho mining district in 1865. The boat came to Fort Union and Fort Benton in 1866. The steamer ran

New Orleans-Red River the winter of 1866 and then ran St. Louis–Tennessee River until she was lost on August 27, 1870, on the Mississippi.

Decatur, a steam towboat rated at 65 tons. She burned while at winter quarters during the winter of 1929–1930 in Missouri. The wreck was removed by the government in 1930.

Deer Lodge, a stern-wheel packet built in Belle Vernon, Pennsylvania, at the L. M. Speer boatyard in 1865. 165' × 35' × 5', rated at 493 tons. The engines were 17.5s built by Robinson, Rae & Company with three boilers (38" × 26'). The steamer was designed by James Dunbar. Captain Thomas W. Rae served as master with H. A. Dohrman as clerk. She was designed for the Missouri River, and had aboard a portable sawmill for sawing her own cordwood en route. She made a total of eleven trips to Fort Benton during her career. The boat struck a snag and sank while headed upbound, 12 miles below St. Joseph, Missouri, in late 1865. The boat was raised and finally dismantled in 1874.

Delaware, a side-wheel packet built for the Missouri River trade at Monongahela, Pennsylvania, in 1850. The boat was rated at 168 tons, with two engines (14.5" × 4.5') and two boilers (22' × 40"), which allowed a working pressure of 135 lbs. Captain Baker served as the boat's master. The first two locomotives that ever came up the Missouri were transported on this boat. She was snagged and lost in Kansas in 1857.

Dells, a stern-wheel packet built in Osceola, Wisconsin, in 1866. 90' × 16.5' × 5.5', with two engines (8" × 2.5') and one boiler (16'x 40"), which allowed a working pressure of 110 lbs. The boat was owned in 1874 by the Kaskaskia River Navigation Company. She was snagged on the Missouri River in Nebraska on October 26, 1878. Two men reportedly jumped overboard and were drowned.

Denver, see DENVER CITY

Denver City (also DENVER NO. 1), a side-wheel packet built at Madison, Indiana, in 1862. 225' × 33' and rated at 300 tons, with two engines (24" × 6.5') and three boilers (24' × 42"), which allowed a working pressure of 137 lbs. She was owned by the Hannibal & St. Joseph Railroad Company, with Captain John Waddell serving as master. She burned at the St. Joseph wharf on May 16, 1867. The hull was not badly damaged; it was used to build a ferry.

Denver No. 2, a center-wheel ferry built in Pittsburgh, Pennsylvania, in 1871. 136' × 24.2' × 6.3'. The hull and engines came from the side-wheel packet the DENVER. She operated at St. Joseph, Missouri, and later at Fort Lincoln. The ferry was destroyed by ice at Fort Lincoln on March 13, 1880.

Derrick Barge No.1, a steam-rigged derrick barge built by the U. S. government in 1877. Such barges were to aid in the removal of obstructions on the upper Missouri River. The boats would both remove and blast large boulders. This barge was lost on the Missouri in Montana in August 1877.

Derrick Barge No.2, a steam-rigged derrick barge built by the U. S. government in 1877. She was working on the upper Missouri River and was pulled out on to the bank for the winter of 1891–1892. The barge burned along the Missouri River shore in Montana during the summer of 1892.

Dew Drop, a stern-wheel packet built at Monongahela, Pennsylvania, in 1857. The boat was rated at 148 tons, with two engines (13.5" × 4') and two boilers (24' × 33"), which allowed a working pressure of 132 lbs. She burned near the mouth of the Osage River on June 12, 1860.

Diana, a side-wheel packet built in 1834 in Louisville, Kentucky, for the American Fur Company. Captain John Shallcross served as master. She was at Cabanne's Post near Council Bluffs, Iowa, in 1834 and at Fort Union in 1835. The boat sank the first time near Lexington, Missouri, in March of 1836, while bound for Council Bluffs. The cargo was saved and put ashore, but the rising river carried most of it away. The steamer was raised and repaired in St. Louis. She was snagged and fatally lost in Missouri on October 10, 1836.

Don Cameron (also noted as the J. DON COMERON), a government steamer built specifically for the Yellowstone River. She was built in 1877 at the Barnore boatyard in Jeffersonville, Indiana. The boat was lost on the Yellowstone River on May 17, 1877.

Dora, a side-wheel packet built in 1872 by J. D. Hibbler and August Woht for the Missouri River trade. The boat was lost in ice at the mouth of Charette Creek, Missouri, on January 22, 1877. She was raised and sold to the Washington Ferry Company, Missouri. The steamer burned when a lamp exploded while in Madison Crossing, 17 miles above St. Louis.

Dorcas, a Missouri River steamer that was lost in Missouri.

Dorothy (also MELUSINA), a side-wheel packet built at Carondelet, Missouri, in 1882. 82.9' × 12.7' × 3.6', rated at 30 tons, with two compound oscillating engines (10" and 14" × 3') and one boiler (16' × 42"), which allowed a working pressure of 180 lbs. The boat was owned by the Pioneer Sand Company of St. Joseph, Missouri. The steamer filled with water while lying up for the night at St. Joseph on March 20, 1920. The watchman slept through the crisis and was drowned. The boiler and capstan were salvaged. This boat was formerly the U. S. Steamer MELUSINA.

Dr. Burleigh, see HIRAM WOOD NO. 1

Duncan S. Carter, a side-wheel packet built at Mound City, Illinois, and St. Louis. 221' × 33', rated at 426 tons, with two engines (20.5" × 7') and three boilers (28' × 40"), which allowed a working pressure of 134 lbs. She was owned by William P. Eads, Jr. and Eardly O. Sayle. She snagged on the Missouri River on August 28, 1859, en route from Weston to St. Louis.

Durock, a side-wheel steamer built for the Missouri River trade in 1850. John McCloy was the boat's master. She struck a snag and sank in Missouri in 1852.

E. A. Ogden, a side-wheel packet built in St. Louis, Missouri, in 1855. 280.5' × 36' × 6', rated at 399 tons. The boat ran on the Missouri River with Captain

Hamilton Lee. The boat was snagged on the lower Missouri River, February 22, 1860, in Missouri.

E. H. Durfee, a stern-wheel packet built in Pittsburgh, Pennsylvania, in 1871. 206' × 35'. The boat's engines were 16s and were built by John Herbertson, of Brownsville, Pennsylvania. She had three boilers (38" × 26') built at the Eberman & McFall yard. The boat was built for Captain William Coulson and others for the Pittsburgh–Fort Benton trade. All total, the boat made it to Fort Benton seven times in her career. In 1876, the boat carried General Miles and six companies of the fifth U. S Infantry to the Indian wars. Later the boat was owned by Captain George G. Keith and others and was used in handling wheat from the lower Missouri to St. Louis. The steamer was overloaded when she sank at the mouth of the Gasconade River on May 31, 1881.

E. M Clendenin, a side-wheel passenger steamer built in 1850. The boat operated in the lower Missouri River trade and sank in Missouri in 1853.

E. M. Ryland, a side-wheel packet built in Brownsville, Pennsylvania, in 1857. The boat was rated at 267 tons. Captain Blount served as master while the boat was in the lower Missouri River trade. She was burned and lost at St. Louis on October 8, 1861.

E. O. Standard, a side-wheel packet built in Metropolis, Illinois, in 1865. The boat was rated at 281 tons. The boat was snagged and lost below Sioux City on May 13, 1865.

Eagle, a stern-wheel ferry boat built in Madison, Indiana, in 1879. 85.9' × 20' × 3.3', with two engines (8" × 2') and one boiler (14' × 44"), which allowed a working pressure of 100 lbs. She was owned by Martha H. Moore, and Meredith T. Moore served as pilot. She burned at Lexington, Missouri, when a gasoline stove exploded on February 26, 1897. The wreck was removed later that year by the C. R. SUTER.

Eclipse, a stern-wheel packet built at California, Pennsylvania, in 1878 at the Ebberman and McFall boatyard. 180' × 30' × 4'. The boat had an iron paddle wheel with a 16' diameter and 22' buckets. She was owned by A. B. Sheperd of Wellsville, Ohio, and Alex V. Caughey, Frank S. Moore and John D. Briggert, all of Allegheney County, Pennsylvania. Between 1878 and 1881, the boat made eleven trips to Fort Benton. In 1881, she was the flagship of a group of boats carrying several thousand Indians from the Yellowstone to agencies in the Dakotas. In later years, she was owned by the Montana Transportation Company under the direction of Isaac P. Baker. The boat was fatally snagged in Iowa on September 3, 1887.

Edgar, a side-wheel ferryboat built in Leavenworth, Kansas, in 1866. 116.1' × 28.9' × 4.6', rated at 127 tons, with one engine (20" × 4') and two boilers (18' × 42"), which allowed a working pressure of 120 lbs. Operated at Leavenworth as a ferry and was owned by W. T. B. Simpson and Mrs. J. R. Sousely. She was lost to ice in Nebraska in 1884.

Edinburgh, a side-wheel packet built in Brownsville, Pennsylvania, in 1854. The boat was rated at 283 tons. She ran on the Missouri River in the St. Louis–St. Joseph trade in 1856. In the late 1850s, she ran to New Orleans and made trips up the Red River. The boat burned on the Mississippi near St. Louis on May 15, 1859.

Edna, a side-wheel packet built in 1840 for the St. Louis–Glasgow trade. Captain Jason McCord was the boat's master. The boat was named for one of his daughters. A boiler exploded on July 3, 1842, at the mouth of the Missouri River, killing fifty-five German emigrants.

Effie Deans, a stern-wheel packet built in Madison, Indiana, in 1863. 157' × 33' × 5', rated at 238 tons. The boat was owned by the Keokuk Packet Company along with Captain Joseph LaBarge, John LaBarge, and others. The boat was named after a Sir Walter Scott character, Effie Deans, in his *Heart of MidLothian.* Captain Joe LaBarge commanded the boat on a trip to New Orleans and up the Missouri to Forts Union and Benton. The boat burned at St. Louis on April 7, 1866.

El Paso, a side-wheel packet built in St. Louis, Missouri, in 1850. 180' × 28', rated at 260 tons with two engines (18.5" × 6.5') and three boilers (22' × 38"), which allowed a working pressure of 160 lbs. In 1852, this boat ascended the Platte River to Guernsey, Wyoming. She was the only steamboat to ever go there. In 1853, she ascended the Missouri to the mouth of the Milk River, the first steamboat to reach that location. She was snagged and lost in Missouri on the lower Missouri River on April 10, 1855. At the time of the sinking, the boat was owned by Bennett, Itzen, and Wineland. The boat's master was Captain Andrew Wineland with Captain William R. Massie serving as pilot.

Elisha Woods, a stern-wheel towboat rated at 98 tons. The steamer was owned by the Woods Brothers Construction Company, of Omaha, Nebraska. The boat overturned and sank in Jackson's Bend on October 26, 1926. Two lives were lost. The U. S. snagboat MISSOURI removed the wreck on the same day.

Eliza Stewart, a side-wheel packet built in St. Louis, Missouri, in 1847. The boat was rated at 169 tons. She ran St. Louis-Galena in 1848, with a few trips on the Missouri as well. In 1849, she ran St. Louis-Keokuk. The vessel burned in a wharf fire at St. Louis on May 17, 1849.

Elk, a side-wheel steamer built in Cincinnati, Ohio, in 1837. The boat was built for the American Fur Company and was rated at 99 tons. The steamer went to Fort Union in 1838. She was snagged and lost in Missouri that same year. The passengers were taken off by Captain Joseph La Barge on the steamer KANSAS.

Ella, a center-wheel ferry built in 1858. She was rated at 72 tons and operated on the Missouri River. She foundered in Kansas on August 3, 1868.

Ella Kimbrough (also GENERAL SHERMAN), a stern-wheel packet built in Jeffersonville, Indiana, in 1877. 145' × 28' × 4', with two engines (12.5" × 4.5') and two boilers (22' × 38"), which allowed a working pressure of 145 lbs. The boat was originally the GENERAL SHERMAN built for the U. S. military for the Yellowstone River. The United States sold the boat to Captain Peter M. Manion who then sold it to Captain T. M. Kinbrough, who named the boat for his wife. The boat was snagged in St. Charles Chute on the Missouri River on September 20, 1884, with a large load of wheat. The ferry JOHN L. FERGUSON salvaged the wheat.

Ella Stewart, an early lower Missouri River boat. Her master was Isaac McKee. The boat burned at St. Louis on May 17, 1849.

Emigrant, a side-wheel packet built in Cincinnati, Ohio, in 1856. The boat was rated at 343 tons. She was owned and operated by Captain William Terrell. The boat ran St. Louis-St. Joseph every 2 weeks. The boat was burned and lost in Missouri on November 19, 1860.

Emilie La Barge, a side-wheel packet built in Mound City, Illinois, in 1869. 218' × 38' × 5.5', rated at 290 tons, with two engines (22" × 6') and three boilers (26' × 42"), which allowed a working pressure of 129 lbs. The steamer was originally built by Captain Joseph LaBarge and others for the Missouri River trade. She was sold in St. Louis on April 12, 1871, to Captain David H. Silver and James Gunsolis. The boat was snagged and lost on June 6, 1874, in Missouri.

Emilie No. 1, a side-wheel packet built in Pittsburgh, Pennsylvania, in 1841. The steamer was rated at 220 tons and had two engines. She was built for use in the fur trade by Pierre Chouteau Jr. and John W. Keiser and was named for Mrs. Chouteau. She journeyed to Fort Union in 1840 and was snagged and lost in Missouri on April 3, 1843.

Emilie No. 2, a side-wheel packet built in St. Louis, Missouri, in 1859. 225' × 32', rated at 388 tons, with two engines (22" × 6') and two boilers (26' × 44"), which allowed a working pressure of 110 lbs. The boat ran on the Missouri River and was owned and commanded by Captain Joseph LaBarge. The steamer was named for his daughter and was the first side-wheeler ever seen at Fort Benton when she arrived there in June 1862. Later, the boat was sold to the Hannibal & St. Joseph Rail Road and was lost in a tornado at St. Joseph, Missouri, on June 4, 1868. The boat was completely destroyed to the hull, which was later floated to Atchison, Kansas.

Emily (also NELLIE KENT and MARY BARNES), a stern-wheel packet built in Osceola, Wisconsin, in 1868. 137' × 24.4' × 4.2'. Originally the boat was named NELLIE KENT, when built by Captain William A. Kent. He sold the packet to the U. S. government in the fall of 1884, and the boat was renamed the MARY BARNES. The boat was converted to a snagboat for U. S. service and was renamed the EMILY. She was lost in the spring ice breakup in North Dakota in 1885.

Emma (also noted as the EMMA No. 2), a stern-wheel packet built in Nebraska near Sioux City, Iowa, on the Missouri River in 1872. 64' × 18' × 3', with one engine and one boiler. Originally, the boat was owned by George and Fay Mattison who used her as a wood carrier. She sank during a storm 20 miles above Omaha, Nebraska, on August 1, 1873. The vessel was repaired and sold to L. C. Lohmen who ran her on the Osage River. The boat was on her way to be dismantled when she was stranded opposite Ewing's Landing bound from Osage to Jefferson City on August 18, 1885. The empty hull was caught by a falling river. Captain George Young was serving as pilot at the time of loss.

Emma Brown, a stern-wheel packet built in Memphis, Tennessee, in 1854. This was a small steamer rated at only 107 tons. The engines on this boat came from the steamer the LAKE OF THE WOODS. The boat was dismantled in 1857.

Empire City, a stern-wheel packet built in California, Pennsylvania, in 1854. 150' × 34.5' × 5.6', rated at 260 tons. Originally owned by James Vandergrift, Isaac Hamilton, C. P. Caughey, Samuel Barr Jr., and William H. Stackhouse of Pittsburgh and David G. Mulford of New York. They operated the boat in the Pittsburgh–St. Louis trade until the outbreak of the Civil War. The boat was sold to Captain Jacob Hazlep of St. Louis and was then impressed into U. S. service as a transport from 1862–1865. The boat was lost in ice at St. Louis on January 12, 1866.

Endors, a small fur trade packet that burned in St. Louis, Missouri, on May 17, 1849. Very little is know about the boat.

Esperanza, a stern-wheel packet built in Brownsville, Pennsylvania, in 1871. 177' × 33.5' × 5.5' with two engines and three boilers (46" × 26'). Operated in the St. Louis–Missouri River trade with Captain Dunlevy commanding. The boat went south during the winter months and ran New Orleans-Red River. In the fall of 1873, the boat was lengthened in St. Louis to 228' and also received larger engines. The boat was operating Cincinnati-New Orleans in 1874. The boat burned on the Mississippi River on October 21, 1874.

Estella, a side-wheel packet built in Shousetown, Pennsylvania, in 1862. 205' × 35' × 6', rated at 414 tons. The boat's hull was built by E. and N. Porter, and the machinery came from the James Rees boatyard. She was originally built for Captain William B. Hazlett and others. In 1862, Hazlett sold the steamer at Cincinnati to Captain John P. Keiser and others of St. Louis. The boat burned in the great St. Louis steamboat fire on October 27, 1862.

Eudora, a side-wheel packet built in Cincinnati, Ohio, in 1847. The boat was rated at 420 tons and ran St. Louis Ouachita River. She burned at the St. Louis wharf on May 17, 1849. This may be the ENDORS (see above).

Euphrasie, a side-wheel packet built for the Missouri River trade before 1840. The boat had a single engine and was named for the wife of George Collier Esq. She was lost in Missouri on September 17, 1840, when she struck a snag. The boat's furniture and engine were removed (the engine went to the steamer OCEANA), but the cargo was a total loss. It was so great a loss that the accident caused the Glasgow Marine Insurance Company to go out of business.

Evening Star, a side-wheel packet built in Freedom, Pennsylvania, in 1864. The boat was rated at 343 tons. The boat was completed in Wellsville, Ohio, where the cabin and machinery were installed. After completion, the boat left for St. Louis under the command of Captain Murphy, entering the Missouri River trade. The boat was almost destroyed on the Missouri River in January 1867; she was traveling close to the steamer W. R. CARTER when she exploded. The steamer was finally lost on August 24, 1869, when she burned at St. Louis.

Excel, a stern-wheel packet built in McKeesport, Pennsylvania, in 1851. 150' × 27' × 5', with two engines (12" × 55") and two boilers (22' × 38"), which allowed a working pressure of 150 lbs. The boat originally ran on the Cumberland River for W. P. Henry & Company. Then the boat was sold to Mr. Miller of St. Louis, who operated it on the Illinois River. Later, Captain Benjamin F. Beasley ran the boat in the Memphis–Hatchie River trade and on the Missouri. It was snagged and lost on the Missouri on March 23, 1856, in Missouri.

Exchange (also TENNESSEE and U. S. Tinclad #38), a stern-wheel packet built in Brownsville, Pennsylvania in 1862. The boat was originally named the EXCHANGE. She became U. S. Tinclad #38, still called the EXCHANGE, on April 6, 1863. The boat was redocumented the TENNESSEE on September 4, 1865. In July 1868, she ran the Evansville–Cairo trade. The boat made a trip up the Missouri River in the spring of 1869 with Captain Joe Wheeler. She was snagged and lost in Nebraska on April 25, 1869, with E. S. Weaver serving as pilot on watch.

Expansion, a stern-wheel packet built in Bismarck, North Dakota, in 1900. 123' × 26' × 3.5'. The boat was owned by the Benton Packet Company. The boat often operated with Captain Grant Marsh as master and pilot. She was lost in ice at Bismarck on March 13, 1910. Part of the hull was later used on the motor vessel EXPANSION.

Express, a side-wheel packet built in West Elizabeth, Pennsylvania, in 1850. The boat was rated at 192 tons. In 1852, the Adams Express Company ran the boat in the Vevay–Madison trade to connect with the new Madison & Indianapolis Railway. Later, the boat went to the Missouri River and was snagged and lost in Kansas on July 15, 1855.

F. F. Hilman, a stern-wheel packet built for the Missouri River trade. The boat was snagged in the 1880s on the Missouri River.

F. J. Nutz, a stern-wheel packet that operated on the Missouri River. The boat struck a snag and broke in two on August 17, 1869, in Kansas.

F. Y. Batchelor, a stern-wheel packet built in Freedom and Pittsburgh, Pennsylvania, in 1878. 180' × 30' × 3.5'. The boat was built at the McCaskey & Kerr boatyard, with Captain C. W. Batchelor overseeing the boat's construction. The machinery was built by Robert Lea. The boat was the only one to arrive at Fort Custer on the Bighorn River in 1878. In August 1878, the boat set a new speed record by running from Bismarck to Fort Buford in 55 hours and 25 minutes, beating the record held by the RED CLOUD by 8 hours. The boat crashed into rocks 16 miles below Forest City, South Dakota, in November 1879. Leighton & Jordan owned the boat until 1885 when she was sold to the Benton Packet Company. The boat made her last trip to Fort Benton in 1890. The boat worked around Bismarck after that and was wrecked by ice while at winter quarters at Running Water, South Dakota, on March 6, 1907.

Fannie Lewis, a steamer that operated on the Missouri. She helped with the salvage operation of the FAR WEST in October 1883.

Fannie Ogden (also FANNY OGDEN), a side-wheel packet built in Madison, Indiana, in 1862. The boat was rated at 417 tons. The boat was originally built for Captain Joseph Kinney who wished to name the boat for one of the three daughters of L. C. Odgen of St. Joseph, Missouri. To help him decide which daughter to name the boat after, he had the girls draw straws; Fanny had the longest. Captain Kinney ran the boat on the Missouri River. In 1863, the boat was owned by Captain John P. Keiser of St. Louis. She was sold again in 1864 to Captain John C. Copelin and others who advertised her for a trip from St. Louis to the gold mines of Idaho. The boat burned in a large steamboat fire at St. Louis on April 7, 1866.

Fanny Barker (also FAWN), a stern-wheel packet built in Cincinnati, Ohio, in 1863. The boat was rated at 174 tons. It was originally built for Barker, Hart & Cook of Cincinnati. In 1863, the boat was impressed into U. S. service and renamed FAWN on April 10. The boat was redocumented as the FANNY BARKER on October 19, 1865. The boat was stranded in Missouri on March 24, 1873.

Fanny Ogden, see FANNIE OGDEN

Far West, a side-wheel packet built at the mouth of Bonnie Femme Creek, below Boonville, Missouri, in 1834. 130' × 20' × 6' with a single engine. The boat was snagged and lost in Missouri in 1836.

Far West, a stern-wheel packet built in Pittsburgh, Pennsylvania, in 1870. 190' × 33', with two engines (15" × 5') and three boilers (22' × 38"), which allowed a working pressure of 130 lbs. The boat was built for Captain Sanford B. Coulson and became one of the more famed steamboats on the upper Missouri River. The boat was commanded by Captain Grant Marsh when she participated in the ill-fated Custer expedition. This boat that was up the Little Yellowstone River and brought the wounded from the battle of Little Bighorn to Fort Lincoln. Later General Miles and Buffalo Bill used the boat for scouting expeditions. The FAR WEST made a total of eighteen trips to Fort Benton and for 2 years operated for the U. S. government on the Yellowstone River. The boat was later sold to Victor Bonnet and Captain Henry M. Dodds. She struck a snag and was lost in Missouri on October 30, 1883, but part of the cargo was salvaged by the FANNIE LEWIS.

Favorite, a side-wheel packet built in Cincinnati, Ohio, in 1859. The boat was rated at 115 tons. She operated on the upper river in 1863, and was to Fort Benton in 1866. The boat was dismantled in 1868.

Fawn, see FANNY BARKER

Fearless, a large stern-wheel towboat built in Pittsburgh, Pennsylvania, in 1865. 160' × 30', rated at 395 tons, with two engines (20" × 8') and five boilers (26' × 40"), which allowed a working pressure of 150 lbs. The boat was owned by the Kansas City Barge Line. The FEARLESS was a large, heavy-draft Ohio or Lower Mississippi River towboat, not at all adapted to the Missouri River. She struck a snag and was lost in Missouri on August 26, 1882. Captain Thomas Poe was master at the time of loss.

Felix X. Aubery, a popular lower Missouri River boat built in 1853. Captain Brierly was the boat's master. The boat sank in Missouri in 1860. Her machinery was removed and installed on the steamer ARAGO. In honor of the man for whom the boat was named, she bore on her hurricane roof, aft of the pilothouse, a figure of a man riding at full speed on horseback.

Fire Canoe, a side-wheel packet built at Ironton, Ohio, in 1854. 160' × 30', rated at 166 tons. The boat operated on the upper Mississippi in 1855 with Captain Baldwin and again in 1856 and 1857 with Captain Spencer. She spent 1858 on the Minnesota River. In 1858, Goddin Brothers Coal Company, out of Leavenworth, Kansas, bought the boat. She was snagged and lost in Kansas on her way to Leavenworth with a load of coal on November 13, 1858. The boat's bell was taken off the wreck and placed in the old Gillis house in Kansas City.

Florence Miller No. 2 (also U. S. Tinclad #34—MOOSE and LITTLE ROCK), a stern-wheel packet built in Cincinnati, Ohio, in 1863. 154' × 32' × 4.5', rated at 189 tons. The boat was sold to the U. S. military on May 20, 1863, and renamed MOOSE Tinclad #34. She was sold into private hands on October 9, 1865, and renamed LITTLE ROCK. The boat was at Fort Benton in 1867. She burned and was lost on December 23, 1867 in Arkansas.

Florence Miller No. 3 (also ORIOLE—U. S. Tinclad #52 and AGNES), a stern-wheel packet built in Cincinnati, Ohio, in 1864. 160' × 33' × 5', rated at 236 tons. The steamer was originally owned by John Swasey and Company. The boat was impressed during the Civil War on December 7, 1864, and renamed ORIOLE Tinclad #52 on March 22, 1865. She was sold on October 14, 1865, back into private hands and renamed AGNES. The boat was to Fort Benton in 1866 and 1867. The boat was snagged and lost on March 3, 1869, in Mississippi.

Florence No. 2, a side-wheel packet built in Elizabeth, Pennsylvania, in 1857. 200' × 34', rated at 399 tons, with two engines (22.5" × 6.5') and three boilers (26' × 43"), which allowed a working pressure of 125 lbs. The boat was built for Captain Joseph Throckmorton and others who ran the boat in the St. Louis–Sioux City trade. The boat made one trip to Fort Stewart 100 miles above the Yellowstone River. She was snagged and sunk at Port William, Kansas, in 1857.

The boat was raised and sold to J. C. Coeplan and others of St. Louis. In 1859, the boat carried opposition goods to Fort Stewart. The boat was fatally snagged and lost on the Missouri in Kansas on March 29, 1864.

Floyd, a stern-wheel steamer built at Bonnets Mill, Missouri, in 1914. 102' × 7' × 3.2', rated at 56 tons with two engines (9" × 4') and one boiler (18' × 44"), which allowed a working pressure of 182 lbs. The boat was owned by Thompson Brothers with Captain Thompson serving as pilot. The steamer hit a clump of submerged piling of an old dyke in Missouri on March 3, 1920. Owing to a rising river, the steamer could not be raised and was abandoned.

Fontenelle, a stern-wheel packet built in Brownsville, Pennsylvania, in 1870. 205.5' × 33.8' × 4.3'. The boat was built for Captain John H. Shaw for the Missouri River trade. All told, the boat made seven trips to Fort Benton and four to Cow Island and Carroll for the Kountz and Peck steamboat lines. The boat was snagged opposite Amazonia, Missouri, in August 1868 and was raised. She snagged a second time 10 miles above St. Joseph, Missouri, on August 21, 1871. The boat was raised again. In 1872, she operated on the Red River. In January 1876, the boat was on the Arkansas River with Captain C. L. Bernnan. The boat spent the winter of 1876–1877 frozen in at Pascals Island, 60 miles above Fort Sully on the Missouri. The boat was finally lost to an ice floe in South Dakota in the spring of 1881.

Frederick, a stern-wheel packet built in Tuscumbia, Missouri, in 1883. 96.4' × 14.3' × 3', rated at 82 tons. The boat ran on the Osage River along with the HULBERT, connecting with the MP Railroad at Osage City. Captain Henry Castrup was the boat's master and Bob Marshall served as pilot. She was sold in 1889 to R. M. Marshall (manager) and ended up towing barges. She sank at Jefferson City, Missouri, on August 10, 1894. The wreck was raised and dismantled.

Frolic, a stern-wheel packet built in Louisville, Kentucky, in 1844. The boat was rated at 126 tons. The boat was owned by the Union Fur Company. She loaded at Pittsburgh in the spring of 1844 with Captain Baldwin, bound for the Missouri River. The boat was headed for Fort Mortimer in 1844, but because of low water made it only as far as Fort George (near Fort Pierre) where the boat stayed for the winter. She finally made it to Fort Mortimer in 1845. The boat burned and was lost at St. Louis on April 17, 1849.

G. A. Thomson, a stern-wheel packet built in Eureka, Wisconsin, and completed in St. Paul, Minnesota, in 1865. The boat was rated at 366 tons. In 1866, the boat was advertised for the New Orleans–St. Louis trade with Captain C. L. Huntoon as master. The boat was logged in at Fort Benton in 1867. She was snagged and lost on the Arkansas River in Arkansas on April 9, 1869. The wreck later burned. James Alexander Frazier of Cincinnati and James H. Kelly of Racine, Wisconsin, owned the boat when she was lost.

G. B. Allen, a side-wheel packet built in Metropolis, Illinois, and St. Louis in

1865. 215' × 34.5' × 5.5', rated at 593 tons. The boat was built for the Missouri River for John P. Keiser and others. She often ran St. Louis-Shreveport. The boat was lost in a St. Louis steamboat fire on March 29, 1869 with several other steamers.

G. M., a small stern-wheel packet built at Arrow Rock, Missouri, in 1906. 89.5' × 17.9' × 3.9', rated at 51 tons with two engines (8.25" × 3.5') and one boiler (12' × 60"), which allowed a working pressure of 200 lbs. The little steamer was owned by Woods Brothers Construction Company of Lincoln, Nebraska, with Captain Wallace Walter serving as pilot. She struck a snag on November 19, 1919, near the Little Sioux River. The machinery was salvaged, and the hull was raised and beached. Ultimately, the hull was lost when an ice floe carried it away.

G. W. Graham, a side-wheel packet built in Elizabeth, Pennsylvania, in 1861. 245' × 39' × 6.5', rated at 508 tons. The boat was named for G. Wash Graham of Halliday & Company, Cairo, Illinois. Captain C. W. Batchelor oversaw the boat's construction . The boat often ran St. Louis-Memphis. The boat was at Fort Union in 1865 and in 1867 to Fort Buford. Shortly after returning from the Missouri River she burned at St. Louis alongside the YELLOWSTONE on July 11, 1867.

Gallatin (originally the CLINCH), a stern-wheel packet built in Kingston, Tennessee, in 1864. 140' × 30', rated at 131 tons. The boat was originally built by the U. S. Quartermaster Corps as a transport during the Civil War and was named the CLINCH. She was renamed the GALLATIN on April 10, 1866, when she was sold into private hands. The boat was operated by Captain Samuel Howe. The boat set a temporary record in 1867 when she ascended the Missouri River 40 miles above Fort Benton to High Wood Creek. The boat made the record-breaking trip solely for the purpose of beating the record set by the PETER BALEN the previous year. The GALLATIN's record stood until 1868 when the TOM STEVENS made it almost to the Great Falls of the Missouri. The boat was snagged and lost in Nebraska on April 16, 1868.

Gem, a stern-wheel packet built at Wheeling, West Virginia, in 1863. 160' × 26' × 4', rated at 145 tons. In 1864, the boat may have had improvements made in Freedom, Pennsylvania. The boat's length was reported increased by 45'; a texas deck was to be added, along with new engines and a new stern-wheel. The boat was lost in Nebraska on November 9, 1869, from unknown causes.

General Brady, a side-wheel packet built for the Missouri River trade in 1843. Captain J. Gunsolis served as the vessel's master. The boat was snagged and lost in Missouri in 1843.

General Bragg, a steamer reported lost on the Missouri River in Missouri. Little is known about this vessel.

General Brooke, a side-wheel packet built in Pittsburgh, Pennsylvania, in 1842. The boat was rated at 143 tons. The boat was sold to Captain Joseph LaBarge in 1845. She traveled to Fort Union in 1845 and again in 1846. The boat burned at St. Louis on May 7, 1849.

General Chas H. Tompkins, a stern-wheel packet built in Pittsburgh, Pennsylvania, in 1878. 181' × 25' × 3.5', rated at 356 tons. The boat was built for William J. Kountz and others for the Missouri River trade. In the spring of 1881, the boat was struck by an ice floe at St. Stephens Mission, South Dakota. The boat drifted 10 miles and lodged at Swan Lake about 1 mile from the river. It took 2 weeks to get the boat back on the river. Later, the boat operated in the Memphis–Arkansas trade. The boat was lost on the Arkansas River.

General Custer, a stern-wheel packet built in Belle Veron, Pennsylvania, and completed at Pittsburgh in 1870. 182' × 28' × 3.8', with two engines (13" × 4') and two boilers (20' × 38"), which allowed a working pressure of 132 lbs. The boat was built for William J. Kountz for the Missouri River trade. She was snagged and lost in Nebraska on October 5, 1879.

General Gaines, a side-wheel packet built in Brownsville, Pennsylvania, in 1849. The boat was rated at 159 tons. She was taken out of packet service in 1855 and taken to St. Joseph, Missouri, to be used as a ferry. She sank in Missouri in 1857.

General Grant, a stern-wheel packet built in Monongahela, Pennsylvania in 1863. The boat was rated at 172 tons, with two engines (13" × 4') and two boilers (20' × 38"), which allowed a working pressure of 132 lbs. Captain John Woodburn ran the boat when she was new and then sold her in March 1864 to Captain Packard. The boat went to Vicksburgh in early 1864 delivering cotton from Louisville. The boat advertised for the "gold mines of Idaho" in 1864 and had so many takers she was compelled to refuse freight. The boat participated in General Sully's Yellowstone River expedition in the summer of 1864. The boat was lost in ice in Nebraska on March 18, 1866.

General Lee, a steam ferryboat lost on the Missouri River in Missouri on February 14, 1883.

General McNeil, a stern-wheel packet in the Missouri River trade. She struck a snag and was lost in Missouri in the 1860s.

General Meade, a stern-wheel packet built in Pittsburgh, Pennsylvania, in 1875. 192' × 30' × 4.3', rated at 171 tons, with two compound engines (8.75" and 23" × 4') and two boilers. The boat was originally built for Captain William J. Kountz for the Missouri River. The boat was snagged opposite Jefferson, Missouri, on September 5, 1884. The boat was raised and later snagged and lost on the Mississippi River on September 4, 1888.

General Sherman, see ELLA KIMBROUGH

General Terry, a stern-wheel packet built in Freedom, Pennsylvania, at the McCaskey & Kerry boat yard in 1878. 178.2' × 31' × 4', with secondhand boilers and used engines. The boat was built for W. A. Byrleigh and John Todd of Miles City, Montana. Unfortunately, the pair had difficulty paying, and James

Rees & Sons Company, filed a lawsuit and took over interest in the boat. The boat was later sold to T. C. Power & Brothers of Fort Benton and operated in their Block P Line. In all, the steamer made seven trips to Fort Benton, the last one in 1887. While transporting troops from Fort Yates, North Dakota, to Kansas City, Missouri, the boat hit a pier of the new Union Pacific bridge at Omaha and sank.

General W. H. Ashley, a side-wheel packet in the Missouri River trade. Captain Jason Sweeney was owner and master. The boat was named after the famous fur trader. She was snagged and lost in Missouri in 1830.

Geneva No. 1, a stern-wheel packet built in Brownsville, Pennsylvania, in 1848. The boat was rated at 121 tons. She often operated on the upper Mississippi River. On December 2, 1852, while taking on wood 4 miles below Alton, Illinois, her three boilers exploded, killing several passengers. The boat was snagged and lost in Nebraska on September 30, 1856. Captain Throckmorton was master at the time of loss.

Genoa, a side-wheel packet built in California, Pennsylvania, in 1854. 170' × 28' × 5', rated at 266 tons. The boat was owned by Robert Campbell, Captain Joseph Throckmorton, and Joseph E. Gorman, all of St. Louis, who operated her on the Missouri River. Captain Thorckmorton served as master. The boat was at Fort Pierre in 1855. The boat was Snagged and lost in Nebraska on September 13, 1856.

George C. Wolf, a stern-wheel packet built in Madison, Indiana, in 1872. 198' × 37.5' × 5.7', with its machinery from the steamer CITY OF PEKIN. The boat was originally built for the Illinois River Packet Company, and named for Claiborne Greene Wolff. She operated in the Illinois River–St. Louis trade and also made runs on the St. Louis–Shreveport route. The boat's master was Captain Lloyd T. Belt. In 1873, the boat's boilers exploded at St. Francis Island, near Helena, Arkansas, on August 22. The LADY LEE towed the wreck to Memphis, and the towboat FUTURE CITY towed it above for rebuilding. In the spring of 1874, the boat was making a Missouri River trip when she was snagged and lost in Missouri on May 2, 1874, with Captain William W. Crapster as master.

George Spangler, a stern-wheel packet built in Madison, Indiana, in 1873. 124' × 25' × 4.2', with two engines (10.5" × 3') and one boiler (22' × 46"), which allowed a working pressure of 120 lbs. The boat was built for Captain Nat William. In 1877, the boat ran the New Orleans–St. Martinsville trade with Captain W. C. Smith. The boat sank in 1879 when she broke away from moorings at Barry's Landing on the Missouri River, 5 miles above Portland, Missouri, and then drifted on the wreck of the MOLLIE DOZIER in Albert Bend and sank. At the time of loss, the boat was owned by A. A. Hibbard and others, with Captain J. Glenn serving as master. The boat was raised and returned to service.

George Washington, a side-wheel single-engined steamer built in 1825. The boat was snagged and lost on the Missouri River in Missouri while on her way to Fort Calhoun, near Council Bluffs, Iowa, in 1826.

George Washington, a side-wheel packet that ran on the Missouri River. She struck a snag and was lost in Nebraska in 1887.

Georgetown, a stern-wheel packet built in Line Island and Pittsburgh, Pennsylvania, in 1852. The boat was rated at 183 tons, with two engines (14" × 4') and two boilers (24' × 39"), which allowed a working pressure of 190 lbs. She was owned by Captain Thomas Poe and others of Georgetown, Pennsylvania. She snagged in the Missouri River on October 12, 1853. The boat was raised and returned to service. She was fatally snagged in Missouri on her way to a military post on May 11, 1855.

Georgie Lee, a stern-wheel ferryboat built at Henley's Ford on the Gasonade River in 1879. The boat was rated at 91 tons, with two engines (9" × 3') and one boiler (17' × 40"), which allowed a working pressure of 120 lbs. The boat was owned by Patrick Jordon and William A. Dollman; Captain George Riddell served as pilot. The boat was lost in ice in Missouri on February 14, 1883.

Glasgow, a side-wheel packet built in New Albany, Indiana, in 1862. 208' × 34.5' × 5', rated at 340 tons, with two engines (22' × 7") and three boilers (26' × 42"), which allowed a working pressure of 130 lbs. The boat partially burned in the St. Louis steamboat fire on July 15, 1864. The board of underwriters auctioned off the burned boats, and the GLASGOW was sold to Captain William P. Lamothe for $6, 200. In 1867, she ran on the Missouri River in the St. Louis & Omaha Packet Company, with Lamothe serving as master. The boat was part of Carter's Red River Line in 1873, running St. Louis-Shreveport. The boat struck the wreck of the steamer MONSOON on the Red River on February 22, 1873, and was a total loss.

Glencoe No. 2, a stern-wheel packet that ran on the Missouri River. She struck a snag and was lost in Nebraska in 1887.

Glenmore (also the JOHN W. THOMAS), a stern-wheel packet built in Jeffersonville, Indiana, at the Howard boatyard in 1897. 160' × 26.5' × 4.2', rated at 208 tons, with two engines (14" × 5') and two boilers (18' × 36"), which allowed a working pressure of 180 lbs. The boat was originally named the JOHN W. THOMAS. She burned at Evansville on Christmas night 1905. The boat was rebuilt and renamed for a popular bourbon marketed by the Glenmore distillery. The boat was later sold for service on the Missouri River. On March 18, 1909, the boat was being repaired at the marine ways in North Kansas City, when the shore eroded and allowed the boat to fall into the river. The boat was a total loss. At the time of the accident, the boat was owned by Booth Baughman, J. J. Pryor, Phil McCrory, and Capt. E. H. Matheus, who was also the boat's master.

Globe, a 150-ton Missouri River steamer built in 1830. Captain Wineland served as master on a trip for the U. S. government in 1830. The boat was snagged and lost on the Missouri River in 1834.

Goddin, a Missouri River steamer. Very little is known about this boat except that she delivered military supplies to Fort Randall in 1855.

Goldfinch (also the NEW ERA), a stern-wheel packet built at Wellsville, Ohio, in 1862. 137' × 29' × 4.5', rated at 157 tons. The boat was immediately sold to the U. S. Navy on October 27, 1862, and became Tinclad #7 - NEW ERA. The boat was sold on August 17, 1865, into private hands. On November 27, 1865, it was renamed GOLDFINCH. The boat was at Fort Benton in 1866. The boat burned on the Missouri River on June 3, 1868.

Governor Allen, a side-wheel packet built at Ironton, Ohio, in 1874. 136' × 26' × 4', rated at 206 tons, with two engines (14" × 5') and three boilers (20' × 36"), which allowed a working pressure of 139 lbs. The boat was originally owned by M. Wise & Company with Captain John H. Farell serving as master. The boat was in Cairo, Illinois, for the winter of 1875–1876 and was then was sold to W. J. Lewis of St. Louis. He had the boat towed to St. Louis by the towboat RAVEN. Lewis ran the boat as a shuttle connecting with the St. Louis–Kansas City & Northern Railway at Dewitt, Missouri. On March 13, 1877, en route from Waverly. Missouri, to Dewitt, the boat snagged and was lost.

Governor Sharkey (also ALONE), a stern-wheel packet built in Madison, Indiana, in 1863. The boat was rated at 211 tons. The boat was sold to the U. S. Quartermaster Corps on completion in 1863. She was to Fort Union and the mouth of the Milk River in 1863. While returning downriver, the boat was impressed into service by the Army at Fort Pierre to shuttle supplies back upriver. The boat finally returned to St. Louis on November 4, 1863. In 1864 the boat was part of General Alfred Sully's Yellowstone expedition. The boat was sold on October 21, 1865, into private hands and renamed GOVERNOR SHARKEY. The boat sank on June 21, 1867.

Grace Huston, a center-wheel ferry built at Missouri City, Missouri, in 1878. 70.7' × 17.9' × 2.6', rated at 27 tons, with one engine (7" × 12") with one boiler (12' × 36"), which allowed a working pressure of 100 lbs. The boat was owned by Broxton H. Thomas. The boat was lost while at winter quarters in ice at Waverly, Missouri, on Febrary 7, 1881.

Grand Jerry (also noted as the GRAND FERRY). This vessel struck a bridge pier at Omaha, Nebraska, on June 10, 1880 and became a total loss.

Gray Cloud (also COLONEL KINSMAN and KINSMAN), a side-wheel packet built in Elizabeth, Pennsylvania, in,1854. The boat was rated at 245 tons. The boat brought military supplies to Fort Pierre in 1855. She was captured by Union forces as the confederate steamer COLONEL KINSMAN in 1862. The boat was renamed the U. S. Q. M. C. KINSMAN on September 30, 1862. In late 1862 she was sold into private hands and renamed GRAY CLOUD. She snagged and was lost on February 23, 1863.

Grey Eagle, a Missouri River steamer that was reported to have struck rocks on the Missouri and was lost on May 9, 1861.

Guidon, a stern-wheel packet built in McKeesport, Pennsylvania, in 1864. The boat was rated at 240 tons. The boat was built under the supervision of Captain C. W. Batchelor. The vessel originally operated in the Pittsburgh–Cincinnati–Louisville trade with Captain J. W. Batchelor. In November 1864, the boat struck two loaded coal boats that were stuck on rocks near Louisville. This boat had a replica of the Statue of Liberty on top of its pilothouse. Later, she ran Memphis-Arkansas River with Captain I. R. Whittaker. In 1867, she loaded out for a trip to Fort Benton from St. Louis. The boat then operated in the Memphis–Arkansas River trade. She was snagged and lost on the Arkansas River on March 23, 1870.

Gus Fowler, a stern-wheel packet built in Jeffersonville, Indiana, at the Howard boatyard in 1880. 160' × 29.5' × 5.6', with two engines (14.75" × 4.75') and two boilers (28' × 42"), which allowed a working pressure of 160 lbs. The boat was originally owned by the Fowler Line of Paducah and replaced the JAMES FISKE, JR., in the Paducah–Carior trade; she ran there 17 years until the DICK FOWLER replaced her. In the summer of 1897, the boat ran Memphis-Friar's Point and was returned to Paducah that September. In March 1898, the boat was sold to the Yazoo City Transportation Company. The boat was sold again, this time to H. L. Jones, who operated the boat on the Missouri River where Captain Alex Lamount was master. The boat was snagged and lost in Missouri on August 22, 1899.

Gus Linn, see COLONEL GUS LYNN

H. C. Coleman, a stern-wheel packet built at St. Louis, Missouri, in 1879. The boat was rated at 9 tons, with two engines (5" × 20") and one boiler (6' × 50"). She was owned by Henry McPherson and C. Williamson. The boat was destroyed on the Missouri River in a boiler explosion on July 7, 1884, in Missouri.

H. C. Nutt, a side-wheel packet built in California, Pennsylvania, and completed at Wellsville, Ohio, in 1870. 180' × 33' × 5', rated at 246 tons, with two engines (20" × 5.5') and four boilers (20' × 48"), which allowed a working pressure of 121 lbs. The boat was owned by the Missouri River Transfer Company. While unloading railcars at Omaha, Nebraska, on July 14, 1871, the boat struck the bridge pier. The boat continued to operated out of Omaha until ca. 1875 when the boat was sold to M. B. Pritchard of Little Rock, Arkansas. The boat ran on the Arkansas River with W. W. Maingault in command. She was out of service by 1878.

H. J. W., a steam towboat owned by the Jefferson City Sand Company of Jefferson City, Missouri. 73.5' × 15.5' and rated at 29 tons. The boat struck a snag and sank on the Missouri River on August 19, 1929, in Missouri. The boiler was salvaged, and then the wreck was removed by the U. S. government.

H. S. Turner (also noted as HENRY S. TURNER), a side-wheel packet built in Cincinnati, Ohio, in 1866. The boat was rated at 763 tons. She ran in the St. Louis & Omaha Packet Company, with Captain James A. Yore commanding in 1867. The boat ran New Orleans-Bayou Sara twice weekly with Captain V. B. Baranco in 1869. She was reported sunk on the Missouri River in 1870, but was raised and repaired. The boat sank at Island 16 on the Mississippi River on January 6, 1871, with Captain J. W. Rusk commanding. Two weeks later, the captain had the boat running again, and he was still using her in New Orleans in 1873. The boat later ran as a regular packet in the Cincinnati–Evansville trade. The boat was dismantled at Cincinnati in 1877.

Haidee, a side-wheel packet built for the Missouri River trade in 1846. The boat was lost at Charbonier Island near the mouth of the Missouri in 1846. In 1849, on her way to Fort Leavenworth, the boat was hung up in ice in Missouri and the passengers and crew had to walk to the Fort.

Halcyon, a side-wheel packet built in 1832 for the Missouri River. The boat was rated at 121 tons. Captain Shepard was in command when the boat was snagged and lost in Missouri on November 11, 1834, upbound from St. Louis to Fort Leavenworth. The hull filled with mud and could not be saved, but most of the cargo was salvaged.

Harry Clyde, a stern-wheel packet built at New Franklin, Missouri, in 1889. 60.9' × 23.3' × 3.3', and rated at 23 tons. The boat was owned by F. J. Hawkins & Brothers with Captain William Townes serving as pilot. The upperworks were destroyed by fire at New Franklin, Missouri, on August 14, 1890. There was no damage to the hull or machinery. The boat was rebuilt and later snagged near Omaha, Nebraska, on April 1, 1891. In 1892, high winds caused waves that swamped the boat in Nebraska on April 1. This time the boat was a total loss.

Harry Lynds, a center-wheel ferry built at White Cloud, Kansas, in 1892. 64' × 18' × 3', rated at 27 tons, with one Engine (7" × 10") and one boiler (7' × 30"), which allowed a working pressure of 160 lbs. The ferry was owned by John H. Lynds. She was snagged and lost in Kansas on August 13, 1899.

Hattie May, a side-wheel packet built in Wheeling, West Virginia, in 1864. The boat was rated at 230 tons. She was at Fort Union on the Missouri River in 1865. The boat was lost in ice at St. Louis on January 12, 1866.

Hattie Weller, a center-wheel ferry built in Metropolis, Illinois, in 1866. The boat was rated at 90 tons, with one engine (14" × 4') and one boiler (18' × 44"), which allowed a working pressure of 130 lbs. The boat was carried downstream from Kansas City, Missouri, by running ice on February 6, 1873, with considerable damage.

Helena No. 1, a stern-wheel packet built in St. Louis, Missouri, in 1866. The boat was rated at 199 tons, with two engines (13.5" × 3.5') and two boilers (26' × 38"), which allowed a working pressure of 139 lbs. The boat was owned by T. C. Power and Brothers out of Fort Benton, Montana, and operated as part of the Block P Line. The boat was at Fort Benton in 1866 and 1867. She was snagged near Bonhomme Island in Missouri on October 16, 1868, with John Stansberry as pilot on watch. The hold cargo (military supplies) was severely damaged, but the deck freight was usable and the boat was raised.

Helena No. 2, a stern-wheel packet built in California, Pennsylvania, in 1878. 194' × 33' × 4.5'. The boat was originally owned by T. C. Power & Brothers, of Fort Benton, Montana. Captain James McGarry served as master. The boat made more than fifty trips to points in Montana with several masters while part of the Block P Line. In 1887, the boat was sold to A. S. Bryan and others of Washington, Missouri. She was snagged in 1887 at lower Bonhomme Island. The boat was raised and returned to service. She was fatally snagged in South Dakota on October 23, 1891, with Ed Anderson as pilot on watch. The vessel's bell was placed in a Washington, Missouri, church steeple. In 1937, the wreck was partially removed by a U. S. government snagboat.

Henry S. Turner, see H.S. TURNER

Henry Wohlt, a stern-wheel packet built in Hermann, Missouri, in 1900. 97.8' × 20' × 3', rated at 67 tons, with two engines (7" × 3.5') and one boiler (16' × 50"), which allowed a working pressure of 165 lbs. The boat was owned by the Hermann Ferry & Packet Company. She was sunk by ice at Boonville, Missouri, on January 1, 1910, and was raised.

Hermann, a side-wheel packet built for the lower Missouri River trade in 1845. Captain Tom Baker was in command when the boat struck a snag and was lost in Missouri in 1846.

Hesperian, a side-wheel packet built in Louisville, Kentucky, in 1857. 218' × 33'. Captain F. B. Kercheval was owner and master with Grant Marsh serving as mate. The boat was in the St. Louis and St. Joseph Union Packet Line in 1858. She burned in Kansas on August 19, 1860.

Highland Mary, a side-wheel packet built in Wheeling, West Virginia, in 1848. The boat was rated at 158 tons. Originally operated in Wheeling-Pittsburgh, in 1849 she served as a ferryboat at St. Joseph, Missouri. In 1850, the boat went to St. Paul with Captain Joseph Atchison. The boat was bought in 1852 by Captain Joseph LaBarge who operated it on the lower Mississippi River. The boat was damaged by fire at St. Louis on July 27, 1853. She was finally lost in ice at St. Louis on February 26, 1856.

Hilman, a steamer reported lost on the lower Missouri River.

Hiram Wood No. 1 (also DR. BURLEIGH), a stern-wheel packet built at Wyandotte, Kansas, in 1865. 100' × 22'. The boat was owned by Captain Crokett who was also the boat's master. She snagged at Bijou Hills, Rosebud Landing, in South Dakota in 1873. Captain Grant Marsh bought the wreck and rebuilt her into a ferryboat. In October 1877, he renamed it DR. BURLEIGH.

Hiram Wood No. 2, a side-wheel ferryboat built in Sioux City, Iowa, in 1880. The boat was rebuilt from the wrecked steamer HIRAM WOOD by Captain Grant

Marsh. She had two engines (11.5" × 4.5") that were cogwheel geared, with two boilers (14' × 42"), which allowed a working pressure of 115 lbs. Captain Andrew Larsen served as pilot. The ferry sank from unknown causes at Sioux City, Iowa, in 1880. The machinery was salvaged and placed on the steamer ANDREW BENNETT.

Homer C. Wright, a stern-wheel packet built in Tuscumbia, Missouri, in 1920. 86.8' × 18.5' × 3.4'. Originally, the boat operated on the Missouri River. Later, she did ferry service for the Union Electric Company out of St. Louis. She was owned by the New St. Louis & Calhoun Packet Corporation when she sank at the foot of Rutger Street in St. Louis in August 1927.

Honduras, a side-wheel packet built in Brownsville, Pennsylvania, in 1853. The boat was rated at 296 tons, with two engines (18" × 6.5") and three boilers (26' × 39"), which allowed a working pressure of 170 lbs. She typically ran Pittsburgh-St. Louis-Missouri River. She sank near Doniphan, Kansas, in 1853 but was raised. The boat was snagged and lost in Illinois on January 25, 1855. She was owned by W. W. Conley and others with Captain M. Conley commanding at the time of loss.

Hope, see T. L. McGILL

Howard, a side-wheel packet built for the Missouri River trade. She was snagged and lost in Missouri in 1838.

Huntsville, a side-wheel packet built in New Albany, Indiana, in 1842. 205' × 29' × 6', rated at 344 tons. The boat was to Fort Union in 1842 and 1843. In 1852, it was owned by Charles W. Harrison, James Pell, L. H. Flernoy, George P. Frazer, and George Warren. The boat was commanded by Captain Charles Pell. She was snagged and lost on the Mississippi in Missouri on August 21, 1854.

Huntsville, a stern-wheel packet built in New Albany, Indiana, in 1864. 159' × 33' × 4.5', rated at 358 tons. She was to Fort Benton in 1866 and 1867. In 1871, she ran New Orleans-Shreveport. While downbound on the Red River 80 miles below Shreveport, the boat broke her tiller line and hit the bank and then sank. The boat had 180 head of cattle on board, many of which were drowned. She was raised and returned to service. She was finally lost on August 26, 1874.

Huron, a stern-wheel towboat built at Le Claire, Iowa, in 1865. The boat had two engines (16.5" × 5.5') and three boilers (22' × 40"), which allowed a working pressure of 144 lbs. Captain Willis Blakely was the boat's master. The boat burned while en route from St. Joseph to St. Louis on October 24, 1871.

Iatan, a side-wheel packet built in Cincinnati, Ohio, in 1858. 221' × 33' × 5.4', rated at 421 tons. The boat was built for Captain H. S. Eaton and others for the Missouri River trade. She ran Mobile-New Orleans in 1865 and participated in the cattle trade out of Shreveport in 1868. She was dismantled in 1868.

Ida Fulton (also the CONVOY No. 2), a stern-wheel packet built in Cincinnati, Ohio, in 1863. 145' × 26' × 4.5', rated at 143 tons. The boat was originally named the CONVOY No. 2 and was sold to the U. S. Quartermaster Corps on

January 12, 1864. She was sold into private hands on January 29, 1867, and renamed IDA FULTON. She was logged in at Fort Benton in 1867. The Diamond Jo Line ran the boat on the upper Mississippi for years. She was finally dismantled in 1884.

Ida Rees, a stern-wheel packet built at Elizabeth, Pennsylvania, in 1863. 156' × 30' × 4.5'. This boat had four rudders and was owned by Thomas M. and James H. Rees of Pittsburgh. Captain Ezekiel Gordon commanded the boat. In 1865 she was on the Allegheny River. She ran Pittsburgh-Cincinnati in 1866–1867 with Captain Joe Brown. In the spring of 1868, she was on the Missouri River at Fort Benton with James Rees. In the fall of 1868, the boat was taken to Galveston, Texas, where she ran on the Sabine River with Captain Thomas Stubblefield. The boat was lost on February 28, 1873, enroute from the Sabine to New Orleans loaded with cotton.

Ida Rees No. 2, a stern-wheel packet built in Pittsburgh, Pennsylvania, by William Latta in 1865. 180' × 30'. The boat was originally owned by Thomas M. and James H. Rees who operated it in the Pittsburgh–Oil City trade on the Allegheny River. During the summer of 1868, she ran Pittsburgh-Brownsville-Geneva on the Monongahela River. The boat was sold to Durfee and Peck, which operated the boat on the Missouri River. She was lost in South Dakota on June 20, 1871, with Captain John Gillan commanding.

Ida Stockdale, a stern-wheel packet built in McKeesport and Pittsburgh, Pennsylvania in 1867. 180' × 32', rated at 377 tons. The boat was built for Captain Jackman T. Stockdale of Allegheny and named for his daughter Ida. The boat's first trip from Pittsburgh was to Fort Benton, Montana with Captain Grant Marsh in charge. All told, the boat made six trips to Fort Benton during her career. She was lost in ice in South Dakota in April 1871, then owned by J. Wesley Jacobs.

Imelda, a stern-wheel towboat that was snagged and lost in North Dakota on the Missouri River in 1870.

Imperial, a stern-wheel packet built in Cincinnati, Ohio, in 1863. The boat was rated at 286 tons. The boat ran in the St. Louis–Nashville trade in 1865. She made a trip to Fort Benton, Montana, in 1867. The boat was lost in ice in South Dakota in 1867. At the time of the loss, the boat was owned by David White, W. S. Harper, and A. S. Rowland, with Captain McComas serving as master.

Intrepid, see BENTON.

Ione, a side-wheel packet rated at 250 tons built for the Missouri River. The boat was snagged and lost in Missouri in 1846.

Iowa, a side-wheel packet built in St. Louis, Missouri, in 1848. 220' × 35' × 7', rated at 454 tons. The boat was at Fort Pierre and Fort Union on the Missouri River in 1849. The boat was lost in ice on March 17, 1856.

Irene, a side-wheel ferry built in Wellsville, Ohio, in 1867. The boat was rated at 117 tons and was a double-ended ferry used at Omaha, Nebraska. She was snagged and lost in Nebraska in February 1877.

Iron City, a stern-wheel packet built in Pittsburgh, Pennsylvania, in 1864. 150' × 28' × 3', rated at 190 tons. The boat was at Fort Benton on the upper Missouri River in 1866. She was snagged on the Red River in Louisiana on February 23, 1868.

Ironton, a side-wheel packet built in Cincinnati, Ohio, in 1850. 157' × 26' × 5.7', rated at 189 tons. The boat's engines were from the steamer NORTHERN LIGHT. The boat was snagged and lost in Missouri on December 24, 1854.

Isabella (also noted as ISABELLA No. 2), a side-wheel packet built in McKeesport, Pennsylvania in 1857. 211' × 32', rated at 361 tons. Captain John P. Keiser, bought an interest in the steamer in 1858 and was master until 1861. The boat made several trips up the Missouri River. She took part in General Sully's 1864 Yellowstone Expedition. The steamer was snagged and lost in Missouri on April 15, 1868.

Island City, a stern-wheel packet built in Fort Byron, Illinois, in 1863. 140' × 30', rated at 139 tons. The boat was owned by Adam Heine, with Captain Alex Lamont serving as master. The boat was with General Sully in 1864 on the Yellowstone expedition. She was snagged and lost in North Dakota in August 1864. The machinery was recovered and taken to St. Louis on the BELLE OF PEORIA.

J. B. McPherson, a government-owned steamer that was lost in Iowa in 1897.

J. Don Cameron, see DON CAMERON

J. G. Morrow, a side-wheel ferry built in Brownsville, Pennsylvania, in 1861. The boat was rated at 163 tons. Her first home port was Memphis, Tennessee. The boat was snagged and lost on the lower Missouri River on September 1, 1861.

J. H. Lacy, a side-wheel packet built at Madison, Indiana, and completed at St. Louis, Missouri, in 1857. The boat was rated at 269 tons and ran the St. Louis–St. Joseph trade up the Missouri River. This boat may have been lengthened; she is later described as 670 tons, 270' × 41' × 8.2'. She was on the Red River in 1864. The boat was snagged and lost in Missouri on October 10, 1867, enroute from Omaha to St. Joseph .

J. H. Oglesby (also JOSEPH H. OGLESBY), a side-wheel packet built Cincinnati, Ohio, in 1856. 225' × 35', rated at 399 tons. The boat was built for Captain Henry A. Ealer and others. She ran Louisville-New Orleans in 1857. The boat was snagged and lost on the Missouri River above Glasgow, Missouri, on August 28, 1858.

J. M. Clendenin, a side-wheel packet built in Louisville, Kentucky, in 1852. 200' × 32', rated at 276 tons, with two engines (20" × 7') and three boilers (26' × 40"), which allowed a working pressure of 160 lbs. The boat was owned by Captain Henry W. Smith, who was also master, and others. The boat was snagged and lost at Bate's Woodyard, Missouri, on the Missouri River on November, 1, 1853. Theodore Bates, the woodyard proprietor, bought the wreck and made a saloon out of the cabin.

J. M Converse, a side-wheel packet built at McKeesport, Pennsylvania, at the Coursin Boatyard in 1856. 225' × 35' × 6' and rated at 417 tons. The boat ran St. Louis-St. Joseph, Missouri, on every other Sunday. She was lost in March 1857 on the Missouri River.

J. M. Richtman, a stern-wheel packet built in Sterling Island, Illinois, in 1899. 121' × 23.5' × 3.9'. The boat was owned by Jacob Richtman and Sons, with Captain J. J. Richtman in command. On Sept. 13, 1900, the crown sheet on the boat's starboard boiler let go, scalding several passengers after the boat left Florence, Nebraska, on the Missouri River. In 1904, the boat was renamed the CONQUEST.

J. P. Gage, a stern-wheel ferry built in Clinton, Iowa, in 1884. 114' × 32' × 5', rated at 198 tons, with two engines (16" × 4.5') and two boilers (20' × 42"), which allowed a working pressure of 140 lbs. The ferry was owned by the St. Charles Ferry & Transportation Company. She snagged and sank on September 7, 1893, at St. Charles and was raised. In 1898, the boat was transferred to Dardanelle, Arkansas.

J. R. Wells, a stern-wheel packet built at Tuscumbia, Missouri, in 1897. 110.6' × 20' × 4', rated at 92 tons, with two engines (10' × 4') and one boiler (18' × 42"), which allowed a working pressure of 177 lbs. The boat was built for Anchor Milling Company of Tuscumbia, and was named for the head of the firm. She ran in the Osage River trade with Captain John W. Adcock in command. The boat was sold in 1909. Stanton & Jones owned the boat when she sank from ice in Missouri on January 30, 1920.

Jacob Richtman (also UNCLE SAM), a stern-wheel packet built at Sterling Island, Illinois, in 1898. 160 × 32 × 5', rated at 360 tons, with two engines (14" × 6') and two boilers (26' × 40"), which allowed a working pressure of 160 lbs. The boat was originally owned by the Richtman family and operated as an excursion steamer. The boat burned at Quincy Bay in 1904. She was rebuilt and renamed UNCLE SAM. By1910, she was owned by the Missouri River Excursion Company with Captain E. H. Matteus in command. On May 18, 1910, the boat collided with a sand barge and sank in Kansas City.

Jacob Sass, a side-wheel packet built in Leavenworth, Kansas, in 1865. The boat was rated at 179 tons, with two engines (12' × 4') and two boilers (14' × 40"), which allowed a working pressure of 120 lbs. She was snagged and lost on the Missouri River in Nebraska in 1869.

James E. Rankin, a stern-wheel packet built in Metropolis, Illinois, at the Alf Cutting Yard in 1871. 142' × 30.5' × 4'; the boat was rated at 249 tons. The boat was originally owned by C. Cole of Cincinnati; he sold it to Sila Hemmiway in April 1877 for use on the Missouri River. The boat was lost after being pulled off a sandbar on the Yellowstone River on October 5, 1877.

James H. Trover (also KATE B. PORTER, also KATE U. S. Tinclad #55), a stern-wheel packet built at Belle Veron, Pennsylvania, in 1864. 160' × 32' ×

4.2', rated at 391 tons. The boat was originally named the KATE B. PORTER. During the Civil War she was KATE—U.S. Tinclad #55. The boat was sold into private hands after the war and renamed the JAMES H. TROVER on March 12, 1866. In a disastrous trip from St. Louis to Fort Benton in June 1867, the boat was grounded several times on sandbars and laid up for repairs five times; the boat caught fire more than once, and the crew got smallpox. The boat was commanded by Captain D. Artee on this trip. The boat made it as far as Trover Point, 30 miles above the Musselshell River in Montana, when the boat needed repairs again. The boat was caught in a falling river and was left high and dry and had to be abandoned on June 21, 1867. The IDA STOCKDALE took the boat's cargo on to Fort Benton.

James Lyon, a stern-wheel packet built in Belle Vernon, Pennsylvania, in 1853. The boat was rated at 187 tons. The boat ran St. Louis-St. Paul in 1855–1858 and was one of the best-known boats on the Mississippi. The boat was snagged and lost on the Missouri River headed upbound in Missouri on December 26, 1858.

James Lyons, a stern-wheel packet that operated in the Missouri River trade. The boat was snagged and lost near the mouth of the Missouri River in 1882.

James Monroe, a side-wheel packet built in 1848. In 1849, the boat was headed up the Missouri River with California-bound emigrants. On arrival at Jefferson City, Missouri cholera broke out on the boat. She was abandoned by the officers and crew who were trying to avoid the disease after it killed most of the passengers. After lying at Jefferson City for several months, the boat was taken back to St. Louis.

Jennie Brown, a side-wheel packet built in Louisville, Kentucky, in 1864. 137' × 23' × 4.5' and rated at 146 tons. The boat ran Cincinnati-Chilo during low water in 1864. The boat was on the Missouri River at Fort Benton in 1866 and 1867. The boat had many owners and was finally sold to Isaac Staples of Stillwater, Minnesota, who dismantled the boat in 1890, using the parts to build the rafter ISAAC STAPLES.

Jennie Lewis, a side-wheel packet built in Paducah, Kentucky, in 1864. The boat operated on the lower Missouri and was rated at 509 tons. Captain Henry McPherson and William W. Ater owned the boat and ran her in the Miami Packet Company. She ran St. Louis–Glasgow–Cambridge trade. The boat was at Fort Benton in 1866. She burned at St. Louis on March 29, 1869, with Captain McPherson in command.

Jo Horton Fall (also VALLEY QUEEN), a stern-wheel excursion boat built in Jeffersonville, Indiana, at the Howard boat yard in 1913. The boat was rated at 156 tons. Originally, she was named JO HORTON FALL. Captain Peter Lee and others bought the boat ca. 1926 and ran excursion trips out of Caruthersville, Missouri, as the VALLEY QUEEN. In 1934, the boat made a Missouri River trip and was sunk in Nebraska on May 17.

Joe Kinney, a side-wheel packet built Madison, Indiana, in 1872. 231' × 38.4' ×

6.8', rated at 739 tons. The boat typically ran St. Louis-Missouri River and in off seasons was occasionally on the Red River. She was owned by the Kansas City Packet Company with Captain George G. Keith in command The boat had a bad habit of running into things. She struck the Boonville bridge, tearing off her texas deck, pilothouse, and chimneys. On March 27, 1876, she struck a pier at the Kansas City bridge and lost a paddle wheel. She was finally lost on April 13, 1882, when she struck the Glasgow bridge.

John Aull, a side-wheel packet built in 1840 for the Missouri River trade. She was named for a prominent merchant of Lexington, Missouri. The boat was lost on the lower Missouri in 1845.

John B. Eaton, a Missouri River steamer that was lost in Missouri during the Civil War.

John Baird, a steamer lost on the lower Missouri at an unknown date.

John Bell, a stern-wheel packet built Louisville, Kentucky, in 1855. The boat was rated at 209 tons. The boat was owned by the U. S. government and was snagged and lost in Missouri on the lower Missouri River in 1861.

John Golong, a side-wheel packet built at Ice Creek, Ohio, in 1844. The boat was rated at 144 tons. In 1844, she ran on the Kanawha River. She was sold to the Baker family who operated her on the Missouri River running St. Louis-Weston. She was snagged and lost in Missouri on March 8, 1846.

John Hancock, a side-wheel packet built for the Missouri River trade in the late 1830s. She had a single engine and was rated at 100 tons. She was lost in Missouri in 1840.

John Hancock, a side-wheel packet built in Cincinnati, Ohio, in 1845. The boat was rated at 293 tons. The boat was snagged and lost on the Mississippi in Missouri on March 25, 1851.

John Heckmann, a stern-wheel packet built at Hermann, Missouri, in 1919. 163.6' × 30.5' × 4.2'. The boat was owned by the Heckman Family, with Captain Ed Heckmann serving as master. In 1922, she was on the Cumberland River up to Nashville and Burksville. The boat was later rebuilt as an excursion boat for the Missouri River. She was lost in ice in Missouri in 1928 after being tied to the river bank by the sheriff of Gasconade County, who was auctioning it off.

John L. Ferguson, a recess-wheel ferryboat built in Grafton, Illinois, in 1876. 111.6' × 25.6' × 3.6'. The boat operated at St. Charles, Missouri, and was still documented in 1886.

John L. Rhoads, see C. C. CARROLL

John L. Roach, a Missouri River steamer that sank in 1886 in Missouri. This may be a misnotation in the historical document. The boat name was probably the JOHN L. RHOADS (see above).

John R. Hugo, a stern-wheel packet built in Evansville, Indiana, in 1879. 127' × 27' × 3', rated at 136 tons, with two engines (12.5" × 3.5') and one boiler (24' × 42"), which allowed a working pressure of 160 lbs. The boat was sold to Captain R. M. (Bob) Marshall and Captain Henry Castrup who ran the boat on the Missouri River for F. G. Schenen & Sons. She burned at Florence, Nebraska, on May 22, 1900, with Captain William L. Thompson as pilot. The hull was recovered and floated down to Osage City, Nebraska, where the machinery was placed on the OSAGE.

John W. Thomas, see GLENMORE

Jos. Kinney, a side-wheel packet built in Madison, Indiana, in 1872. 231' × 38.4' × 6.8', rated at 739 tons, with two engines (22" × 7') and three boilers (26' × 39"), which allowed a working pressure of 139 lbs. The boat was built by Joseph Kinney. George Keith commanded the boat in the St. Louis–Kansas City trade. This boat had a habit of running into bridges. She struck the Boonville bridge and the Kansas City bridge, and was finally lost when she collided with the Glasgow bridge on April 13, 1888, becoming a total loss.

Jos. L. Stephens, a center-wheel ferry built in Jeffersonville, Indiana, at the Howard boat yard in 1887. 103' × 29.4' × 4.2', rated at 85 tons, with two engines (10" × 3.5') and one boiler (16' × 48"), which allowed a working pressure of 100 lbs. The ferry was originally owned by L. E. Mohle and operated out of Boonville, Missouri. He boasted that she could handle twelve wagons. The ferry burned at Kansas City on October 31, 1909 and was then owned by Mary E. Brent. The boat was rebuilt and later burned at Cairo, Illinois, on January 8, 1912.

Joseph H. Oglesby, a side-wheel packet built at Cincinnati, Ohio, in 1856. 225' × 35', rated at 399 tons. The boat was built for Captain Henry A. Ealer and others. The boat ran Louisville-New Orleans in 1857. The boat ran the Missouri River in 1858. She was snagged and lost in Missouri on August 28, 1858.

Josephine, stern-wheel packet built in Freedom and Pittsburgh, Pennsylvania, in 1873. 183' × 31' × 4'. She was originally owned by the Coulson and Marratta families. Captain Grant Marsh personally supervised the boat's construction. The boat was named for the daughter of General David S. Stanley. In 1873, the boat was on the Yellowstone River with General Custer. In 1874 and 1875, she was often at Fort Benton or on the Yellowstone River. All told, the boat made more than fifty trips to Montana Territory. The boat was sold in 1885 to become a U. S. snagboat. In 1894, the steamer was sold again, this time to Joseph Leach who planned to reconvert her back to a packet. He never got the chance, the boat was lost in an ice floe at Running Water, South Dakota, on March 8, 1907. The machinery was salvaged and shipped to Alaska for use on a Yukon River steamer.

Josie L. K., a stern-wheel ferry built in Chamberlain, South Dakota, in 1884. 71.4' × 14.5' × 3.5', rated at 27 tons, with two engines (8" × 12") and one boiler (9' × 48"), which allowed a working pressure of 185 lbs. The boat was owned by Captain Joseph Giesler of the Yankton Bridge & Ferry Company, which operated her at Yankton, South Dakota. The boat was cut down by ice in South Dakota on April 1, 1920.

Judith (also NORTHERN PACIFIC NO.2.) , a stern-wheel packet built at Mound
City, Illinois, in 1881. 184.4' × 33.2' × 4.4', rated at 685 tons, with two engines
(14" × 5") and two boilers (26' × 44"), which allowed a working pressure of
159 lbs. She was originally the railroad transfer, NORTHERN PACIFIC NO.2.
The boat was rebuilt into a packet by the Benton Transportation Company for
the Missouri River. She was later sold to Captain John E. Massengale and
Augustus W. Block. The boat was snagged and lost in Missouri on July 29,
1888.

Julia No. 1, a side-wheel packet built in Elizabeth, Pennsylvania, in 1846. The
boat was rated at 234 tons. The boat was originally built for Captain Joe Convers
who sold the boat in 1848 to Captain John W. Keiser of the American Fur
Company. The boat operated on the Missouri River until she was snagged and
lost on September 14, 1850, in Missouri. J. M. Converse was master at the time
of loss.

Julia No. 2, a 7-ton steamer that operated on the lower Missouri River. She was
reported lost in Nebraska. The wreck was later raised and dismantled in 1866.

Kansas, a side-wheel packet built in St. Louis, Missouri, in 1847. The boat was
rated at 276 tons. Ran on the Missouri River. Captain Joe LaBarge often commanded. She was snagged and lost in Nebraska on April 25, 1853.

Kate B. Porter, see JAMES H. TROVER

Kate Edward, a 504-ton steamer that ran on the Missouri River. She was snagged
and lost in Missouri on August 11, 1859.

Kate Howard, a side-wheel packet built in Jeffersonville, Indiana, at the Howard
boatyard in 1857. 235' × 35' × 6', rated at 504 tons, with two engines (24' × 7')
and three boilers (28' × 46"), which allowed a working pressure of 117 lbs. The
boat's machinery came from the N. J. EATON. She ran on the Missouri River,
St. Louis-St. Joseph, with Captain Joseph Nanson in command. She was snagged
and lost on the Missouri River on August 4, 1859. The boat was downbound
from St. Joseph for St. Louis with Captain Nanson as master and Joe Fecto
serving as pilot.

Kate Kearney, a stern-wheel packet built at Belle Vernon and Pittsburgh, Pennsylvania in 1864. 196' × 40' × 5.5', rated at 445 tons. The boat was originally built
for the St. Louis & Keokuk Packet Company, which used it primarily as a
freight boat (she had a very small cabin). The boat was on the Missouri in 1865
at Fort Union, North Dakota. In 1870, the boat was purchased by Captain Grant
Marsh and the Goodin & Brothers coal firm of Lexington, Missouri. The boat
was lost on the Mississippi River in 1871.

Kate Kinney No. 1, a side-wheel packet built in Cincinnati, Ohio, in 1864. The
boat was rated at 508 tons. She ran mainly on the Missouri River in the St.
Louis–Omaha trade for the Omaha Line. Captain Joseph Kinney was the boat's
master. She was partially burned in the steamboat fire at St. Louis on March 2,
1868. She was finally burned and lost in Indiana on October 29, 1872.

Kate Swinney (also KATE SWEENEY), a side-wheel packet built in Jefferson, Indiana at the Howard boatyard in 1852. 180' × 30' × 6.5', rated at 328 tons, with two engines (19' × 7') and three boilers (26' × 40"), which allowed a working pressure of 140 lbs. She was built for a St. Louis tobacco merchant and named for his daughter. In 1854, she was operating on the Missouri River for the American Fur Company with Captain Joe Fecto serving as pilot. The boat was to Fort Pierre in 1854 and to Fort Union in 1855. The boat was snagged and lost in South Dakota on August 1, 1855. The deck crew started walking to Sioux City, Iowa and were killed by Indians on the way. In 1873, the wreck was exposed when the river shifted.

Katie, a center-wheel ferry built in 1867. The boat was rated at 29 tons. She was snagged and lost on the Missouri River in South Dakota on May 31, 1877, with Captain Grant Marsh in command.

Katie Fisher, see STATIE FISHER

Katie P. Kountz, a stern-wheel packet built in Elizabeth, Pennsylvania, at the Latta yard in 1871. The boat had two Hartupee compound engines (10" and 23" × 4.5') and two boilers (22' × 38"), which allowed a working pressure of 132 lbs. The boat was built for Captain William J. Kountz and the K. P. Kountz Transportation Comapny. Although it made three trips to Fort Benton and two trips to Carroll, Montana, the boat was not well suited for the upper Missouri River. She was too large and slow for the mountain trade. In 1874, it took all season for the boat to make one trip to Carroll. In 1876, she went into the Mississippi trade. She sank several times and was finally fatally burned on the Mississippi River on November 1, 1883.

Keith, a steam stern-wheel towboat owned by the U. S. Engineers Department, Kansas City District. 128' × 26', rated at 153 tons. The boat foundered and sank in Missouri on May 26, 1927. The boat's captain, Edgar L Friemonth, his wife, and their four-month-old daughter drowned when the boat capsized. The boat was raised and rebuilt. The boat was finally lost on August 15, 1933, on the Missouri River.

Key West, a stern-wheel packet built at Elizabeth, Pennsylvania, in 1857. The boat was rated at 169 tons. This was an American Fur Company boat. She accompanied the CHIPPEWA to Fort Benton in 1860, establishing that place as the effective head of navigation on the Missouri River. She was at Fort Union and Fort Benton in 1862. In the off-season, the boat ran New Orleans-Arkansas River. She burned and was lost in Arkansas on December 27, 1862.

Key West (also NEW IBERIA), a stern-wheel packet built in Pittsburgh, Pennsylvania, in 1871. 200' × 33' × 5.4'. She was originally owned by a consortium including Sanford Coulson. Later, she was used by the American Fur Company (as the third KEY WEST in their fleet) on the Missouri River. Captain Grant Marsh was in command when the boat explored the Yellowstone River with General Sheridan in 1873. The boat made it as far as the mouth of the

Powder River. All told, this boat made twenty-three trips to Montana points with the Coulson Line. In 1882, she was renamed the NEW IBERIA. In 1885, she ran New Orleans-Bayou Tech and was advertised as an "electric light" steamer.

Key West No. 2, a stern-wheel packet built in Ottisburgh, Pennsylvania, in 1860 (Ways notes she was built in California and Pittsburgh). She was rated at 206 tons. In 1861–1862, she ran the Pittsburgh–Cincinnati trade. She was sold to the American Fur Company in 1862 for a trip up the Yellowstone River. She snagged and sank in Illinois on October 26, 1863.

Keystone, a side-wheel packet built in Brownsville, Pennsylvania, in 1853. The boat was rated at 307 tons. Thomas I. Goddin was master when the boat was on the lower Missouri in 1855 and 1856. In 1856, the boat carried John W. Geary, the third territorial governor of Kansas, to Fort Leavenworth, Kansas, on September 9. The boat ran Pittsburgh-St. Louis in 1857 and was off the lists in 1863.

Kit Carson, a side-wheel packet built in Elizabethtown, Pennsylvania, in 1848. 165' × 28.5' × 6.3' and rated at 280 tons. The boat was designed for the St. Louis–Glasgow trade on the Missouri River. She was named for the famed mountain man. The boat was a very elaborate for her time. She burned and was lost in the great steamboat fire at St. Louis on May 17, 1849.

Lacon, a stern-wheel packet built in Freedom and Pittsburgh, Pennsylvania, in 1862. 159' × 28' × 4', rated at 250 tons. The boat was owned by Captain John N. Bofinger and F. Blair Symmes of St. Louis. In 1862, she was advertised for the Missouri River Mountain trade with Captain Frank Maratta commanding. She later went to the Illinois River. On May 10, 1863, the boat was impressed for U. S. service as a transport between St. Louis and Vicksburg. She was dismantled at Le Claire, Iowa, in 1872. The boat's machinery went to the rafter STILLWATER, and the hull was converted into a barge.

Lady Grace, a stern-wheel packet built at Madison, Indiana, in 1865. 159' × 33' × 5', rated at 387 tons, with two engines (15.5" × 4.5') and three boilers (22' × 36"), which allowed a working pressure of 140 lbs. In 1866, she was sold to W. S. Wheeler of Vicksburg to run the New Orleans–Shreveport trade. In the spring of 1867, the boat made a trip up the Missouri in the mountain trade from St. Louis. The boat was sold in August 1867 to Captain Dave Haney, who loaded the boat for New Orleans. In the spring of 1868, she ran the Cincinnati–Evansville trade. She was later bought by Captain W. C. Watts and D. Blackmore at a U. S. marshal sale. In the spring of 1869, the boat loaded at Cincinnati for a mountain trip up the Missouri River but was halted at St. Louis when the Board of Underwriters refused the boat's insurance. She eventually went to Omaha, Nebraska, and ran excursions. She burned and was lost in Nebraska on January 7, 1870.

Lady Lee, a stern-wheel packet built in Pittsburgh, Pennsylvania, in 1871. 176' ×

35' × 5.5', rated at 417 tons, with two engines (16' × 6') and three boilers (24' × 40"), which allowed a working pressure of 125 lbs. In 1871, ran Pittsburgh-Cincinnati with pilots John Shouse and Andy Bunting. She also ran in the Carter Line, St. Louis-Red River, with Captain G. F. Shields as master. The boat was owned by the Illinois & St. Louis Packet Company in 1874. In 1881, the boat was part of the Star Line running St. Louis-Missouri River with Captain Bill Ball commanding and was lengthened to 227'. The boat was lost to wind and a snag in Missouri on March 29, 1882.

Lake of the Woods, a side-wheel packet built at Naples, Illinois, in 1847. The boat was rated at 86 tons. The boat's boilers and machinery came from the NEW HAVEN. Captain James Dozier often commanded the boat. The boat was snagged on her way to Fort Union near the mouth of the Cheyenne River in 1847. She was dismantled in 1853 with the engines going into the EMMA BROWN. In 1884, a steamboat wreck was visible at low water on the Ohio River. Pilot Henry Porter of the CITY OF ST. LOUIS identified the wreck as the LAKE OF THE WOODS. He said it was a single-engined boat that was later owned by Thad Jacobs and commanded by Captain W. Wood. He recalled that the wreck's engines went to the EMMA BROWN.

Lancaster, a side-wheel packet built in Liverpool, Illinois, in 1866. The boat was rated at 175 tons with two engines (12" × 4') and two boilers (20' × 42"), which allowed a working pressure of 120 lbs. The boat was snagged and lost in Missouri on the Missouri River in 1866. The wreck was still visible during low water in 1927.

Lancaster No. 4, a side-wheel packet built at Cincinnati, Ohio, at Dan Morton's boatyard in 1861. The boat was rated at 218 tons. The boat was originally built for the Cincinnati–New Richmond trade. The boat was impressed during the Civil War to carry troops and supplies. She was with the United States on the Tennessee River in 1862. The boat ran New Orleans-Vicksburg in June 1864, with Captain M. J. McCullough in command. The boat loaded for the Missouri River trade in the fall of 1864. She struck a log and sank in Missouri on November 18, 1864, while still under U. S. charter.

Last Chance, a stern-wheel packet built in St. Louis, Missouri, in 1865. 142' × 30' × 3.5', rated at 222 tons. The boat was designed for the Missouri River trade. She was owned by W. G. and M. S. Mepham of St. Louis in 1867. That year, the boat ran St. Louis-Fort Buford, North Dakota, with Captain O. B. Hunter in command. She was sold in 1870 to Captain C. S. Peck and others for the Tennessee River where she ran Chattanooga-Knoxville. She collided with the R. P. CONVERSE on March 6, 1872, near Dayton, Tennessee. The boat was dismantled in 1873, and many parts were used in building the R. M. BISHOP.

Last Chance, a stern-wheel packet built at Burlington, Iowa, in 1870. 98.2' × 17.8' × 3', rated at 50 tons, with two engines (11' × 3.5') and one boiler (18' × 42"), which allowed a working pressure of 83 lbs. The boat originally came out with a scow bow and was changed to model bow, ca. 1878, by McCaffrey & Rambo. The Le Clair Navigation Company, organized in 1872, used this boat to help rafts over the rapids above Keokuk. It sold the boat in August 1886 to Captain H. J. King of Chamberlain, South Dakota. He ran the boat in the Sioux City–Chamberlain trade. The boat was snagged and lost in Nebraska in 1899.

Leanora, see LEONORA

Leavenworth, a side-wheel packet owned by the Dresser Sand Company of Leavenworth, Kansas. 80' × 16', rated at 42 tons. The boat foundered in a wind storm on the Missouri on May 27, 1918, in Missouri.

Leni Leoti, a stern-wheel packet built in Freedom and Pittsburgh, Pennsylvania, in 1863. The boat was rated at 174 tons. In 1864, the boat ran Pittsburgh-Louisville and made trips to Nashville in 1865. She ran Wheeling-Parkerburg in 1866 and Pittsburgh-Parkerburg in 1867. The boat departed St. Louis for the upper Missouri in 1868, where the bodies of several woodchoppers were discovered at a wood stop in Montana. Captain John D. Adams bought the boat at Little Rock, Arkansas, in 1869. The boat was snagged and lost on the Arkansas River downbound for New Orleans on May 10, 1869, while operating for the Memphis & Arkansas River Packet Company.

Leodora, a side-wheel packet built in Alton, Illinois, in 1864. 164' × 25' × 5', rated at 158 tons. The boat was loaded out for the Missouri River trade in 1864. She went aground and then burned in South Dakota on May 21, 1866. The boilers were recovered in 1870–1871 by digging through sand accumulated over the wreck. In 1895, Mr. Werner, a Missouri River salvor, attempted to salvage the boat but came up with very little.

Leonora (also noted as LEANORA), a stern-wheel packet built at Woodland, Virginia, in 1861. 180' × 32', rated at 285 tons with two engines (15.5" × 4.5') and three boilers (24' × 36"), which allowed a working pressure of 128 lbs. She was built for Captain Michael Davis and named for his daughter. In 1862, he sold the boat to Captain Richard Calhoon for the Missouri River. The boat was destroyed by fire in Nebraska on May 29, 1867 (or 1866) with Captain Timothy Packard in command.

Lewis F. Linn, see LOUIS F. LINN

Lexington, a side-wheel packet built in 1844 at St. Louis, Missouri. 135' × 22', rated at 200 tons, with a single engine and two boilers. Captain William Littleton was the boat's master. The boat struck a snag and sank in September 1845 at Frankfort, Missouri. The wreck was raised and taken to St. Louis.

Lexington (Originally VICTORIA, also ABRAHAM—U.S. Army), a side-wheel packet built in Elizabeth, Pennsylvania, in 1858. 277' × 41' × 6', rated at 405 tons. She was originally named VICTORIA and was captured by Union forces on June 6, 1862, and renamed ABRAHAM. She was used as a U. S. Quartermaster Corps wharf boat. She was sold on March 16, 1866, into private hands and renamed LEXINGTON. The boat was on the Missouri River to Fort Benton in 1866. She ran Cincinnati-New Orleans in 1867. She was destroyed by a tornado at Vicksburg in 1868. The boat was rebuilt and was finally burned and lost in Louisiana on February 3, 1869.

Libby Congo (also noted as the LIBBY CONGER), a stern-wheel packet built in Metropolis, Illinois, and Dubuque, Iowa, in 1878. 168' × 29.5' × 4.5'. The boat was owned by the Diamond Jo Line. She made a trip up the Missouri River as far as Bismarck, North Dakota. The boat was lost in a tornado at St. Louis on May 26, 1896.

Liberty, a side-wheel packet built for the Missouri River trade in 1830. She was owned and commanded by J. B. Moussette. The boat was snagged and lost in Missouri on October 24, 1831.

Light Western, a side-wheel ferryboat built at Oldenburg, Missouri, in 1874. 83.3' × 16.4' × 2.7', rated at 40 tons, with two engines (8' × 12") and one boiler (10' × 36"), which allowed a working pressure of 100 lbs. She was owned by Henry Wohlts. She was lost in ice on the Missouri River on December 17, 1879, in Missouri.

Lillie Martin, a stern-wheel packet built at Freedom, Pennsylvania, in 1863. 159' × 33' × 4', rated at 210 tons. Before 1864, the boat was up the Red River. She was then sold and was up the Missouri River to Fort Benton in 1865 and 1866. She later ran St. Louis-Memphis until she broke in two and burned on the Mississippi River on February 4, 1867, in Missouri.

Lillie Maud, a stern-wheel ferry built in DeWitt, Missouri, in 1889. 53' × 11' × 3.5', with one engine (6" × 12") and one boiler (4.5' × 40"), which allowed a working pressure of 120 lbs. The ferry was owned by Samuel B. Casebolt. On July 8, 1891, after being laid up for some time, the boat sank at Brunswick, Missouri. The wreck was raised and dismantled.

Lilly, a side-wheel lighthouse tender built at Louisville, Kentucky, in 1875. 178' × 28' × 4', rated at 507 tons. The boat struck a snag and sank near Wellington, Missouri, on October 17, 1911. She was raised and was snagged again and lost in Missouri on November 24, 1911, on the Missouri River. The machinery and equipment were salvaged.

Lilly, a stern-wheel packet built in Louisville, Kentucky, in 1864. The boat was rated at 256 tons, with two engines (15" × 5') and two boilers (22' × 42"), which allowed a working pressure of 120 lbs. The boat was at Fort Benton in 1867. She struck a snag and was lost in Nebraska on October 24, 1868, while upbound on the Missouri from St. Louis to the Grand River.

Little Dick, a center-wheel ferry built in Rocheport, Missouri, in 1876. 98.6' × 27.6' × 3.2' and rated at 63 tons with one engine (16" × 5'). She was owned by David L. and Fannie B. Kaiser, with Captain David L. Kaiser serving as master. The boat was lost in Missouri on May, 8, 1881, after the river fell rapidly and left the ferry on the bank. Attempts to get the boat back in the river with the boat's spars failed, and the boat crashed off the bank and sank in the river.

Little Mail, a side-wheel steamer with a single engine built for the Missouri River trade. She was snagged and lost in Missouri in November 1845.

Little Maud, see WESTON

Little Missouri, a side-wheel packet built in Cincinnati, Ohio, in 1846. The boat was rated at 198 tons. Captain Bob Wright was in command when the boat was snagged and lost in the Missouri River on April 1848 in Missouri.

Little Red, a side-wheel steamer built for the Missouri River trade. She was named after U. S. Senator David Barton, the first senator elected from Missouri, who had flaming red hair. The boat was snagged and lost in Missouri in 1840.

Little Rock (also FLORENCE MILLER No. 2 and U. S. Tinclad #34 MOOSE), a stern-wheel packet built in Cincinnati, Ohio, in 1863. 154' × 32' × 4.5' , rated at 189 tons. She was originally named the FLORENCE MILLER No. 2. The boat was impressed into service during the Civil War on May 20, 1863, and became U. S. tinclad #34 MOOSE. She was sold on October 9, 1865, into private hands and renamed LITTLE ROCK. The boat was to Fort Benton in 1867. She burned and was lost on December 23, 1867, in Arkansas.

Livingston (also noted as M. LIVINGSTON), a side-wheel packet that ran on the Missouri River. 120' × 20'. She ran Sioux City- Fort Benton in 1868. She sank in an ice floe in 1868 in South Dakota. The boat was raised and returned to service. She was dismantled in 1882 with her machinery going to the ferryboat BENNETT.

Lizzie Campbell, a stern-wheel ferry built in Jeffersonville, Indiana, she was owned by J. R. Sousley and others, with Captain W. T. B. Simpson as master. The boat was lost in Nebraska in 1883.

Lizzie Reid, a stern-wheel packet built at Forest City, South Dakota, in 1896. The boat was owned by the Northwestern Transportation Company. She was burned and lost in South Dakota on July 12, 1901.

Lizzie Warden, a stern-wheel ferryboat built in Independence, Missouri, in 1868. The boat was owned by Brambal, Miner, and others. She was lost in South Dakota in 1873.

Lloyd, a stern-wheel ferryboat built at Norborne, Missouri, in 1902. 67.2' × 18' × 3.7' and rated at 26 tons. The boat was lost in an ice floe while lying at winter quarters in Missouri on January 25, 1910.

Louis F. Linn (also noted as LEWIS F. LINN), a side-wheel packet built at Pittsburgh, Pennsylvania, in 1844. The boat was rated at 163 tons. The boat operated on the upper Mississippi in 1844. She was reported snagged and lost on the Missouri River in 1848–1849 in Missouri. Captain W. C. Jewett was master at the time of loss.

Louisa, a side-wheel packet built at Cairo, Illinois, in 1864. 130' × 30' and rated at 250 tons with two engines (12" × 4.5') and one boiler (26' × 42"), which allowed a working pressure of 185 lbs. She ran St. Louis-Fort Leavenworth, Kansas in 1864. The boat burned and was lost on the Missouri River in 1868 in Missouri.

Louisville, a stern-wheel packet built in Wheeling, West Virginia, in 1863. 180' × 33' and 288 tons with two engines (14" × 4') and two boilers (26' × 45"), which allowed a working pressure of 155 lbs. The boat was owned by Captain Davis White in 1864. In 1864, the boat headed up the Missouri River for the Yellowstone region when she was snagged and lost between Sioux City and Fort Randall in May 1864. Captain Abe Wolf was the boat's master. She was later raised and repaired.

Low Water, a stern-wheel boat built for the Missouri River trade in 1856. She was rated at 176 tons. The boat was lost in Missouri on November 27, 1857.

Luella, a stern-wheel packet built in Pittsburgh, Pennsylvania, in 1866. The boat was rated at 258 tons. She made three trips to Fort Benton, Montana, in 1866 and 1867. She was known as the "treasure ship of the Montana gold rush" for carrying down miners and their fortunes. Captain Grant Marsh and Captain William J. Kountz both commanded the boat. She was dismantled in Pittsburgh in 1868.

Lynchburgh, a side-wheel packet built for the Missouri River trade in 1842. She struck a sang and was lost on her maiden voyage in Missouri on March 27, 1842.

M. Livingston, see LIVINGSTON

M. S. Mepham, a side-wheel packet built at Elizabeth, Pennsylvania, in 1864. 236' × 38' × 7.5', rated at 683 tons. William Latta built the hull, and the machinery was by James Rees. The boat was built for the St. Louis–Leavenworth trade on the Missouri River with Captain A. A. Shaw. The boat was very elaborate and popular with passengers. In 1867, she ran Louisville-New Orleans. The boat burned and was lost at St. Louis on March 2, 1868.

Magenta, a side-wheel packet built in Mound City, Illinois, in 1863. 215' × 35', rated at 424 tons, with two engines (20.5" × 6.5') and two boilers (26' × 46"), which allowed a working pressure of 125 lbs. The boat was built for the Missouri River and was owned by F. M. Dozier, C. C. Chouteau, Ben Johnson, and Frank Constant. She was snagged and lost in Missouri on May 22, 1863.

Majors, see A. MAJORS

Malta, a side-wheel packet built for the American Fur Company in 1839. 140' × 22' × 5', rated at 114 tons. Captain Joseph W. Throckmorton was master when the boat sank in Missouri in August 1841.

Mandan, a side-wheel packet built at St. Louis, Missouri, in 1847. The boat was rated at 204 tons. She ran the Missouri River trade and once snagged at the mouth of the Gasconade River. She was burned and lost on May 17, 1849, in the great St. Louis steamboat fire.

Mandan, a stern-wheel iron hulled snagboat built at St. Louis, Missouri, in 1891. 138' × 24' × 4.7'. She was built for Missouri River service and originally had no machinery, but was towed to snag locations. The boat worked all along the upper Missouri including above Fort Peck, Montana, and some on the Yellowstone

River. She was dismantled at the U. S boatyard in Gasconade, Missouri after 1925. The hull was taken to Bluffton Island Chute and was sunk there.

Marcella, a side-wheel packet built in Louisville, Kentucky, in 1863. 180' × 32' × 8', rated at 300 tons. The boat was advertised for the Missouri River in 1864 with Captain Sousley in command. Grant Marsh first saw the Missouri River on this boat. The boat operated on the Missouri River until she was sold to Captain T. G. Ledbetter of New Orleans. She was dismantled in 1874.

Mariner (also RACHAEL MILLER and REINDEER), a stern-wheel packet built at Cincinnati, Ohio in 1863. 180' × 33' and 212 tons. The boat was originally named RACHAEL MILLER. She was impressed into U. S. service on May 25, 1863, and renamed REINDEER U.S. Tinclad #35. The boat was sold to private hands and renamed MARINER on October 5, 1865. She operated on the Missouri River and was snagged and lost in Nebraska on May 9, 1867.

Marion (also SILVER LAKE No. 2), a stern-wheel packet built at Wellsville, Ohio, in 1861. She was originally named SILVER LAKE NO.2. She was sold to the U.S. Quartermaster Corps in 1861. The boat was sold to private hands, and the rig was changed to side-wheel on October 7, 1865. The new steamer was renamed MARION. The boat was on the Missouri River headed to Fort Benton, Montana, when she sank on a sandbar in Montana and was lost in August 1866. Captain William D. Shanks was master at the time of the loss. Much of the vessel was salvaged.

Marjorie, a stern-wheel ferry built at Osage, Missouri, in 1908. 74' × 21' and 54 tons, with two engines (7" × 2.5') and one boiler (12' × 40"), which allowed a working pressure of 110 lbs. She was owned by the Lafayette County Ferry Company. The boat was destroyed by fire on the Missouri River on July 8, 1917 in Missouri.

Mars, a side-wheel packet built at Cincinnati, Ohio, in 1856. 180' × 34' and rated at 329 tons with two engines (20' × 7') and three boilers (28' × 40"). The boat had several encounters with the military in 1861 and 1862. Later, the boat was owned by a St. Louis group who ran the boat in the Memphis–Ohio River trade and then on the Missouri River. The boat was snagged and lost on the lower Missouri on July 8, 1865, in Missouri.

Martha, a side-wheel packet built at St. Louis, Missouri, in 1847. The boat was rated at 180 tons. She was built for Captain Joseph La Barge and others for the Missouri River trade. On the boat's first trip up the Missouri, LaBarge took along his wife who is reportedly the first white woman in Dakota Territory. The boat burned in the steamboat fire at St. Louis on May 17, 1849.

Martha Stephens, a stern-wheel packet built at Osage, Missouri, in 1883. The boat was rated at 192 tons, with two engines (10' × 3.5') and one boiler (14' × 48'), which allowed a working pressure of 130 lbs. She was owned by Captain Henry McPherson who was also master. She was snagged and lost on the Missouri River on August 9, 1884 in Missouri.

Mary, a side-wheel packet built in Cincinnati, Ohio, in 1847. The boat was rated at 276 tons. In the spring of 1849, the boat carried Mormons up the Missouri River. The boat burned and was lost at St. Louis on July 28, 1849.

Mary Barnes, see EMILY

Mary Bell, a center-wheel ferryboat built at Layensville, Missouri, in 1876. 70' × 12' × 2.6' and rated at 50 tons, with one engine (6' × 12") and one boiler (80' × 30'), which allowed a working pressure of 90 lbs. The boat was owned by W. B. Milam and William Sturgis. The boat was snagged and lost on the Missouri River in 1878 in Missouri.

Mary Bennett, a stern-wheel packet that ran on the Missouri River. Captain Jim Clarke was master when the boat was lost in ice in Iowa in 1869.

Mary Bryan, a 97-ton steamer, 115' × 28', which was laid up and dried out on the Missouri River on October 12, 1897, in Missouri.

Mary Cole, a side-wheel ferryboat built in Cincinnati, Ohio, in 1849. She was rated at 93 tons. The boat was snagged and lost in Nebraska on April 22, 1855.

Mary E. Bennett, a stern-wheel packet built at Covington, Nebraska, in 1888. 21 tons. 64' × 14' × 2.5' and rated at 21 tons, with two engines (7.25" × 34") and one boiler (16' × 38"), which allowed a working pressure of 150 lbs. She was owned by Richard Talbot. The boat sank in ice at Sioux City, Iowa, on March 4, 1894, and was raised and repaired. The boat was finally lost on the Missouri River on October 15, 1898, when she struck a snag.

Mary H., a center-wheel ferryboat that operated on the Missouri River. She was owned by Captain Hostetter. She was lost in Missouri in 1906.

Mary J. Arnold, a stern-wheel ferryboat built in Muscatine, Iowa, in 1868. 94.4' × 24.8' × 3.7', rated at 61 tons, with two engines (9.5' × 3') and two boilers (14' × 38"), which allowed a working pressure of 150 lbs. The boat was owned by Leonard Arnold, with Captain James Tetlow as pilot. She was lost in ice on March 12, 1875, but was raised and repaired. She operated at Brownsville, Nebraska (below Omaha), from 1875 through 1876. The boat was snagged and lost in Nebraska on February 20, 1880.

Mary McDonald, a side-wheel packet built at St. Louis, Missouri, in 1866. She was rated at 563 tons, with two engines (20' × 5') and three boilers (24' × 38"), which allowed a working pressure of 142 lbs. She was on the Missouri River at Fort Benton, Montana, in 1866 and 1867 for the St. Louis & Omaha Packet Company. In 1870, she made trips on the Ouachita River with the Ouachita River Packet Company. The boat burned and was lost on the Missouri River on June 12, 1873, in Missouri with Captain George Keith in command.

Mary McGee, a center-wheel ferry built at Nordaway Slough, Missouri, in 1869. 108.5' × 32.6' × 4.6', rated at 135 tons, with one engine (15.75" × 4.5') and one boiler (20' × 42"), which allowed a working pressure of 110 lbs. The boat was owned by W. Micklewort and E. S. Sharp with Captain W. Micklewort serving as master. She was lost in ice in Nebraska on April 6, 1877.

Mary Tompkin, a lower Missouri River boat built in 1841. She was advertised for regular trips between St. Louis and St. Joseph.

Matamora, a steamer reported sunk on the Missouri River in 1873.

Mattie Bell, a stern-wheel packet built at Rockeport, Missouri, in 1875. 173.5' × 26.2' × 4.2', rated at 240 tons, with two engines (13" × 4.5') and two boilers (26' × 38"), which allowed a working pressure of 137 lbs. The boat ran in the Star line, St. Louis–Kansas City trade. The boat was snagged at the foot of Cora Island on the Missouri River on August 25, 1879. She was raised and sold to the St. Louis, Naples & Peoria Packet Company. She sank in winter quarters at St. Louis on Janaury 30, 1888.

Mattie Lee, a center-wheel ferryboat built at Grafton, Illinois, in 1881. 110' × 28' × 4', rated at 104 tons, with one engine (15' × 4.5') and one boiler (20' × 48"), which allowed a working pressure of 119 lbs. The boat was owned by D. N. and John Burrus; Captain D. N. Burrus was master with Captain Ed Herndon as pilot. The boat was snagged 1 mile below Miami, Missouri, on November 12, 1888. She was raised and repaired and finally lost in ice in Missouri on February 19, 1894.

May Bryan, a center-wheel ferryboat built at Jeffersonville, Indiana, in 1875. 115' × 28' × 4.5', at 97 tons, with one engine (16" × 5') and one boiler (22' × 44"), which allowed a working pressure of 114 lbs. The boat was owned by the Washington Ferry Company. She was lost when the hull dried out at Washington, Missouri, on October 12, 1897. The wreck is still visible at low water at the Missouri Pacific Railway depot at Washington, Missouri.

May Stewart, a stern-wheel packet built at Dubuque, Iowa, in 1905. 91.6' × 22.8' × 3.9' and 62 tons, with two engines (10' × 4') and one boiler (16' × 48"), which allowed a working pressure of 200 lbs. The boat was owned by the Stewart-Pack Sand Company. The boat was reported damaged on May 23, 1907, when she struck a pier at the Atchison, Kansas bridge.

Melusina, see DOROTHY

Messenger Boy, a stern-wheel packet that ran on the Missouri River. The boat was lost in 1881 in Nebraska when she was caught in a falling river. The river quickly cut a new channel leaving the steamer almost three quarters of a mile from the river.

Metamora (also noted as METTAMORA), a side-wheel packet built at Peoria, Illinois, in 1864. Rated at 190 tons. The boat first operated on the Illinois River and then went to Omaha to transport railroad passengers. In 1873, the boat was bought at Omaha by Captain J. A. Ware. He used the boat between Boonville, Missouri, and Kansas City. The boat was snagged and lost in Missouri on September 27, 1875.

Mike Bauer, a stern-wheel packet built at Brunswick, Missouri, in 1892. 65' × 9.1' × 3.3' and 20 tons, with two engines (7" × 2.5') and one boiler (8' × 60"), which allowed a working pressure of 150 lbs. She was owned by the Frankenfield

Sand and Fuel Company. The boat was lost when she struck the Kansas City bridge on May 31, 1903.

Mill Boy, a stern-wheel ferry built in Hermann, Missouri, in 1893. 89.2' × 18.8' × 2.8' and 41 tons, with two engines (8" × 2') and one boiler (18' × 44"), which allowed a working pressure of 125 lbs. She was owned by Frank Blaske and others. She was destroyed by ice in winter quarters on the Missouri River on January 1, 1910, in Missouri.

Miner, a stern-wheel packet built in Pittsburgh, Pennsylvania, in 1866. Rated at 299 tons. The Boat was owned by the North Western Fur Company and was logged in at Fort Benton, Montana in 1866 and to Fort Buford, North Dakota, in 1867. She was dismantled in 1875.

Mink, see ALEX MAJORS

Minnie, a stern-wheel packet built at McKeesport, Pennsylvania, in 1865. 156' × 32.5' × 5' and 445 tons. The boat was built for Captain A. H. Shaw and Mepham & Brothers of St. Louis for the St. Louis–White River trade. She made a Missouri River trip in 1868. The boat was snagged and lost on the Missouri on November 18, 1873, in Kansas.

Minnie, a stern-wheel boat built at Winona, Minnesota, in 1888. The boat had two engines (3" × 4") and one boiler (36" × 24"), which allowed a working pressure of 120 lbs. She was owned by Bush & Sons and Gustave E. Messmer. She was lost to a snag in Kansas in 1892.

Minnie Heerman (also noted as MINNIE HERMAN), a stern-wheel packet built at Reeds Landing, Minnesota, in 1879. 131' × 30' × 2.6' and 169 tons. She was snagged in South Dakota on August 23, 1887. The cargo was salvaged by the GENERAL CHAS. H. TOMPKINS.

Minnie Thomas, a stern-wheel packet built at Boonville, Missouri, in 1881. 66' × 22' and 20 tons, with one engine (8' × 10') and one boiler (11' × 30'), which allowed a working pressure of 100 lbs. The boat was owned by W. S. Thomas. She sank in Missouri on July 1, 1899. She was raised and dismantled.

Missouri (also MINNIE H), a stern-wheel packet built at Reeds Landing, Minnesota in 1880. 133' × 25' × 3'. She was originally named the MINNIE H (see MINNIE HERMAN above). In government service and renamed the MISSOURI. The boat was later owned by T. C. Power & Brothers and operated on the Missouri River in their Block "P" Line. The boat was at Fort Benton in September 1888. This was the last packet there and marked the end of regular steamboating at that location. She struck a rock on the Missouri River on October 4, 1889, in North Dakota.

Missouri, a lower Missouri River steamer built in 1828 by James McCord. The boat was rated at 110 tons. She was snagged and lost in Missouri on May 1, 1831.

Missouri, a side-wheel, single-engine steamer that ran on the Missouri River. Captain Bennett was master. She was snagged and lost in Missouri in 1869.

Missouri Belle, a Missouri River steamer built in 1830 by Captain Littleton. She was the first Missouri River boat to have a steam whistle. In the fall of 1834 she went to the Mississippi River. On October 24, 1834 while enroute from New Orleans to St. Louis, the steamer collided with the BOONSLICK and sank.

Missouri Mail, a side-wheel packet built for the Missouri River trade in 1857. She was lost in Kansas from unknown causes in 1858.

Mittie Stephens, a stern-wheel packet that ran Boonville-Rocheport. Captain Henry McPherson was owner and master. She was snagged and lost on August 7, 1884 in Missouri.

Mollie Dozier, a side-wheel packet built at St. Louis, Missouri, in 1865. 225' × 34' and 384 tons, with two engines (17.5" × 5") and three boilers (26' × 36"), which allowed a working pressure of 140 lbs. The boat was owned and commanded by Captain Frank Dozier who operated her on the Missouri River. The boat was at Fort Benton on June 1, 1866. She was snagged and lost in Missouri on October 3, 1866.

Mollie Moore, a stern-wheel packet built at Elizabeth and Pittsburgh, Pennsylvania, in 1870. 238' × 44.4' × 5.3' and 601 tons. She was owned by Captain George D. Moore, William J. Kountz, and others. She was lost when she settled on rocks in a falling river in South Dakota in 1881.

Monona, a side-wheel packet built in St. Louis, Missouri, in 1843. She ran St. Louis-Galena in 1845 with Captain Nick Wall. The boat sank on the Missouri opposite Little Washington on October 30, 1846. She was raised and repaired. She was fatally lost in Illinois on October 24, 1847.

Monongahela, a side-wheel packet built at Pittsburgh, Pennsylvania in 1863. Rated at 74 tons, with two engines (13.5" × 4.5') and two boilers (24' × 42"), which allowed a working pressure of 135 lbs. She was lost at Leavenworth, Kansas, on February 11, 1870. The boat was condemned and awaiting dismantling when she sank. She was owned by Henry J. Hanley and others at the time of loss.

Montana, a side-wheel packet built in Shousetown, Pennsylvania in 1864. 210' × 33' × 5.7' and 431 tons. She was on the Missouri River at Fort Benton, Montana, in 1866. The boat was sold downriver in 1867 and dismantled in 1879.

Montana, a stern-wheel packet built in California and Pittsburgh, Pennsylvania, in 1879. 250' × 48.8' × 5.5' and 959 tons. She was owned by Coulson & Company. She made numerous trips to Fort Benton and other Montana points throughout her career. The boat was lost when she hit a pier of the St. Charles bridge on June 22, 1884.

Moose, see LITTLE ROCK

Morning Star, a side-wheel packet built at Elizabeth, Pennsylvania, in 1856. 230' × 34' × 5.5' and 465 tons. She was built for the St. Louis & St. Joseph Union Line and the Missouri River trade. She burned at St. Louis, on June 21, 1859.

Morning Star, a stern-wheel packet built at Boonville, Missouri, in 1877. 66 tons, with two engines (10' × 3') and one boiler (18' × 40"), which allowed a working pressure of 130 lbs. She was owned by D. A. Stine and R. D. Willis. The boat was snagged 4 miles below Jefferson City, Missouri, on February 23, 1880. She was raised and repaired. She was finally lost in ice lying in winter quarters at Jefferson City, Missouri, on February 5, 1881.

Mountaineer, a side-wheel packet built at Metropolis, Illinois, in 1867. 205' × 34' × 5.5' and 584 tons, with two engines (20' × 7') and three boilers (24' × 44"), which allowed a working pressure of 122 lbs. The boat was built for Duncan S. Carter of St. Louis for the St. Louis–Omaha trade. The boat was logged in at Fort Benton in 1867 and sank and was raised twice on the Missouri River. She was dismantled in 1875.

Mt. Sterling, a stern-wheel packet built at Hermann, Missouri, in 1910. 60.3' × 12.3' × 2.2' and 22 tons with two engines (6" × 2') and one boiler (6' × 46"), which allowed a working pressure of 186 lbs. She was owned by the Buchanan Sand & Supply Company. The boat was lost in a windstorm in Missouri on May 8, 1917 on the Missouri River.

Mud Hen, a center-wheel ferryboat built at Nebraska City, Nebraska, in 1869. 30 tons, with one engine (12.5" × 3.5') and one boiler (20' × 36"), which allowed a working pressure of 110 lbs. She was owned by F. F. Pratt and others. The boat was destroyed when her boiler exploded on July 24, 1872 in Nebraska.

Mustang, a side-wheel packet built at St. Louis, Missouri, in 1848. 128 tons. She was snagged and lost on the Missouri River on October 9, 1850 in Missouri.

N. J. Eaton, a side-wheel packet built in Louisville, Kentucky, in 1856. She was to run St. Louis-Brunswick up the Missouri River, once a week. The boat was snagged and lost on her first trip on April 9, 1856, with Joseph S. Nanson in command. The boat's engines went to the KATE HOWARD in 1857.

Nadine, a stern-wheel packet built at Howards Ferry, Missouri, in 1872. Rated at 23 tons, with two engines (8" × 3') and one boiler (10' × 36"), which allowed a working pressure of 110 lbs. She was owned by Nicholas W. Smith who ran her on the Missouri River. She was snagged and lost enroute from St. Charles to St. Louis on September 10, 1878.

Nellie, see PRINCESS

Naiad, see PRINCESS

Naomi, a side-wheel packet built at Pittsburgh, Pennsylvania, in 1839. 165 tons. She was snagged and lost on the Missouri River in 1840 in Missouri.

Ne Plus Ultra, a side-wheel packet built at Cincinnati, Ohio, in 1874. Rated at 248 tons, with two engines (28" × 7') and three boilers (32' × 40"), which allowed a working pressure of 125 lbs. She ran New Orleans -St. Louis in 1851. She was snagged on the Missouri River at Council Bluffs, Iowa, on May 6, 1854, with Captain Richard Phillips in command. She was raised and dismantled in 1855.

Nebraska City, a side-wheel ferryboat built at Wellsville, Ohio, in 1859. 70 tons. The ferry operated at St. Joseph, Missouri. She was off the lists in 1869.

Ned Tracy (also D. A. JANUARY), a side-wheel packet built at Cincinnati, Ohio, in 1857. 225' × 34' and 440 tons. She was originally named the D. A. JANUARY and ran St. Louis–St. Joseph on the Missouri River. The boat was sold to U. S. Quartermaster Corps. on June 1, 1864, and used as a hospital boat. She was sold back into private hands on February 1, 1866, and renamed NED TRACY. The boat was logged in at Fort Benton, Montana, in 1866. She was snagged and lost in Illinois on December 18, 1867.

Nellie Rogers, a stern-wheel packet built at California and Pittsburgh, Pennsylvania, in 1862. 178' × 32' × 4.6' and 249 tons. The boat was on the Missouri River at Fort Union, North Dakota, in 1863 and to Fort Benton, Montana, in 1864. She returned to Fort Benton in 1866. The boat was converted to a barge in 1872.

New Haven, a side-wheel packet built at Pittsburgh, Pennsylvania, in 1841. Rated at 86 tons. The boat ran on the Missouri River. She was to Fort George and Fort Mortimer in 1843. She sank and was lost on January 24, 1847. Her machinery and boilers went into the LAKE OF THE WOODS.

New Iberia, see KEY WEST

New Lucy, a side-wheel packet built at St. Louis, Missouri, in 1852. 225' × 33' and 416 tons, with two engines (22' × 8') and four boilers (28' × 40"), which allowed a working pressure of 165 lbs. She was originally built for the Keokuk Packet Company. She was later sold and ran on the Missouri River. She was burned and lost in Missouri on November 22, 1857, with Captain R. DeVinney in command.

New Orleans, a early Missouri River boat that was 306 tons. She was snagged and lost in Missouri on September 12, 1842.

New Sam Gaty, a side-wheel packet built at Louisville, Kentucky, in 1860. 367 tons with the engines from the SAM GATY. She was owned by Captain F. P. Johnson, who was also master, and others. The boat burned and was lost while downbound on the Missouri on June 28, 1868, in Missouri.

New St. Paul, a side-wheel packet built at Wheeling, West Virginia, in 1851. She was rated at 265 tons, with two engines (18' × 6') and three boilers (24' × 40"), which allowed a working pressure of 170 lbs. She was rebuilt at New Albany, Indiana, in 1855–1856. Captain James Bissell was the boat's owner and master. She was snagged and lost on the Missouri River on August 9, 1857 in Missouri.

Nick Wall, a stern-wheel packet built at Pittsburgh, Pennsylvania, in 1869. 180' × 33' × 5' and 338 tons. Her machinery was from the PEERLESS. The boat was named for the famed Missouri River captain. She was owned by Captain Thomas Poe and others who ran the boat on the Missouri River. While en route to Fort Benton, Montana, the boat struck a snag near Wyoming, Iowa, on April 26, 1869. She was raised and was back at Fort Benton in 1870. The boat was snagged and lost in Arkansas on December 18, 1870, with a number of passengers. The wreck floated 3 miles downriver when the SEMINOLE happened along and took off survivors.

Nile, a side-wheel packet built at Pittsburgh, Pennsylvania, in 1866. 200' × 34' × 5' and 454 tons. The boat ran on the Missouri River. She went to Council Bluffs, Iowa, in 1866 and then loaded for Fort Benton, Montana, in 1867 and again in 1868 with Captain Grant Marsh in command. She was to Fort Benton again in 1869 but was then lost at St. Louis in a storm on April 8, 1874. The boat was then owned by Daniel S. Stover, M. D. Munson, and James H. Hamilton. They were using the boat as a railroad transfer in south St. Louis at the time.

Nimrod, a side-wheel packet built at St. Louis, Missouri, in 1844. 156' × 25' × 5.7' and 210 tons. The boat was built for Captain Joseph Throckmorton, Pierre Chouteau Jr., and John B. Sarpy, all in the fur trade. In 1844 she made "mountain" runs up the Missouri River for the American Fur Company. She was sold in 1846 for the lower Mississippi River and changed owners several times before she was finally lost at New Orleans on August 6, 1850.

Nodaway, a side-wheel packet that was built for the Missouri River in 1840. 145' × 24' and 203 tons, with a single engine. She was owned by Captain John J. Roe and others with Captain Celeghron serving as master. She was lost in Missouri in 1844.

Nora, a stern-wheel packet built in California, Pennsylvania, in 1864. 159' × 30.5' × 4.8' and 214 tons. She was owned by boat builder James Rees and Samuel Shuman. She was snagged and lost in Nebraska on May 30, 1867, with Captain William Shedden commanding. The SILVER LAKE NO. 4 took the passengers to Sioux City, Iowa.

North Alabama (also the VIRGINIA BARTON), a side-wheel packet built at Brownsville and Pittsburgh, Pennsylvania, in 1864. 160' × 32' and 219 tons. Originally she was named the VIRGINIA BARTON. She was sold to the U. S. Quartermaster Corps. in 1864. After the war she was sold to Barton Able and others of the Northwest Transportation Company for use on the Missouri River. She was snagged and lost in South Dakota on October 27, 1870 with Captain A. Townsend in command. The boat was briefly exposed by a shift in the river in 1906.

Northern Pacific No. 2, see JUDITH

Nugget, a stern-wheel packet built in Monongahela, Pennsylvania, in 1860. 129' × 3.5' with two boilers. The boat was owned by L. B. Hine, Adam Hine, and R. H. Martin, who ran her mainly on the Upper Mississippi River. In late February 1864, she sank in the Arkansas River with a cargo from St. Louis mainly from M. S. Lapham & Brothers. The steamer was raised and repaired, and on June 1, 1864, she was sold to the U. S. Quartermaster Corps. She was next sold at public sale on March 19, 1866 and renamed NUGGET. The boat entered the Upper Missouri River trade promptly after the sale. She was snagged and lost in Nebraska on April 22, 1866.

Nymph No. 2, a stern-wheel packet built at Portsmouth, Ohio, in 1864. 147' × 24' × 4' and 149 tons. The boat was built by Captain Henry Davies of Portsmouth. She was at Fort Benton, Montana, in 1867. The boat was sunk at Chain of Rocks on the Missouri River at Sibley, Missouri, on March 3, 1868.

O. K. (also BURKESVILLE), a stern-wheel packet built at Cincinnati, Ohio, in 1898–1899. 116.5' × 17.1' × 3.8'. She was originally named BURKESVILLE. She was owned by the Burkesville & Burnside Transportation Company, operating on the Cumberland River. She was sold in 1904 to Captain Oscar Knapp of Dubuque who renamed her the O. K. He sold the boat in June 1905 to the Charles Stevens Transportation Company of Mondak, Montana. In the fall of 1905, she made trips up the Yellowstone to Glendive, Montana, and in the spring of 1906 made her first appearance at Fort Benton. She ran Milk River-Fort Benton during the summers of 1906–1907, carrying groceries and hardware for trading with ranchers and Indians. She burned at Fort Benton on June 30, 1908. The wreck can still be seen at low water.

Oceana, a Missouri River steamer built in 1836 for the American Fur Company. Captain Miller was the boat's master. Father De Smet reportedly came up the Missouri from St. Louis to Westport on this boat in 1841. She was lost in 1843.

Octavia, a side-wheel packet built at St. Louis, Missouri, in 1866. She was rated at 595 tons. The boat was loaded for Fort Benton, Montana, with Captain Joe LaBarge in 1867 and again in 1868. In the fall of 1868, the boat was sold to the United States. She was lost sometime in 1871.

Oddfellow, a stern-wheel packet lost on the Missouri River in August 1850 in Missouri.

Oddity, a 112-ton steamer built in 1841. She was snagged and lost on the Missouri River on October 3, 1846, in Missouri.

Omaha, a side-wheel packet built at Madison, Indiana, in 1856. 206' × 30' × 5' and 307 tons. Sioux City, Iowa, got its start with the arrival of this boat, which was carrying everything needed to start a new town. She ran St. Joseph-Council Bluffs weekly with Captain J. E. Barrow. She was lost in ice at St. Louis on December 16, 1865.

Omaha City, a side-wheel packet built at Freedom, Pennsylvania, in 1857. She was rated at 147 tons. The boat ran on the Missouri River out of Omaha, Nebraska. She was lost in ice at St. Louis on January 12, 1866.

Omega, a side-wheel packet built at Pittsburgh, Pennsylvania, in 1840. She was rated at 144 tons. She came to Fort Union, North Dakota, in 1843 with John J. Audubon and company who came to study the wildlife of the west. She was dismantled in 1849.

Onawa, a stern-wheel packet built for the Missouri River trade. She was snagged and lost in Iowa in 1880.

Only Chance, a side-wheel packet built at Alton, Illinois, in 1865. The boat was rated at 219 tons. She ran St. Louis-Missouri River and was to Fort Benton in

1866 and 1867. The boat was damaged in a steamboat fire at St. Louis on March 29, 1869. She was repaired and later sank in Arkansas on November 23, 1869.

Ontario, a stern-wheel packet built at California, Pennsylvania, in 1864. 156.3' × 32' × 5.8' and 265 tons, with two engines (15" × 5') and three boilers (22' × 38"), which allowed a working pressure of 132 lbs. She originally ran Pittsburgh-St. Louis. The boat was sold to John C. Copeland and others for the Missouri River with Captain David Haney commanding. She was snagged and lost in Nebraska on September 25, 1866.

Oriole, see FLORENCE MILLER NO. 3

Orion, a stern-wheel packet built for the Missouri River trade. She was snagged and lost in Missouri in 1864.

Osage, a side-wheel steamer that was built for the Missouri River in 1845. She was snagged and lost in Missouri in 1848.

Osage, a stern-wheel packet built at Osage City, Missouri, in 1900. 100' × 19.8' × 3.5'. Her engines came from the JOHN R. HUGO. She briefly ran on the Osage and Missouri Rivers and was then sold to the Houston Lumber Company, of Vicksburg. She was sold again and then dismantled in 1917.

Osage Valley, a 166-tons steamer built for the lower Missouri River trade in 1840. Captain Young commanded. She was stranded and lost at St. Louis on October 5, 1842.

Osceola, a stern-wheel packet built at Osceola, Wisconsin, in 1874. 130' × 22' × 45'. She was built by Emil Munch. The boat sank at Peters Landing 40 miles below Memphis upbound from St. Francis River to Memphis with 300 bales on February 27, 1876. The boat was raised and sold to General Mark D. Flower in 1877 for a trip up the Yellowstone River. She was lost in a tornado on June 22, 1877, on the Yellowstone while stopped so the passengers could chase a stallion. The hull was towed back downriver and was lost in striking water at Kansas City.

Otto, a side-wheel packet built at Jefferson, Indiana, in 1832. She was rated at 163 tons. The boat was leased by William Sublett and Robert Campbell (fur traders) in 1833. They sent the boat to the newly constructed Fort William (3 miles east of Fort Union) in 1833, but she only reached Fort Pierre. Keelboats were required to make the rest of the journey with the freight. The boat was lost in Lake Pontchartrain, Louisiana, on January 6, 1836.

P. T. Miller, steam ferry built at Metropolis, Illinois in 1867. She was 67 tons. In 1874, she was owned by the Jefferson City Steam Ferry Company. In 1875, she was lost on the Missouri River in ice.

Pathfinder, a stern-wheel packet built at Clinton, Iowa, in 1898. 85' × 20' × 3.6' and 62 tons. She was owned by the Buchanan Sand & Supply Company. The steamer was out of commission at St. Joseph, Missouri, when a bar formed under her stern causing her to break in two on November 13, 1916.

Paul Jones, a steamer built in 1848 with Captain J. B. Dales serving as master. She sank on the Missouri River below Independence. She was raised but was finally wrecked in ice at St. Louis on February 27, 1856.

Peerless, a stern-wheel packet built at Hermann, Missouri, in 1893. 96.6' × 21.4' × 3.5' and 60 tons, with two engines (8" × 3") and one boiler (16" × 42"), which allowed a working pressure of 160 lbs. She was owned by the Hermann Ferry & Packet Company. The boat was sunk by ice at St. Charles, Missouri, on December 30, 1903. She ran the Illinois River in 1905 and was in the Vicksburg area until 1924–1925.

Peninah, a stern-wheel packet built at Pittsburgh, Pennsylvania, in 1868. 180' × 30' and 421 tons. She was owned by Captain William J. Kountz and others and was named for his wife. They ran her in the Missouri River mountain trade. In all she made twenty trips to Montana. She sank at Sioux City, Iowa, on April 5, 1875. The wreck was raised and taken to Yankton, South Dakota, for repairs, but she broke loose from her moorings in high water and drifted 2 miles to Stone's farm where she lodged on the shore. Nat Sykes, a boat builder, spent 3 weeks getting the boat back in the river. When he finally succeeded, a cyclone came along and tore off the boat's cabin.

Peoria Belle, see BELLE PEORIA

Peter Balen, a stern-wheel packet built in Pittsburgh, Pennsylvania, in 1866. She was rated at 545 tons. The boat was built for the mountain trade and made her first trip to Fort Benton, Montana, in 1866. The boat made a $70,000.00 profit on that first trip. She returned to Fort Benton in 1869 and had to double-trip to get her cargo there. On the return trip back downriver, the boat burned in Montana on July 22, 1869. She was owned by M. S. Mepham and others at the time of loss. Planks were later salvaged from the wreck and used in building a patrol cabin in the northwest part of the C. M. Russell Game Range.

Petrel, a stern-wheel packet built at Burlington, Iowa, in 1875. She was 37 tons, with two engines (10" × 3.5') and one boiler (18' × 42"), which allowed a working pressure of 110 lbs. She was built for the Missouri River trade and was owned by Phillip Hendricks & Company. She was sunk by ice on January 3, 1883, in Missouri.

Pin Oak, a stern-wheel packet built at Hermann, Missouri, in 1888. 95' × 17.5' × 2.2' and 43 tons, with two engines (8" × 2.5') and one boiler (17' × 40"), which allowed a working pressure of 125 lbs. She was owned by the Hermann Ferry & Packet Company and was used on the Gasconade River. The boat was sold in 1896. She sank in Missouri on July 29, 1896, after turning over.

Pirate, a side-wheel packet built in Pittsburgh, Pennsylvania, in 1837. She was rated at 128 tons. The boat operated for the American Fur Company. She was on the Missouri River at Fort Union in 1839. She was snagged and lost in Nebraska in 1842.

Platte, a side-wheel packet built at Pittsburgh, Pennsylvania, in 1838. She was rated at158 tons. The boat was on the upper Missouri in 1838. She was snagged and lost on September 7, 1841.

Platte Valley, a side-wheel packet built at Jeffersonville, Indiana, at the Howard boatyard in 1857. 220' × 33' × 5'. She was built for the Missouri River trade and in 1859 ran St. Joseph–Kansas City connection with the Hannibal and St. Joseph Railroad. She was later in the St. Louis-Vicksburg trade. She struck the wreck of the Confederate gunboat JEFF THOMPSON below Memphis on January 18, 1867, and was a total loss.

Platte Valley, a center-wheel ferryboat built at Farley, Missouri, in 1872. The boat had one engine (10" × 3') and one boiler (18' × 36"), which allowed a working pressure of 100 lbs. She was owned by T. W. Nolan. The boat was snagged and lost in Kansas on May 29, 1879.

Plow Boy No. 1 (also PLOUGH BOY), a side-wheel packet built at St. Louis, Missouri, in 1848. 165' × 32' and 275 tons. She was built by Isaac McKee. The boat ran St. Louis-Missouri River. She was snagged and lost on October 6, 1848 in Missouri.

Plow Boy No. 2, a stern-wheel packet built at Stillwater, Minnesota, in 1876. Rated at 36 tons. The boat burned on the Missouri River on July 7, 1877, in Missouri.

Plow Boy No. 3, a center-wheel packet built at Sioux City, Iowa, in 1884. 70' × 18' × 3' and 29 tons, with one engine (7" × 12") and one boiler (10' × 34"), which allowed a working pressure of 140 lbs. The boat operated on the lower Missouri River and sank there several times. She was fatally snagged and lost on May 6, 1897, in Missouri. The boiler and engines were salvaged.

Pocahontas, a side-wheel packet built for the Missouri River trade in 1835. Captain McCord was master when the boat was snagged and lost on August 11, 1840, in Missouri.

Pocahontas, a side-wheel packet built at Cincinnati, Ohio, in 1857. 180' × 32' and 163 tons. She ran Louisville-Nashville in 1862. The boat was on the Missouri River in 1866 when she was snagged and lost in South Dakota on August 9, 1866.

Pocahontas, a side-wheel packet built in 1865. 180' × 32'. She was in the Fort Benton, Montana, trade. The boat was lost in Nebraska on August 10, 1866.

Pontiac, a side-wheel packet built at Cincinnati, Ohio, in 1846. She was rated at 250 tons. The boat was snagged and lost on the Missouri River on April 10, 1852, in Kansas. Captain Tom Baker was in command at the time of loss.

Portsmouth, a stern-wheel packet built at Ravenswood, Virginia, in 1857. 160' × 32' and 169 tons. The boat was snagged and lost on the Missouri River on February 2, 1860, in Missouri.

Post Boy, a side-wheel packet built in 1865. The boat ran St. Louis-Omaha with the Missouri River Packet Company.

Prairie Rose, a stern-wheel wheel packet built at Brownsville, Pennsylvania, in 1854. She was rated at 247 tons. The boat was in the St. Louis–St. Paul trade in

1855 with Captain Maratta. She then ran Cincinnati–Memphis with Captain James S. Wise in 1861. The boat was impressed during the Civil War and was up the Missouri River in 1864 to Leavenworth, Kansas. She was lost in ice at the foot of Biddle Street, St. Louis on January 12, 1866.

Prairie State, a side-wheel packet built at Wellsville, Ohio, in 1863. Rated at 184 tons. The boat was bought in March 1864 by Captain Frank Dozier and others of St. Louis for the Missouri River. She was at Fort Union, North Dakota, in 1865. Later she was at Mobile, Alabama, and then off the lists by 1872.

Princess (also U.S. Tinclad #53–NAIAD), a stern-wheel packet built at Freedom, Pennsylvania, in 1863. 156.9' × 30.3' × 4.4' and 85 tons. The boat was built for Captain Frank Maratta and Captain George W. Cullem. They sold her to the U. S. Navy on March 3, 1864. She was converted into Tinclad #53 and renamed NAIAD. She was sold into private hands in 1865 to B. F. Beasley and others. They rebuilt the boat and changed the name back to PRINCESS on October 21, 1865. She ran St. Louis-Arkansas River in 1866. The boat was fatally snagged in Missouri on the Missouri River on June 1, 1868, enroute to Fort Benton, Montana.

R. J. Lockwood, a side-wheel packet built at St. Louis, Missouri, in 1864. 210' × 34' × 5' and 418 tons. She operated on the Missouri River and was used for U. S. transport service in 1864–1865. On March 4, 1866, her boilers exploded below Memphis coming from New Orleans. The boat was dismantled in Pittsburgh in 1870.

R. M. Bishop, a stern-wheel packet built at Cincinnati, Ohio, in 1866. She was rated at 298 tons. The boat was lost in high wind in Nebraska on July 15, 1867. The mate, Andy Goff, was drowned.

R. W. Dugan, a stern-wheel packet built at Cincinnati, Ohio, in 1873. 160' × 32' × 3' and 421 tons with two engines (13.5" × 4') and two boilers (26' × 40"), which allowed a working pressure of 146 lbs. She originally ran Cincinnati-Memphis. Later, Captain Joseph Kinney ran the boat in the St. Louis–Kansas City trade. Captain William L. Heckmann Sr. acquired the boat in 1874 and ran her St. Louis-Rocheport. Captain Kinney got the boat again in March 1876 for the Jefferson City Transportation Company and ran St. Louis-Jefferson City. The boat was snagged and lost in Missouri on October 31, 1878.

Rachael Miller, see MARINER

Radnor, a side-wheel packet built for the Missouri River trade. Captain J. T. Douglas was the boat's master. The boat was snagged and lost in Missouri bound for Fort Leavenworth, Kansas, in 1846.

Red Cloud, a stern-wheel packet built at Jeffersonville, Indiana, at the Howard boatyard in 1873. 228' × 34.5' × 5.2' and 355 tons. She was originally owned by the Evansville & Tennessee River Packet Company. She was sold in 1877 to I. G. Baker and Company of Fort Benton, Montana, which had the boat lengthened to 228' in the winter of 1877–1878. The boat spent her career in the mountain trade. She was snagged and lost in Montana on July 11, 1882, with Captain John A. Williams in command. The roof bell was salvaged, and Isaac G. Baker presented it to the Episcopal church in Bismark in 1882. The wreck was relocated by John Wener, a salvor, in 1926.

Reindeer, see MARINER

Rialto, a stern-wheel packet in the Missouri River trade. She was snagged and lost in Missouri in 1864.

Richard, a steam towboat owned by the Kansas City Bridge Company. She struck a snag on August 24,1931, at mile 272.8 and sank. The boat was beached and later raised and repaired.

Richmond, a stern-wheel packet built at Louisville, Kentucky, in 1866. 142' x 34' x 4' and 359 tons. She originally ran New Orleans-St. Louis. The boat was logged in at Fort Benton, Montana, in 1867. She was sold in 1868 and ran New Orleans-Shreveport. The boat sank and was lost on the Red River on December 3, 1869.

Roanoke, a stern-wheel packet built at California, Pennsylvania, in 1864. 156' x 32.2' x 5.8' and 266 tons. She originally ran Pittsburgh-Louisville then was sold in 1864 to Captain James Shedden who took the boat to St. Louis. She was at Fort Union and Fort Benton, Montana, in 1865. The boat was lost on the Missouri River on December 17, 1867, in Missouri.

Rob Roy (also SAM BOREE), a stern-wheel packet built at Lafayett, Indiana. She was rated at 107 tons, with two engines (7.25" x 34") and one boiler (20' x 42"), which allowed a working pressure of 137 lbs. The boat was originally named the SAM BOREE and was on the Wabash River in 1878. She was at St. Louis in 1882 and renamed ROB ROY. She was owned by Henry McPherson who ran her on the Missouri River. The boat was snagged 6 miles below Rocheport, Missouri, on July 26, 1883. She was raised and repaired and at Memphis in 1888. She was registered at Cincinnati in 1898.

Robert Campbell, a side-wheel packet built at Hannibal, Missouri, in 1849. She was rated at 268 tons and was named for the noted fur trader. Captain William Edds served as master. She was up the Missouri River to Fort William (Fort Mortimer) in 1851 and to Fort Union in 1853. The boat burned at the St. Louis wharf fire on October 13, 1853.

Robert Campbell No. 2 (also called ROBERT CAMPBELL JR.), a side-wheel packet built at Jeffersonville, Indiana, at the Howard boatyard in 1860. 226' x 41' x 6' and 421 tons. She ran St. Louis-New Orleans with Captain John S. Shaw. In 1863, Captain Joe La Barge loaded the boat for Fort Benton, Montana, but had to turn back at the Yellowstone River because of low water. She was sold to Captain McCloy and others for Vicksburg on her return from the Missouri. The boat burned on the Mississippi on September 28, 1863.

Robert Campbell No. 3, a stern-wheel packet built for the Missouri River trade in 1882. She burned at the St. Louis levee on October 15,1883.

Robert Emmet, a stern-wheel packet built at Memphis, Tennessee, in 1864. She was rated at 178 tons. She was snagged and lost on the Missouri River on November 3, 1864, in Missouri. Colonel Poser's regiment of 350 men was aboard when the accident happened.

Rose of Helena, a stern-wheel packet built at Dubuque, Iowa, at the Iowa Iron Works in 1886. She had a steel hull 54' × 10'. She was owned by Nicholas Higler of Montana. The boat was shipped in pieces to Townsend, Montana, where she was assembled and launched. She eventually became a sightseeing boat. She was lost in the backwaters of Holter Dam just above Gate of the Mountains, Montana, in 1906.

Rosebud, a stern-wheel packet built at California, Pennsylvania, in 1877. 177.4' × 31.3' × 4'. She was originally owned by S. B Coulson, D. W. Maratta, and others of the Benton Transportation Company. The boat was outfitted for the upper Missouri River and made more than fifty trips to Fort Benton over her career. The boat was bought by the Block P Line (T. C. Power & Brothers, of Fort Benton) in 1884. She made trips to Fort Benton in 1888 and 1889 after the railroad had arrived, and was then sold to the Benton Packet Company. She ran on the lower Missouri until she sank in South Dakota on June 16, 1896.

Rowena, a side-wheel packet built at Elizabeth, Pennsylvania, in 1847. She was rated at 230 tons. The boat was snagged and lost on the Missouri River on March 12, 1850, in Missouri. Captain William C. Jewett was master at the time of loss.

Roy Lynds (also noted as ROY LINDS), a side-wheel ferryboat built at Jeffersonville, Indiana, in 1887. 87' × 25' × 3.6' and 64 tons, with two engines (9" × 3') and one boiler (18' × 42"), which allowed a working pressure of 161 lbs. She was owned by the Lexington Ferry, Coal, and Transportation Company. She was lost in ice in Missouri on February 5, 1897.

Rubicon, a side-wheel packet built at Shousetown and Pittsburgh, Pennsylvania, in 1866. 200' × 36' × 6' and 637 tons. She was on the Missouri River headed for Fort Benton, Montana, in 1866 but had to turn back at the Milk River because of low water. The boat was converted to a barge in 1873.

Ruth, a steamer reported burned on the Missouri River in Montana on August 2, 1883.

S. B. Oddfellow, a side-wheel packet (also reported as a stern-wheel) that operated on the Missouri River. She was snagged and lost in Missouri in August 1850 or 1859.

S. C. Pomeroy, a stern-wheel ferryboat built at Brownsville, Pennsylvania, in 1863. She was 205 tons, with one engine (20' × 6') and two boilers (22' × 42"), which allowed a working pressure of 100 lbs. The boat was based at Kansas City, Missouri, and owned by S. C. Charliss. She sank on the Missouri River on March 23, 1877, with Captain William H. Cline as master.

Sacramento, a side-wheel packet built at Cincinnati, Ohio, in 1848. 182' × 27.5' ×

5.8' and 221 tons. She was lost on the Missouri River in 1849 in Missouri with Captain Robert Becker, master. She was raised and returned to service but was off the lists in 1855.

Sallie List, a stern-wheel packet built at Elizabeth, Pennsylvania, in 1860. She was rated at 212 tons. The Hannibal and St. Joseph Railway used the boat on the Missouri River. She was snagged five miles above Kickapoo, Kansas, on May 5, 1863. She was raised and operated on the Red River in 1864 and the lower White River in 1866. The boat was snagged and lost on February 21, 1868, in Alabama. She was owned by the Mobile Trade Company at the time of loss.

Sallie West, a stern-wheel packet built at Louisville, Kentucky, in 1853. She was 286 tons, with two engines (16" × 4.5') and three boilers (22' × 36"), which allowed a working pressure of 139 lbs. The boat was owned by the Hannibal and St. Joseph Railroad Company. She was lost on the Missouri River in Kansas on May 5, 1859.

Saluda, a side-wheel packet built at St. Louis, Missouri, in 1846. 179' × 26.7' and 223 tons. She ran St. Louis-St. Joseph. In 1850, she struck a snag and sank 5 miles below Rocheport, Missouri. She was raised and rebuilt. The boat's boilers exploded on April 9, 1852, in Missouri on her way to Council Bluffs with Mormon emigrants.

Sam Borll, see ROB ROY

Sam Cloon, a side-wheel packet built at Cincinnati, Ohio, in 1851. She was rated at 301 tons. At New Orleans in 1851, on the lower Mississippi in 1853, and also on the Missouri in that year. She was lost in ice at St. Louis on February 27, 1856.

Sam Gaty, a side-wheel packet built at St. Louis, Missouri, in 1853. 210' × 36' and 294 tons. She was owned by the St. Louis Packet Company with Captain John Baldwin, master. She burned on the Missouri River on June 27, 1858, in Missouri.

Santa Fe, a stern-wheel ferryboat built at Glasgow, Missouri, in 1919. 65' × 20.5' × 2.9'. Snagged and lost in Missouri in 1931.

Seitz, a Missouri River steamer that was lost in Iowa on the Missouri.

Selkirk, a stern-wheel packet built at McCauleysville, Minnesota, in 1871. 110' × 24' × 3' and 119 tons. She was lost in North Dakota in the Missouri River when she collided with a bridge on October 25, 1886.

Senator, a stern-wheel ferryboat built at Yankton, South Dakota. 120' × 26' and 118 tons. She was owned by the Yankton Steam Ferry Company. She was destroyed by fire in South Dakota on July 5, 1858.

Senator, a stern-wheel ferry built at Yankton, South Dakota, in 1882. 115' × 28' × 4'. She was owned by the Yankton Steam Ferry Company. The boat was sunk by ice on February 5, 1885. She was repaired and finally lost on March 11, 1887, in ice on the Missouri River in South Dakota.

Settler, a Missouri River steamer that was reported at Fort Union in 1865.

Seventy-Six, a side-wheel packet in the Missouri River trade. 181' × 25.5'. Captain John Gunsaullis was master when in 1876 she struck rocks and sank in Missouri.

Shamrock, a stern-wheel steamer in the Missouri River trade. She sank in 1863 in Missouri.

Shoal Water, a side-wheel packet built in the 1820s. She was lost on the Missouri River in 1828 in Missouri.

Shoal Water, a side-wheel packet on the Missouri River. She was snagged and lost in Missouri near the mouth of the river in 1863.

Shreveport, a side-wheel packet built at Louisville, Kentucky, in 1860. 155' × 28' × 4.4' and145 tons. She was an opposition boat under LaBarge, Harkness & Company in 1862 and 1863 to Fort Benton, Montana. The boat was impressed by the Army near Fort Pierre to carry supplies back upriver in 1863. She was back on the upper Missouri in 1866 and was dismantled in 1871.

Silver Bow, a side-wheel packet built at Pittsburgh, Pennsylvania, in 1869. 212' × 32' × 5.5' and 335 tons. She was on the Missouri River at Fort Leavenworth in 1869. The boat then joined the Carter Line, running St. Louis-Shreveport. She sank on the Mississippi in 1871 and was raised. The boat was fatally lost in ice at St. Louis on February 26, 1872. Parts were used in building the BELLE OF SHREVEPORT in 1873.

Silver Lake No. 2, see MARION

Silver Lake No. 4, a stern-wheel packet built at California, Pennsylvania, in 1863. 155' × 33' × 5.5' and 224 tons. She was at Fort Benton, Montana, in 1867 and was frozen in by ice above Sioux City, Iowa, in 1877. The boat was off the lists in 1879.

Sioux City, a side-wheel packet built at Cincinnati, Ohio, in 1857. 218' × 33' × 5.8' and 379 tons. She operated on the Missouri River. The boat ran trips up Red River in 1860 and was in U.S. transport service in 1863–1864. She was lost in the ice breakup at St. Louis on February 26, 1867.

Sioux City No. 2, a side-wheel packet built at California, Pennsylvania, in 1870. 162.5' × 30' × 3.4'. The boat was originally owned out of Sioux City, Iowa, and made a Fort Randall trip in 1870 direct from Pittsburgh. In 1871 she was sold to the St. Louis & Arkansas River Packet Company. She sank on the Arkansas River in October 1871 but was pumped out and repaired. In 1882, the boat was sold to J. H. Durfee for operations on the Missouri River again. The boat was lost on March 19, 1873, in an ice gorge in South Dakota.

Sonora, a side-wheel packet built at St. Louis, Missouri, in 1851. 220' × 32' × 5.5' and363 tons. She ran St. Louis-Missouri River, with Captain Joseph LaBarge commanding. The boat was logged in at Fort Union, North Dakota, in 1852. She was on the Red River with Captain William Terrell in 1853 and back at Fort Union in 1854. The boat was lost in ice on the Missouri River on February

26, 1856, in Missouri. The machinery and brass were taken out in 1916, and the wreck was still visible during the low water of 1927. The U. S. dredge KEOKUK removed the wreck from the river in 1949.

Sophie M. Gardner, a stern-wheel packet built at Point Pleasant, West Virginia, in 1912. 118.6' × 25.3' × 3.5' and 91 tons, with two engines (11.75" × 4') and one boiler (18' × 56"), which allowed a working pressure of 230 lbs. She was owned by Marshall Rust of Kansas City, Missouri, with Captain William Struttman as pilot. The steamer was lost on the Missouri River after recieving a heavy load of coal. She was being driven upriver in a windstorm when a hog chain brace came loose and punctured the hull on April 3, 1917 in Missouri.

South Dakota, a stern-wheel packet built at Running Water, South Dakota, in 1899. 137.5' × 19.4' × 4.5' and 96 tons, with two engines (10" × 4') and one boiler (20' × 44"), which allowed a working pressure of 178 lbs. She was owned by Joseph Leach Sr. The boat burned and was lost on the Missouri between Running Water and Yankton, South Dakota, on May 10, 1902.

Southwester, a side-wheel packet built at Jeffersonville, Indiana, at the Howard boat yard in 1857. 217' × 36' × 6.5' and 418 tons. She was built for the Boonville Missouri Steamboat Company. The boat ran in the St. Louis & St. Joseph Union Line in 1858 and ran New Orleans-St. Louis in 1861. The boat was lost to ice on the Mississippi in Missouri in 1865.

Spray, a stern-wheel packet built at Allegheny City, Pennsylvania, in 1864. Rated at 232 tons. She was on the Missouri River to Fort Berthold in 1865. She went to a U. S. marshal sale at Cincinnati in 1868 and was sold to Captain Vincent Shinkle. Later she was in the Cincinnati–Nashville trade. She was lost in a boiler explosion on February 17, 1871, in Indiana.

Spread Eagle, a side-wheel packet built at Brownsville, Pennsylvania, in 1857. 210' × 36' × 6' and 389 tons, with engines (22" × 7') and three boilers (24' × 44"), which allowed a working pressure of 114 lbs. The boat was built by Captain Ben Johnson who sold her on arrival at St. Louis to Captain Joseph LaBarge and the American Fur Company. She spent her career on the Missouri River. The boat offloaded freight at Fort Union, North Dakota, for 4 years, and was at Fort Benton, Montana, in 1862. She was snagged and lost in Missouri on March 20, 1864.

St. Ange, a side-wheel packet built at St. Louis, Missouri, in 1849. 200' × 36' × 6' and 254 tons. This boat was built complete on the ways rather than finished while afloat. She operated on the Missouri River with Captain Joseph LaBarge for the American Fur Company. The boat was named for St. Ange de Bellerive, the first French military governor of upper Louisiana. Father De Smet was aboard in 1851 when cholera broke out on the boat and a fellow priest died. The boat was lost in ice at St. Louis on February 2, 1854.

St. Anthony, a side-wheel packet built at Belle Vernon, Pennsylvania, in 1846. 157' × 24' × 5' and 184 tons. In 1844, she ran Galena-St. Peters with Captain A.

G. Montford. The boat ran Pittsburgh-Wheeling briefly in 1848 and in February 1849 departed for St. Louis. The boat burned on the Missouri on March 25, 1851 in Missouri. Captain Jim Gonsaullis was in command.

St. Charles, a side-wheel packet rated at 127 tons. She ran in the Missouri River trade and was burned and lost on July 21, 1836, in Missouri.

St. Johns, a stern-wheel packet built at Wheeling, West Virginia, in 1864. 174' × 36' × 5' and 309 tons. The boat was on the Missouri River at Fort Benton, Montana, in 1865, 1866, and 1867. The boat was lost in 1875, owned at the time by the St. Louis & Illinois Packet Company.

St. Louis Oak, a side-wheel packet built at St. Louis, Missouri, in 1842 and rated at 108 tons. The boat ran St. Louis-Galena-Dubuque. She was snagged and lost on the Missouri River with Captain Dozier in command in1847.

St. Luke, a side-wheel packet built at St. Louis, Missouri, in 1868. 210' × 36' × 7' and 720 tons with two engines (22" × 6') and three boilers (26' × 40"), which allowed a working pressure of 135 lbs. She was built by Captain Joe Kinney for the St. Louis-Missouri River. The boat was painted yellow and as a result was called the "Yellow Hammer." She was owned by the Missouri River Packet Company. The boat was lost when she hit the bridge at St. Charles, Missouri, on May, 2, 1875. Captain Thomas Townsend was pilot on watch.

St. Mary, a side-wheel packet built at St. Louis, Missouri, in 1855. 204' × 35' × 4.5' and 295 tons, with two engines (24" × 6') and two boilers (24' × 46"), which allowed a working pressure of 116 lbs. The boat was on the Missouri River with Captain Joseph LaBarge in 1855. In 1856, the boat went up the Missouri carrying 900 passengers aboard on one trip. The boat was snagged and lost enroute from St. Joseph to Omaha on September 4, 1859, in Nebraska.

St. Paul, a side-wheel packet built at St. Louis, Missouri, in 1847. She was rated at 358 tons, with two engines (18.5" × 8') and three boilers (28' × 40"), which allowed a working pressure of 140 lbs. The boat typically ran St. Louis-New Orleans. She was snagged and lost on the Missouri River, in 1852, with Captain J. H. Cole in command.

St. Peters, a side-wheel packet built at Pittsburgh, Pennsylvania, in 1836 and rated 119 tons. Captain Chouteau commanded the boat for the American Fur Company. When the boat was at Fort Union in 1837, she brought smallpox to the upper river tribes, which killed about half of their number. The boat was dismantled in 1838.

Star of the West, a side-wheel packet built at McKeesport, Pennsylvania, in 1855. Rated at 435 tons. The boat ran in the Missouri River trade, St. Louis-St. Joseph. She burned at St. Louis on April 22, 1858.

Statie Fisher, a center-wheel ferryboat built at Jeffersonville, Indiana, at the Howard boatyard in 1875. 122' × 28' × 4' and 106 tons, with one engine (16.5" × 5') and one boiler (22' × 42"), which allowed a working pressure of 100 lbs. The Howard yard lists the boat as the KATIE FISHER. The boat was owned by the Jefferson

City Ferry Company, of which Phil E. Chappelle was president. She was sunk in ice on February 1, 1888, at Jefferson City, Missouri. She was raised and sunk again by ice during the winter of 1893 in Missouri.

Sully, a stern-wheel packet built at St. Louis, Missouri, in 1867. She was rated at 280 tons, with two engines (15.5" × 5') and two boilers (22' × 40"), which allowed a working pressure of 115 lbs. The boat ran in the Missouri River trade. She was snagged and lost in Missouri on October 22, 1869, with Captain C. A. Cunningham in command.

Sultan, a side-wheel packet built at McKeesport, Pennsylvania, in 1854. 185' × 31' × 6.5' and 349 tons. She ran biweekly with Captain John McCloy St. Louis-Omaha. She was snagged in Missouri in 1857, but was raised and returned to service. The boat frequently made Cincinnati–St. Louis trips. Enroute St. Louis to New Orleans, she burned on the Mississippi River in Missouri on April 2, 1858.

Sunset, a stern-wheel packet built at Pittsburgh, Pennsylvania, in 1865. She was rated at 103 tons, with two engines (14" × 4') and two boilers (20' × 40"), which allowed a working pressure of 134 lbs. The boat was owned by Austin M. Tate and A. R. Davenport (also master). She was snagged and lost below Sioux City, Iowa, on July 18, 1869 on the Missouri River.

Sunshine, a side-wheel packet built at Elizabeth, Pennsylvania, in 1860. Rated at 354 tons. She ran St. Louis-St. Paul in 1861 with Captain Willard. In September 1861, she went to the Missouri River where the Confederates captured her at Glasgow, Missouri, and required the boat to transport their troops across. In June 1863, she was fired on near Waverly, Missouri. The boat burned at St. Louis on July 13, 1864.

Susan, a stern-wheel packet built at Rock Island, Illinois, in 1896. 128.4' × 34.2' × 5.1' and 198 tons, with two engines (15.5" × 4') and one boiler (24' × 48"), which allowed a working pressure of 160 lbs. She was snagged and lost in Nebraska on the Missouri River on September 16, 1907. The boat was owned by Captain G. M. Sively.

T. L. Crawford, a side-wheel packet built at Warsaw, Missouri, in 1858. Rated at 155 tons. She was snagged and lost on the Missouri River on December 12, 1860 in Missouri.

T. L. McGill, a side-wheel packet built at New Albany, Indiana, in 1862. 238' × 36' × 7' and 598 tons, with two engines (24.5" × 7') and four boilers (26' × 42"), which allowed a working pressure of 148 lbs. The hull was from the former T. L. MCGILL. The boat came out named HOPE, but for legal reasons T. L. MCGILL was restored. She typically ran St. Louis-New Orleans but also made trips up the Missouri. The boat was owned by Captain Thomas W. Shields and D. H Silver. She burned on the Mississippi near Memphis on January 16, 1871.

T. T. Hillman, a stern-wheel packet built at Paducah, Kentucky, in 1875. 196 tons, with two engines (10.5" × 4') and two boilers (14' × 38"), which allowed a working pressure of 122 lbs. She was built for the Cumberland River between Eddyville and Canton. Later, she ran Cairo-New Madrid. The boat was snagged on a bar in the Missouri River on August 23, 1882, in Missouri. She was owned and commanded by Captain J. A Stine.

Tacony, a side-wheel packet built at Paducah, Kentucky, in1864. 179' × 32' × 5.5' and 390 tons. The boat ran on the Missouri River. She was deliberately sunk at Fort Peck, Montana, in 1870. She was originally owned by the Lexington Railroad & Transportation Company with Captain D. C. Riter, master. A. J. Edwards purchased the TACONY for $350.00 at auction. He decided to wreck the hull and sell the machinery and furnishings to other boats. A portion of the hull was pulled up during the construction of Fort Peck Dam in 1935.

Tamerlane, a side-wheel packet built at St. Louis, Missouri, in 1846 and rated at 122 tons. She was snagged and lost on the Missouri River in 1848 in Missouri. She was raised and was to Fort William on the Missouri in 1849. The boat was fatally snagged at St. Louis on November 16, 1849.

Telegraph, a Missouri River boat rated at 313 tons. She foundered and was lost on the Missouri River on February 14, 1852, in Missouri.

Tempest No. 2, a stern-wheel (also reported as side-wheel) built at Pittsburgh, Pennsylvania in 1863. Rated at 364 tons. She was originally designed for the Louisville and Cumberland River. She was snagged and lost in South Dakota in 1865.

Tennessee, see EXCHANGE

Thomas Morgan, a stern-wheel packet built at Hobbs Mills on the Missouri River in 1866. 106' × 18' × 3.5' and 97 tons, with two engines (8" × 16") and one boiler (12' × 48"), which allowed a working pressure of 96 lbs. She was owned by Morgan Baker and Hall. She was lost and then raised at Leavenworth, Kansas, on February 15, 1866. The boat's boiler exploded in Nebraska on November 10, 1877.

Thomas Jefferson, a side-wheel packet owned by the U. S. government. She was lost on the Missouri River in June 1819 in Missouri. She participated in the Long Yellowstone expedition. This was the first steamboat wrecked in the Missouri River.

Tidy Adula, a ferryboat commanded by Captain Blackiston. She sank on the Missouri River in 1868.

Timour No. 2, a side-wheel packet built at St. Louis, Missouri, in 1849. She was rated at 232 tons. The boat ran on the Missouri River. She burned at St. Louis in 1849 and was rebuilt. The boat's boilers exploded on the Missouri River on August 20, 1854, in Missouri. She was owned by Captain Edunm F. Dix, Charles F. Eckler , and others at the time of loss. The wreck was exposed in 1927 during low water.

Tom Brierly, a side-wheel ferryboat built at Elizabeth, Pennsylvania, in1856. Rated at 163 tons. She operated on the Missouri River and was lost there in 1868.

Tom Rodgers, a stern-wheel ferryboat built at Grand River, Missouri, in 1870. Rated at 67 tons, with one engine (12' × 3') and one boiler (14' × 46"), which allowed a working pressure of 100 lbs. She burned while laid up for the night on the Missouri River on May 5, 1887. She was owned by J. M. Green and others.

Tom Stevens, a stern-wheel packet built at St. Louis, Missouri, in 1866. 134' × 28' × 3.5' and 170 tons. She ran on the Missouri River and was the boat that went to the Great Falls of the Missouri, the highest point ever reached by steamer, on July 15, 1868. The point of arrival is marked on a rock in which the pilot, Frank A. Murray, carved his name. The boat was dismantled in 1878, and the hull was used as a barge.

Trapper (also ANTELOPE), a side-wheel packet built at Louisville, Kentucky, in 1838. Rated at 132 tons. This was an American Fur Company boat. She first appeared at Fort Union, North Dakota, in 1838. She was renamed TRAPPER on February 27, 1841. The boat was dismantled in 1843 with her machinery going to the NIMROD.

Trenton, a side-wheel packet in the Missouri River fur trade. She was built in 1832 and was snagged and lost on April 3, 1833 in Missouri.

Tropic, a side-wheel packet built at Brownsville, Pennsylvania, in 1853. 225' × 23' and 242 tons. The boat operated as a Lighting Line packet. The boat was snagged and lost on the Missouri River on October 14, 1857, in Missouri. Captain Joe Nansen was master at the time of loss.

Twilight, a side-wheel packet built at Jefferson, Indiana, in 1857. 215' × 33' × 6' and 335 tons. She was owned by John P. Keiser, J. Henery, C. M. Sombart, and H. W. McPherson, with Captain William Massie as master. The boat was snagged and lost on the Missouri River on September 10, 1865, in Missouri. The vessel has been the subject of numerous salvage attempts and is currently being petitioned for salvage. The state of Missouri is fighting the request, and the case is now in the hands of a Missouri judge.

Tyler, a stern-wheel packet in the Missouri River trade. She was lost on the Missouri River in 1878 or 1879 in Missouri. Captain Al Dodd was pilot.

U. S. Grant, a 20-ton steamer lost on the Missouri River in Nebraska in March 1866.

U. S. Lilly, lost on the Missouri River in the vicinity of Centaur Bend.

U. S. Mail, a side-wheel packet built at Elizabeth, Pennsylvania, in 1852. 181' × 27' × 6' and 196 tons. She ran St. Louis-Missouri River after 1853 with Captain M. E. Lucas. The boat ws snagged and lost in Kansas in June 1857.

Umpire, a stern-wheel packet built at Nashville, Tennessee, in 1854. She was 124 tons, with two engines (13.5" × 3.5') and two boilers (20' × 35"), which allowed a working pressure of 120 lbs. The boat burned on the Missouri River on June 12, 1860, in Missouri with Captain Lewis Baldwin in charge.

Uncle Sam, see JACOB RICHTMAN

Undine, a center-wheel ferryboat built at Mound City, Indiana, at 1873. 112' × 30' × 2' and 72 tons, with one engine (17" × 4') and two boilers (14' × 36"), which allowed a working pressure of 110 lbs. The ferry was owned by the Lexington Ferry, Coal, and Railroad Transportation Company with Captain T. J. Anderson, master. The boat sank in Missouri on September 5, 1889, as a result of the oakum leaking out of the boat's seams.

Undine, a side-wheel ferry (also reported as center-wheel ferry) built at Wellsville, Ohio, in 1868. 115' × 30' × 4' and 76 tons. She was owned and operated by Captain William Braithwaite. She was lost at Bismarck, North Dakota, in ice on April 13, 1886. This steamer was built out of the steamer DENVER.

Urilda, a stern-wheel packet that ran on the Missouri River. 112' × 30' and 72 tons. She was lost in Missouri on September 5, 1889 on the Missouri River.

Urilda, a stern-wheel packet built at Monongahela, Pennsylvania, in 1863. Rated at 168 tons. The boat ran the Pittsburgh–Oil City trade on the Allegheny River in 1863. Ran Ohio River trade in 1864 and then back to Allegheny. She left Pittsburgh for Fort Benton, Montana, on April 9, 1868, with Captain G. J. Hazlett. She was owned in part by William J. Kountz. The boat was snagged and lost on the Missouri River on April 23, 1869, with John C. Ball, pilot.

Valley Queen, see JO HORTON FALL

Vermont, a 158-ton steamer built in 1835. She was snagged and lost on the Missouri River on September 11, 1841, in Missouri.

Vice President, a stern-wheel packet built at Madison, Indiana, in 1872. 164' × 34' × 5' and 197 tons, with two engines (18" × 5.5') and four boilers (22' × 42"), which allowed a working pressure of 125 lbs. C.W. Holdrege was managing owner with Captain Overton Butt as master. She was inspected at Nebraska City on the Missouri in 1880. Later the boat was run on the Mississippi at Cape Girardeau, Missouri. She burned on Febraury 14, 1892.

Victoria, see LEXINGTON

Vienna (also CITY OF PLATSMOUTH), a stern-wheel packet built at Plattsmouth, Nebraska, in 1879. 89.6' × 24' × 2.3' and 73 tons, with two engines (8" × 14") and one boiler (12' × 40"), which allowed a working pressure of 110 lbs. Formerly steamer CITY OF PLATTSMOUTH. She was snagged and lost on the Missouri on December 10, 1889, owned at the time by E. Schleff and others; Henry Zeiblin was the pilot. Part of the cargo was salvaged.

Vint Stillings (also WILLIE CADE), a center-wheel ferryboat built at Metropolis, Illinois, in 1881. 131' × 31' × 4' and 177 tons with one engine (20" × 5') and two boilers (22' × 42"), which allowed a working pressure of 125 lbs. She was owned by Seltzer Brothers based at Leavenworth, Kansas. Later she was renamed VINT STILLINGS. The boat was lost in ice while in winter quarters at Sioux City, Iowa, during the winter of 1897–1898.

Viola Belle, a side-wheel packet built at Pearl Landing, Illinois, in 1865. 200' × 3' × 5' and 345 tons. The boat made five trips to Fort Benton, Montana, during her career. She was lengthened 25' and got a new bow at Daggett's Dock, St. Louis, in 1868. The boat was owned by the Northwestern Transportation Company. She was snagged and lost on August 21, 1871, on the Missouri River in Kansas.

Virginia Barton, see NORTH ALABAMA

W. H. Russell (also noted as WILLIAM H.), a side-wheel packet built at Madison, Indiana, in 1865. 204' × 34' × 5.5' and 405 tons. She ran St. Louis-Missouri River with Captain Joseph Kinney. The boat was named for a founder of the Pony Express. Burned at St. Louis in a large steamboat fire on October 27, 1862. Machinery went to the T. LO MCGILL.

W. J. Behan, a stern-wheel packet built at Jeffersonville, Indiana, in 1873. 160' × 33' and 288 tons. She originally ran New Orleans-Shreveport in the New Orleans & Red River Transportation Company, in 1876. The boat was sold to the Fort Benton Transportation Company in 1878 and was lost in ice at Bismark, North Dakota on March 28, 1884.

W. W. Walker, a side-wheel (reported also as stern-wheel) built at Industry, Pennsylvania, in 1867. Rated at 237 tons, with two engines (20" × 6.5') and four boilers (22' × 38"), which allowed a working pressure of 121.5 lbs. Owned by John I. Blair and others. She was snagged and lost in Nebraska on November 14, 1874.

Wakendah, a side-wheel packet built at Elizabethtown, Pennsylvania, in 1846. 160' × 27' and 193 tons. She ran on the Missouri River, owned in part and commanded by Captain J. M. Convers. Sank at the mouth of Fishing River on the Missouri on April 2, 1846. Off the list in 1848.

Walk-in-the-Water, a side-wheel ferryboat built at New Albany, Indiana, in 1850. Rated at 118 tons. She operated on the Missouri River. Out of service in 1855.

Walk-in-the-Water, a side-wheel packet that was in the Missouri River trade. She was lost on the Missouri by snag in the late 1880s in Missouri.

Walter B. Dance, a side-wheel packet built at Paducah, Kentucky, in 1866. 200' × 34' × 5.7' and 571 tons. The boat was on the upper Missouri at Fort Benton in 1866 and 1867. She was dismantled in 1871.

War Eagle, a side-wheel packet built at Cincinnati, Ohio, in 1858. 223' × 35' × 6' and 446 tons. This boat was designed for the Missouri River. Joseph and John B. LaBarge owned the boat. She was at Fort Union, North Dakota, in 1863. She was burned at St. Louis on August 24, 1869.

Warsaw, a small steamer built for the Missouri River trade. She was snagged and lost on the Missouri on March 25, 1846, in Missouri.

Washington, a Missouri River steamer built in 1837. She burned in Missouri in 1840 on the Missouri River.

Washington, a side-wheel ferryboat built at Freedom, Pennsylvania, and Wellsville, Ohio, in 1867. 90' × 19' and 53 tons. She spent a long career on the Missouri River. She was burned and lost there on April 10, 1880, in Missouri. She was owned at the time by August Woht of Hermann, Missouri.

Watossa, a stern-wheel packet built at Brownsville, Pennsylvania, in 1857. 127 tons. Her first home port was Kansas City, Missouri. She was snagged and lost on the Missouri River on September 26, 1858, in Missouri.

Watson, a stern-wheel towboat that was lost on the Missouri River in Missouri. Captain Reneke was master.

Waverly, a side-wheel packet built at Metropolis, Illinois, and St. Louis, Missouri, in 1866. 200' × 34' × 5.5' and 280 tons. It was owned by John P. Keiser, Thomas Raigin and Captain Thomas W. Rha, who operated it on the Missouri River. She was at Fort Benton, Montana, in 1867. She was snagged and lost while downbound Omaha to St. Louis on November 24, 1867. The machinery was salvaged and placed on the SILVER BOW.

Welcome, a side-wheel packet built at Shousetown, Pennsylvania, in 1863. 214' × 36' × 6' and 449 tons. She was on the upper Missouri River at Fort Union in 1864. The boat burned and was lost at New Orleans in August 1871.

Wenona, a side-wheel packet built at St. Louis, Missouri, in 1852. 247 tons. She ran on the Missouri River and was snagged twice. She was fatally lost in 1855 in Missouri. The boat was owned by Robert Barclay, John McClurg, and W. D. Murphy. Off the lists in 1857.

West Wind, a side-wheel packet built at Elizabeth, Pennsylvania, in 1859. 215' × 33' × 5.7' and 350 tons. Built for Captain Samuel Lewis for the Missouri River. In the fall of 1864, she was in U.S. Service. Brought troops down and landed them at Glasgow, Missouri. The town was attacked and captured by General John B. Clark and General Joseph G. Selby while the boat lay there, and she burned the following night, October 16, 1864.

Western, a stern-wheel packet built at Pittsburgh, Pennsylvania, in 1872. 212' × 34' and 475 tons. She was owned by the Western Transportation Company and ran the Missouri River. All told she made nine trips to Fort Benton, Montana. She was cut down by ice during the great gorge at Yankton, South Dakota, on March 27, 1881.

Weston, a side-wheel packet built for the Missouri River trade in 1843. She burned and was lost on the Missouri River on March 20, 1844, in Missouri with Captain William Littlejohn, master,

Weston (also LITTLE MAUD), a stern-wheel packet built at Running Water, South Dakota, in 1901. 110' × 30' × 4.5' and 89 tons. She was originally named LITTLE MAUD and was owned by the Benton Packet Company. She was snagged and lost in North Dakota on September 7, 1909.

Whirlwind, a Missouri River steamer built in 1845. 180' × 30' × 5'. Captain Dodge served as master. She was the first double engined boat on the Missouri.

White Cloud, a side-wheel packet built at McKeesport, Pennsylvania, in 1857. 200' × 35' × 5.5' and rated at 345 tons. Ran St. Louis-St. Paul in 1857. In 1858, she was running up the Missouri River for the Great Mail and Transportation Company. She served as a transport during the Civil War. The boat was sunk in ice at St. Louis on February 12, 1867.

William Baird, a stern-wheel packet built at Elizabeth, Pennsylvania, in 1855. She was rated at 286 tons. She was upbound on the Missouri River on April 19, 1858, when she struck a snag in Missouri. The boat was on the way to Sioux City, Iowa, with 160 passengers.

William H., see W. H. RUSSELL

William L. Lewis (also noted as WM. J. LEWIS), a side-wheel packet built at Metropolis, Illinois, in 1866. 125' × 36' × 3.8', 503 tons. She was at Fort Benton, Montana, in 1866 and 1867. Snagged and sank April 2, 1873.

Willie Cade, see VINT STILLINGS

Winona, a side-wheel packet built for the Missouri River in 1847. She sank in Missouri on November 10, 1855, on the Missouri.

Yankton, a center-wheel ferry built at St. Louis, Missouri, in 1866. She was rated at 32 tons. She was snagged and lost in 1870 in South Dakota. She was owned by Bramble, Miner, & Foster.

Yellow Stone, a side-wheel packet built at Louisville, Kentucky, in 1830. 130' × 19' × 5.5', 144 tons. Built by the American Fur Company. To Fort Tecumseh on June 19, 1831. She was the first boat to go as high up the river as the mouth of the Yellowstone in 1832. Prince Maximiliam came up the river in this boat in the spring of 1833.

Yellowstone No. 2, a side-wheel packet built at Cincinnati, Ohio, in 1864. 206' × 30' × 5.5' and 378 tons. She operated on the Missouri River. The boat was to Fort Union carrying fifty soldiers of Company I—30th Wisconsin Infantry in 1864 and then continued on to Fort Benton. In 1865, Company B—1st U. S. Volunteer Infantry Regiment, better known as the Galvanized Yankees, offloaded at Fort Union; the boat went on to Fort Benton. She burned at St. Louis on July 11, 1867.

Yellowstone No. 3, a stern-wheel packet built in Jeffersonville, Indiana, in 1876. She was owned by Dr. Achilles Lamme of Bozeman, Montana. She made three trips to Fort Benton, Montana, between 1876 and 1878. She was lost on the Yellowstone River in late May 1879.

Yorktown, a side-wheel packet built at Freedom, Pennsylvania, in 1864. She was rated at 253 tons. The boat was at Fort Benton, Montana, in 1867. She was dismantled in 1869.

Zephyr (also noted as ZEPHER), a stern-wheel packet built at Brownsville, Pennsylvania, in 1864. 140' × 29' × 3.8' and 158 tons, with two engines (19.5" × 4.5') and three boilers (34' × 36"), which allowed a working pressure of 140 lbs. She ran Pittsburgh-St. Louis 1864. The boat logged in at Fort Benton, Montana, in 1867. The boat then operated out of Memphis for the Arkansas River with Captain Ben Johnson. She went up the river in Missouri and loaded railroad ties for an Arkansas delivery, when it sank on rocks in Missouri on July 20, 1870.

References

Adams, William H., 1977, *Silcott, Washington: Ethnoarchaeology of a Rural American Community*. Reports of Investigations No. 54. Laboratory of Anthropology, Washington State University, Pullman.

Allen, Sam, 1992, *Joinery Basics*. Sterling Publishing, New York.

Barlow, Ronald S., 1991, *The Antique Tool Collector's Guide to Value*. Windmill Publishing Company, El Cajon, California.

Bass, George F. (Editor), 1988, *Ships and Shipwrecks of the Americas*. Thames and Hudson, London.

Bates, Allen, 1968, *The Western Rivers Steamboat Cyclopoedium*. Hustle Press, Leonia, Ohio.

Binkley, Peter, 1998, September 5, personal communication.

Blackburn, Graham, 1974, *The Illustrated Encyclopedia of Woodworking Hand Tools, Instruments, and Devices*. Simon and Schuster, New York.

Blee, Catherine Holder, 1991, *Sorting Functionally Mixed Artifact Assemblages with Multiple Regression: A Comparative Study in Historical Archaeology*. Doctoral dissertation, University of Colorado, Boulder.

Blum, Stella (Editor), 1985, *Fashions and Costumes from* Godey's Lady's Book. Dover Publications, New York.

Borger, Mona, 1983, *Chinas for Study and Admiration*. Borger, San Francisco, California.

Brazier, Helen H. (Editor), 1953, Missouri River Journey, 1866. *Montana Magazine of History*, 3(3):32–38.

Brittain, Judy, 1979, *Needle Craft*. Bantam Books, Toronto, Ontario.

Carson, Gerald, 1961, *One for a Man Two for a Horse*. Bramhall House, Clarkson N. Potter, New York.

Cassler, Michael M., 1999, *Steamboats of the Fort Union Fur Trade*. Fort Union Association, Williston, North Dakota.

Chamberlin, T. C., 1965, The Method of Multiple Working Hypotheses. *Science*, 148:754–759.

Chappell, Phil E., 1905, A History of the Missouri River. *Transactions of the Kansas State Historical Society*, 9:237–316.

Chittenden, Hiram Martin, 1897, List of Steamboat Wrecks on the Missouri River from the Beginning of Steamboat Navigation to the Present Time, *Annual Report of the Chief Engineers, U. S. Army* Serial Set 3631-3636. Government Printing Office, Washington, DC.

227

Chittenden, Hiram Martin, 1903, *History of Early Steamboat Navigation on the Missouri River: Life and Adventures of Joseph La Barge.* Arthur H. Clark Company, Cleveland, Ohio.

Columbia [Missouri] *Statesman,* March 14, 1856.

Conlin, Joseph R., 1993, *The American Past: A Survey of American History to 1877.* Harcourt Press, Fort Worth, Texas.

Corbin, Annalies, 1998, Shifting Sand and Muddy Water: Historic Cartography and River Migration as Factors in Locating Steamboat Wrecks on the Far Upper Missouri River. *Historical Archaeology,* 32(4):86–94.

Corbin, Annalies, in press, Steamboat Archaeology on the Missouri River: Searching for the Forgotten Past. In *The International Handbook of Underwater Archaeology,* edited by Carol V. Ruppe and Janet F. Bartstead. Kluwer Academic/Plenum, New York.

Cumming, Valerie, 1982, *Gloves.* Drama Book, New York.

Daily [St. Louis, Missouri] *Intelligencer,* 1864.

Daily [St. Louis] *Missouri Democrat,* March 10, 1865, March 17, 1865.

Davenport [Iowa] *Gazette,* April 13, 1865.

Deetz, James, 1965, *Invitation to Archaeology.* National History Press, Garden City, New York.

Deetz, James, 1977, *In Small Things Forgotten: The Archaeology of Early North American Life.* Doubleday, New York.

Farrell, Jeremy, 1985, *Umbrellas and Parasols.* B. T. Batsford, London.

Ferguson, Leland, 1977, *Historical Archaeology and the Importance of Material Things.* Society for Historical Archaeology, Columbia, South Carolina.

Fike, Richard E., and H. Blaine Phillips, II, 1984, *A Nineteenth Century Ute Burial from Northeast Utah.* Cultural Resource Series, No. 16, Utah State Office, Salt Lake City Bureau of Land Management.

Fort Benton [Montana] *Press,* February 1, 1882.

Fonteroy, Julieanna, 1995, August 1, personal communication.

Freeman, Ruth S., 1962, *American Dolls, Encyclopedia.* Century House, Watkins Glen, New York.

Gaynor, Jay, 1995, August 11, Personal communication.

Granville, Stuart, 1867, *Diary and Sketchbook of a Journey to "America" in 1866 and Return Trip up the Missouri River to Fort Benton, Montana, Virginia City Montana Post.* Reprinted at Dawson's Book Shop, Los Angeles,1963.

Hardesty, Donald L., 1988, *The Archaeology of Mining and Miners: A View from the Silver State.* Society of Historical Archaeology, Special Publication Series No. 6, Tucson, Arizona.

Harris, Marvin, 1968, *The Rise of Anthropological Theory.* Thomas Y. Crowell, New York.

Hawley, David, [1991], The Raising of the Shipwreck Arabia. Manuscript on file, *Arabia* Steamboat Museum, Kansas City, Missouri.

Hawley, David, 1995, *The Treasures of the Steamboat* Arabia. *Arabia* Steamboat Museum, Kansas City, Missouri.

Hawley, Greg, 1998, *Treasure in a Corn Field.* Paddle Wheel Publishing, Kansas City, Missouri.

Historical Society of Montana, 1876, Steamboat Arrivals at Fort Benton, Montana, and Vicinity. In *Contributions to the Historical Society of Montana,* 1, pp. 317–325, Rocky Mountain Publishing Company, Helena.

Hodder, Ian, 1984, Burials, Houses, Women and Men in the European Neolithic. In *Ideology, Power, and Prehistory,* edited by D. Miller and C. Tilley, pp. 51–68. Cambridge University Press, Cambridge.

Honour, Hugh, 1961, *Chinoiserie: The Vision of Cathay.* E. P. Dutton, New York.

Hunter, Lewis C., 1949, *Steamboats on Western Rivers: An Economic and Technological History.* Harvard University Press, Cambridge, Massachusetts.

Impey, Oliver, 1977, *Chinoiserie: The Impact of Oriental Styles on Western Art and Decoration.* Charles Scribner's Sons, New York.

Jackson, Donald, 1985, *Voyages of the Steamboat Yellow Stone.* Ticknor and Fields, New York.

Jarausch, Konrad H., and Kenneth A. Hardy, 1991, *Quantitative Methods for Historians: A Guide to Research, Data, and Statistics.* University of North Carolina Press, Chapel Hill.

Jefferson [Missouri] *Inquirer,* March 8, 1856, September 13, 1856.

Johnson, Cathy, 1994, *Living History: Drawing on the Past.* Graphics/Fine Arts Press, Excelsior Springs, Missouri.

Kane, Lucille M. (Editor), 1951, *Military Life in Dakota: The Journal of Phillippe Regis de Trobriand,* 1864. Minnesota Historical Society, St. Paul.

Kansas City [Missouri] *Enterprise,* September 6, 1856.

Kansas City [Missouri] *Star,* January 20, 1896.

Kansas City [Missouri] *Times,* September 19, 1856, December 29, 1871.

Karklins, Karlis, 1992, *Trade Ornament Usage among the Native Peoples of Canada: A Source Book.* Studies in Archaeology and History, National Historic Sites Park Service Environment, Ottawa, Ontario.

Kebabian, Paul B., 1978, *American Woodworking Tools.* New York Graphic Society, Boston.

Kidd, Kenneth E., and Martha A. Kidd, 1970, *A Classification System for Glass Beads for the Use of Field Archaeologists.* Canadian Historic Sites, *Occasional Papers in Archaeology and History* (1), National Historic Sites Park Service Environment, Ottawa, Ontario.

Lass, William E., 1962, *A History of Steamboating on the Upper Missouri.* University of Nebraska Press, Lincoln.

Ledbetter, N. Marie, 1981, *Tailoring: Traditional and Contemporary Techniques.* Reston Publishing, Reston, Virginia.

Liberty [Iowa] *Weekly Tribune,* September 19, 1856.

Lytle, William M., and Forrest R. Holdcamper, 1975, *Merchant Steam Vessels of the United States, 1790–1868.* Steamship Historical Society of America, New York.

McClellan, Elizabeth, 1977, *Historic Dress in America, 1800–1870.* George W. Jacobs, Philadelphia.

McDonald, W. J., 1927, The Missouri River and Its Victims. *Missouri Historical Review* 21:215–242, 455–480, 581–607.

Mercer, Henry C., 1960, *Ancient Carpenters' Tools.* Bucks County Historical Society, Doylestown, Pennsylvania.

Merck, Fredrick, 1963, *Manifest Destiny and Missouri in American History.* Alfred A. Knopf, New York.

Missouri [St. Louis] *Republic,* June 1, 1867.

Montana [Helena] *Post,* April 22, 1865.

Moss, James E. (Editor), 1963, Ho! For the Gold Mines of Montana, Up the Missouri in 1865: The Journal of William H. Gallaher. *Missouri Historical Review,* 57:2–163.

Mullan, Captain John, 1865, *Miner's and Traveler's Guide to Oregon, Washington, Idaho, Montana, Wyoming and Colorado via the Missouri and Columbia Rivers.* Wm. M. Franklin, New York. Reprinted Arno Press, 1973.

National Archives, Record Group 41, Records of the Bureau of Marine Inspection and Navigation, Public Enrollment 3, Port of Pittsburgh, General Services Administration. National Archives, Washington, D.C.

National Archives, Record Group 41, Records of the Bureau of Marine Inspection and Navigation, Public Enrollment 12, Port of St. Louis, General Services Administration. National Archives, Washington, D.C.

National Archives, Record Group 41, Records of the Bureau of Marine Inspection and Navigation, Public Enrollment 17, Port of St. Louis, General Services Administration. National Archives, Washington, D.C.

National Archives, Record Group 41, Records of the Bureau of Marine Inspection and Navigation, Public Enrollment 42, Port of Pittsburgh, General Services Administration. National Archives, Washington, DC.

National Archives, Record Group 41, Records of the Bureau of Marine Inspection and Navigation, Public Enrollment 72, Port of Wheeling, General Services Administration. National Archives, Washington DC.

The [Omaha] *Nebraskian,* December 2, 1857.

Ostasien, Abteilung, 1983, Letter from Berlin, Germany, to Allan Montgomery, December 15. Transcript of file at DeSoto National Wildlife Refuge, Missouri Valley, Iowa.

Overholser, Joel, 1987, *Fort Benton: World's Innermost Port.* Falcon Press Publishing Company, Helena, Montana.

Peterkin, Ernest W., and D. A. Saguto, 1989, *Workshop on Historical Footwear.* Paper presented to the Society of Historical Archaeology, Baltimore, Maryland.

Peterson, Harold L., 1958, *American Knives, the First History and Collectors Guide.* Charles Scribner's Sons, New York.

Peterson, William J. (Editor), 1945, The Log of the *Henry M. Shreve* to Fort Benton. *Mississippi Valley Historical Review,* 31:537–578.

Petsche, Jerome E., 1974, *The Steamboat Bertrand: History, Excavation, and Architecture.* National Parks Service and U.S. Department of the Interior, Washington, D.C.

Petsche, Jerome E., 1982, Letter from Missouri Valley, Iowa, to Sister M. L. Martinez, November 4. Transcript on file at DeSoto National Wildlife Refuge, Missouri Valley, Iowa.

Petsche, Jerome E., 1983, Letter from Missouri Valley, Iowa, to Dave Walter, April 9. Transcript on file at DeSoto National Wildlife Refuge, Missouri Valley, Iowa.

Pollak, Emil, and Martyl Pollak, 1983, *A Guide to American Wooden Planes and Their Makers.* Astragal Press, Morristown, New Jersey.

Prat, Julius W., 1933, "John O'Sullivan and Manifest Destiny." *New York History,* 14:213–234.

Renfrew, Colin, 1984, *Approaches to Social Archaeology.* Harvard University Press, Cambridge, Massachusetts.

Renfrew, Colin, and Paul Bahn, 1991, *Archaeology: Theories, Methods, and Practice.* Thames and Hudson, New York.

Robbinson, Deane, 1918, Steamboat Wrecks in South Dakota. *South Dakota Historical Collections,* 9:393–402.

Ross, Lester A., 1990, Trade Beads from Hudson's Bay Company Fort Vancouver (1829-1860), Vancouver, Washington. *Beads,* 2:29–68.

Russell and Erwin Manufacturing Company, 1865, *Illustrated Catalogue of American Hardware of the Russell and Erwin Manufacturing Company.* Association for Preservation Technology, 1980. Reprinted from the 1865 edition, published by the manufacturer.

Saguto, D. A., 1995, August 11, Personal communication.

Schlereth, Thomas J. (Editor), 1982, *Material Culture Studies in America.* American Association for State and Local History, Nashville.

Schlissel, Lillian, 1982, *Women's Diaries of the Westward Journey.* Schocken Books, New York.

Schwantes, Carlos, 1999, *Long Day's Journey: The Steamboat and Stagecoach Era in the Northern West.* University of Washington Press, Seattle.

Settle, Raymond W., and Mary Lund Settle (Editors), 1971, *Overland Days to Montana in 1865: The Diary of Sarah Raymond and Journal of Dr. Waid Howard.* Arthur H. Clark Company, Glendale, California.

Sprague, Roderick, 1981, A Functional Classification for Artifacts from 19th and 20th Century Historical Sites. *North American Anthropologist,* 2(3):251–261.

Sprague, Roderick, 1984, Glass Trade Beads. In *A Nineteenth Century Ute Burial from Northeast Utah,* 2, edited by Richard E. Fike and H. Blaine Phillips, pp. 69–70. Utah State Office, Bureau of Land Management, Cultural Resource Series No. 16, Provo.

Sprague, Roderick, 1991, Glass Trade Beads: A Progress Report. In *Approaches to Material Culture Research for Historical Archaeologists,* edited by George L. Miller, Oliver R. Jones,

Lester A. Ross, and Teresita Majewski, pp. 141–159. Society for Historical Archaeology, Tucson, Arizona.

SPSS Inc., 1990, *SPSS Reference Guide.* SPSS Inc., Chicago.

St. Joseph [Missouri] *Commercial Cycle,* September 12, 1856.

St. Louis [Missouri] *Republican,* September 9, 1856, September 10, 1856.

Steward, Julian H., 1976, *Theory of Culture Change: The Methodology of Multilinear Evolution.* University of Illinois Press, Urbana.

Stone, Lyle M., 1974, *Fort Michilimackinac, 1715–1781: An Archaeological Perspective on the Revolutionary Frontier.* Publications of the Museum, Michigan State University, East Lansing.

Sunder, John E., 1965, *The Fur Trade on the Upper Missouri, 1840-1865.* University of Oklahoma Press, Norman.

Swann, June, 1982, *Shoes.* Drama Book, New York.

Switzer, Ronald R., 1974, *The Bertrand Bottles: A Study of 19th-Century Glass and Ceramic Containers.* National Park Service, U. S. Department of the Interior, Washington, D.C.

Thomas, David Hurst, 1986, *Refiguring Anthropology: First Principles of Probability and Statistics.* Waveland Press, Prospect Heights, Illinois.

Thomas, David Hurst, 1990, *Archaeology.* Holt, Rinehart and Winston, Fort Worth, Texas.

Timmons, R., and Sons, 1820, *Tools for the Trades and Crafts, 1790–1820.* Reprinted from the original, published by Kenneth Roberts for E.A.I.A., 1976.

Trail, E. B., [1940s], Ruth Ferris Collection, "E. B. Trail" folder, Herman T. Potts Inland Waterways Collection, St. Louis Mercantile Library, St. Louis, Missouri.

Tri-Weekly [St. Louis] *Missouri Democrat,* April 16, 1865.

Tylor, Edward Burnett, 1871, *Primitive Cultures,* 1 and 2. Murray, London.

Upham, H. D., 1865, Upham Letters from the Upper Missouri, 1865. *The Frontier,* 13:315–317.

Vyzralek, Frank E., 1970, Riverboat Wrecks in North Dakota Waters. *Plains Talk.* Newsletter of the State Historical Society of North Dakota, Bismarck: State Historical Society of North Dakota.

Ways, Frederick, Jr., 1983, *Way's Packet Directory, 1848–1983.* Ohio University Press, Athens.

Weinberg, Albert K., 1935, *Manifest Destiny.* Johns Hopkins University Press, Baltimore, Maryland.

Wheatley, William McCoy, 1865, "Letters, 1865–1866," Robert W. Binkley Collection, London, Ontario.

Wheeling [West Virginia] *Daily Inteligencer,* November 26, 1864.

White, Leslie A., 1959, *The Evolution of Culture: The Development of Civilization to the Fall of Rome.* McGraw-Hill, New York.

Winther, Oscar Osborn, 1964, *The Transportation Frontier Trans-Mississippi West, 1865–1890.* Holt, Rinehart and Winston, New York.

Woman's Institute Library of Dressmaking, 1926, *Sewing Materials.* Woman's Institute of Domestic Arts and Sciences, Scranton, Pennsylvania.

Worrell, Estelle Ansley, 1979, *American Costume, 1840–1920.* Stackpole Books. Harrisburg, Pennsylvania.

Worrell, Estelle Ansley, 1980, *Children's Costume in America, 1607–1910.* Charles Scribner's Sons, New York.

York, K. A., 1984, *Civil War Ladies Sketchbook,* 3. House of York, Elgin, Illinois.

Index

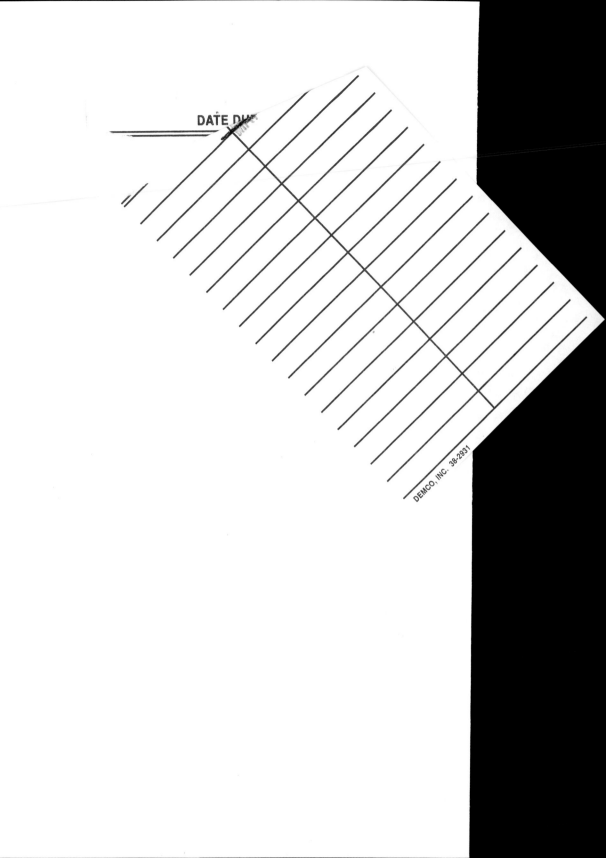

DATE DUE

DEMCO, INC. 38-2931